COME *from the* SHADOWS

the LONG *and* LONELY
STRUGGLE *for* PEACE *in*
AFGHANISTAN

TERRY GLAVIN

COME FROM THE
SHADOWS

Douglas & McIntyre
D&M PUBLISHERS INC.
Vancouver/Toronto/Berkeley

Douglas & McIntyre
An imprint of D&M Publishers Inc.
2323 Quebec Street, Suite 201
Vancouver BC Canada V5T 4S7
www.douglas-mcintyre.com

Cataloguing data available from Library and Archives Canada
ISBN 978-1-55365-782-8 (cloth)
ISBN 978-1-55365-783-5 (ebook)

Editing by Barbara Pulling
Copyediting by Lara Kordic
Jacket and text design by Naomi MacDougall
Map by Eric Leinberger
Jacket photograph © Veronique de Viguerie/Getty Images
The photo depicts a Kuchi woman of the Niazi tribe, Kandahar, 2004.
Printed and bound in Canada by Friesens
Text printed on acid-free paper
Distributed in the U.S. by Publishers Group West

We gratefully acknowledge the financial support of the Canada Council
for the Arts, the British Columbia Arts Council, the Province of British
Columbia through the Book Publishing Tax Credit and the Government
of Canada through the Canada Book Fund for our publishing activities.

Oh, the wind, the wind is blowing,
through the graves the wind is blowing,
freedom soon will come;
then we'll come from the shadows.

—"The Partisan," Leonard Cohen, 1969

The wind blows through the graves,
freedom will return.
We will be forgotten. We will return to the shadows.

—"Le Complainte du Partisan," Emmanuel d'Astier de la Vigerie
   and Anna Marly, 1943

CONTENTS

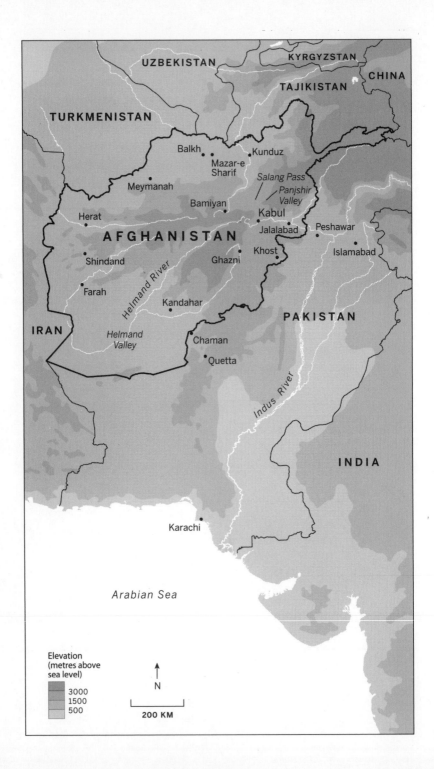

UZBEKISTAN

KYRGYZSTAN

TAJIKISTAN

CHINA

TURKMENISTAN

Balkh

Kunduz

Mazar-e
Sharif

Salang Pass

Panjshir
Valley

Meymanah

Bamiyan

Kabul

Herat

Jalalabad

Peshawar

AFGHANISTAN

Khost

Islamabad

Shindand

Ghazni

Helmand River

Farah

Kandahar

PAKISTAN

Helmand
Valley

Chaman

Quetta

IRAN

Indus River

INDIA

Karachi

Arabian Sea

Elevation
(metres above
sea level)

3000
1500
500

N

200 KM

one

WELCOME TO ABSURDISTAN

"Indifference to objective truth is encouraged by the sealing-off of one part of the world from another, which makes it harder and harder to discover what is actually happening. There can often be a genuine doubt about the most enormous events. For example, it is impossible to calculate within millions, perhaps even tens of millions, the number of deaths caused by the present war. The calamities that are constantly being reported—battles, massacres, famines, revolutions—tend to inspire in the average person a feeling of unreality. One has no way of verifying the facts, one is not even fully certain that they have happened, and one is always presented with totally different interpretations from different sources ... Probably the truth is discoverable, but the facts will be so dishonestly set forth in almost any newspaper that the ordinary reader can be forgiven either for swallowing lies or failing to form an opinion. The general uncertainty as to what is really happening makes it easier to cling to lunatic beliefs."

—from George Orwell's "Notes on Nationalism," in *Polemic*, October 1945

T HE LITTLE CITY of Daste Barchi is not on any official map, and there are no road signs to tell you how to find it. To get there, you look for a particular dirt track that seems to come out of nowhere from behind the bombed-out hulk of the Duralaman Palace on the outskirts of Kabul. You follow the track into the foothills of the snow-covered Paghman Mountains. It becomes a rutted, westward-twisting dirt road for about an hour or so, and then it begins to weave through Jabarhan, a teeming place of tiny, flat-roofed mud brick houses and narrow alleyways alive with children and flocks of sheep and chickens. Just when you think you're lost, and the road could not get any narrower, you are in Daste Barchi.

Daste Barchi means Barchi Desert. It is not a desert. It is a city. Perhaps as many as a million people live in Daste Barchi and its environs. The people are mainly Hazaras, from Afghanistan's Shia minority. These are the people you see at first light down in Kabul, sweeping the streets and pulling handcarts heavy with cauliflowers and pomegranates. They're the day labourers, the house servants, the people who take out Kabul's washing. Without them, Kabul would come apart. The area encompassing Daste Barchi lies within an administrative unit called Police District 13. Apart from what some people manage to procure from diesel generators, there is no electricity. There is no running water. The residents of Police District 13 are classified as Internally Displaced Persons. Daste Barchi does not officially exist.

It is in places like Daste Barchi that the terrain I set out to explore in this book appears in sharp relief. This is the landscape between the Afghanistan that animates debates in Western democracies and the places "outside the wire," as the entire country is often bizarrely and euphemistically described. Having spent fifteen years of my life working for daily newspapers, I'm well acquainted with the distance that can exist between the way the world really is and the way accounts of that world enliven the public imagination. But between the real Afghanistan and the imaginary one, there is a chasm. I travelled to Kabul and Kandahar in 2008, and to Kandahar again in 2009. In 2010 I was back in Afghanistan twice, with Abdulrahim Parwani, a friend from Canada, a colleague and fellow journalist whose story will figure prominently in this book. We went to Daste Barchi in the spring of 2010 to learn about a story that casts light down into that chasm. It involves an event that had come to be called the Battle of Marefat High School.

In the activist polemics of North America's wealthy, privileged students, Afghanistan shows up as a project of American imperialism, an effort by "us" in the capitalist West to impose our hegemonic, democratic values on "them." It brooks only one response: troops out. At Marefat High School, in a cold and poorly lit classroom, the students have decorated the walls with oil paintings of some of the great champions of values that do not draw such distinctions between "them" and "us." The students painted the portraits themselves: Jean-Jacques Rousseau, René Descartes, Rosa Parks, Isaac Newton, Albert Einstein, Ali Akbar Dehkhoda, Immanuel Kant, Abraham Lincoln, Voltaire, Baruch Spinoza and Jawaharlal Nehru. This may seem a mere incongruity, a touching detail, a small matter. It isn't. It's not just a mark of the distance between the imaginary Afghanistan and the real one, either. It's what the Battle of Marefat High School was all about.

Marefat High School is supported almost entirely by the poor of Daste Barchi. The school's focus is on humanism and civic education. The school is accredited by the Afghan government, but it has had a rocky relationship with the education ministry, owing to the students' demands for fully co-educational classes. The roughly three thousand students who attend the school are encouraged to use the Internet, set up personal web pages and communicate with the outside world. Elected class councils and discipline councils allow students to evaluate teachers, tutor one another and manage their own affairs, right down to the amount of the fines levied for overdue library books. The school is governed by a board of trustees elected by parents, students and teachers. There is also an independent student parliament. The idea is that these forms of self-government will encourage students to get into the habit of taking charge of their own lives. This requires practice, hard work and a lot of give and take. It is the art that is known in the West as democracy.

The battle at the school began on the morning of April 15, 2009, when a mob of dozens from Kabul arrived screaming for Marefat principal Aziz Royesh. "I was right here," Royesh told me, as we stood in the rutted, muddy alley outside the school. "The school is a dirty nest of Christians, communists and prostitutes," the mob shouted. "There are boys and girls together. Royesh is an apostate; Royesh must die." In the school courtyard, several boys ran to the doors and quickly locked them. "I ran into my house, right there," said Royesh, pointing across the narrow alley. "The school fought back. The boys didn't run away. They barred the door. They called the police." The battle was more of a riot, but it lasted most of the day. The school was pelted with rocks. Windows were broken. The local police were useless. It took riot police firing into the air to break things up.

The Battle of Marefat High School was directly related to a story that showed up in headlines all over the world, in a version that went something like this: In April 2009, to the great consternation of his Western backers and international human rights organizations, Afghan president Hamid Karzai approved a "rape law," which would forbid women from refusing sex to their husbands and require them to obtain permission from a male relative before leaving the house, as a sop to the country's Shia minority. Afghanistan's Shias wanted to entrench Taliban-like misogynist brutality within a Shia-specific marriage law that would be separate from laws applying to the Sunni majority. Some Afghan women staged a protest in Kabul but were shouted down and threatened by a much larger group of violent counter-protesters. Moral of the story: It all goes to show that we should stop propping up Karzai's warlord regime and pull our soldiers from the country. Troops out.

The problem with the story is that it was pretty much the opposite of the truth. The sternest opponents of the "rape law" included Shia clerics. Mohammad Mohaqiq, one of Afghanistan's most influential Shia parliamentarians, called the law "an offence to the Hazaras." The contents had actually been written in Tehran a couple of years before. The law's champion was Iran's senior ayatollah in Afghanistan, the powerful Mohammad Asif Mohseni. The international human rights outfits in Kabul mainly kept quiet about it all until it was almost too late. Among the Hazara women leading protests against the law were student parliamentarians from Daste Barchi. The mob that showed up at the school came straight from Mohseni's opulent mosque and madrassa complex in Kabul. If there is a moral to this story, it would be something like this: Afghans want more democracy, less misogyny, and more democratic international intervention to help hold their government accountable. In their demonstrations against the "rape law," Afghans were not chanting "troops out."

This wasn't a story about imperialists from the Western democracies trying to cope with an intractable Muslim puppet government that was refusing to behave respectably. It was more accurately a story about wealthy Iranian-backed bullies pushing around poor Afghan Shias who were standing up for the universal values the West dubiously claims as its own.

The closer you look at the Afghanistan that has animated Western debates in the decade since September 11, 2001, that's the sort of thing you find. It is as though some undiagnosed trauma from the gruesome, live-broadcast spectacle of that September morning had gone on to induce a kind of mass psychosis, a "sealing-off of one part of the world from another," as Orwell put it.

In April 2011, during its 219th week on the *New York Times* non-fiction bestseller list, celebrity philanthropist Greg Mortenson's *Three Cups of Tea,* a book that purports to set out a schools-based formula for winning the "war on terror" in Afghanistan and Pakistan, was exposed as a fairytale. Journalist Jon Krakauer and a CBS *60 Minutes* crew revealed that Mortenson's account of his exploits was largely a work of fiction. Krakauer, a journalist who is not afflicted with what Orwell politely described as an "indifference to objective truth," discovered that Mortenson had fabricated his most gripping yarns, not least a tale of being captured and held hostage by a strangely jolly group of Taliban fighters. "The image of Mortenson that has been created for public consumption is an artifact born of fantasy, audacity, and an apparently insatiable hunger for esteem," Krakauer found. "Mortenson has lied about the noble deeds he has done, the risks he has taken, the people he has met." On it goes, in painful detail.

Mortenson's "phony memoir," with its various editions, its sequel and its children's book version, bilked enormous sums of money from unsuspecting donors to build schools that were not built, or were built and left empty or turned out to have been built by someone else. Some of his schools were indeed functioning, but Mortenson's Central Asia Institute issued bogus financial statements and misused millions of dollars, including payments for fancy hotels and flights in private jets for Mortenson's lucrative speaking engagements. Tellingly, all along, few Afghans had ever even heard of the world-famous Mortenson. Hardly anyone in Afghanistan involved in education had ever come across his Central Asia Institute. And yet, Mortenson's *Three Cups of Tea* was a *Time Asia* Book of the Year winner.

Something similar has been at work with regard to another bestseller about Afghanistan by another globetrotting celebrity. Malalai Joya's polemical autohagiography, *A Woman among Warlords: The Extraordinary Story of an Afghan Who Dared to Raise Her Voice,* tells the story of an Afghan parliamentarian so courageous that the BBC bestowed the title "bravest woman in Afghanistan" upon her. Joya's book is not what you would call a work of fiction, but in 2010, the year *Time* chose her for inclusion on its list of the 100 most influential people in the world, she was only dimly remembered in Afghanistan as a former MP who once made an angry speech, got kicked out of Parliament and then left the country. A decade after September 11, throughout Europe and North America, especially among people who considered themselves staunchly progressive, Malalai Joya was a larger-than-life, heroic figure. But among Afghanistan's human rights activists and women's rights leaders, Joya was remembered with a mix of pity and contempt.

All over the English-speaking world, there was something about September 11 that seemed to cause otherwise intelligent people to give vent to all sorts of unhinged declarations. A mere two weeks after al-Qaida's July 7, 2005, suicide bombings in London claimed the lives of fifty-two innocents, London mayor Ken Livingstone declared: "The Americans recruited and trained Osama bin Laden, taught him how to kill, to make bombs, and set him off to kill the Russians and drive them out of Afghanistan." Six years later, when a U.S. Navy SEAL team killed bin Laden in Abbottabad, Pakistan, the famous American documentary filmmaker Michael Moore typed the news into his Twitter account this way: "The monster we created—yes, WE—in the 1980s by ARMING, FUNDING, & TRAINING him in the art of terror agnst the USSR, finally had 2 b put down." But the United States did no such thing. The CIA never organized, trained, armed or funded bin Laden or al-Qaida. During the anti-Soviet jihad, bin Laden was a deranged millionaire construction-industry magnate whose al-Qaida outfit was a marginal presence in Afghanistan. Neither al-Qaida nor the Taliban (which didn't even exist during the 1980s) were ever U.S. allies or CIA assets. But there was nothing unusual about Livingstone's pronouncement, or about Moore's bizarre outburst. These are the kinds of things you hear from all sorts of people, all the time.

Another commonplace fiction shows up when you type "Afghanistan" and "graveyard of empires" into Google: 259,000 results. "It's the mother of all clichés," writes Christian Caryl, a veteran journalist and a senior fellow at the Center for International Studies at the Massachusetts Institute of Technology. "Almost no one can resist it. It's wielded by everyone from thoughtful ex-generals to vitriolic bloggers. It crops up everywhere from Russia's English-language TV channel to scruffy Pakistani newspapers to America's stately National Public Radio." Caryl warns: "If we really want Afghans to attain the future they deserve, clinging to a fake version of their history won't help."

It's not just "their history" that has gotten so absurdly faked, and getting Afghanistan's story backwards or sideways is not confined to the Americans or the English. The Canadian case is especially illustrative, because unlike Britain and the United States, Canada did not muddle things with passionate and furious arguments about Iraq. Canada wasn't a member of the Anglo-American "coalition of the willing" in Iraq. Still, Canada ended up a flotsam-cluttered back eddy for the most manic of the prevailing Euro-American fables floating around about Afghanistan.

It had gotten so that in January 2008, New Democratic Party leader Jack Layton could utter these words, with a straight face, without even having to worry that someone in Canada's national news media would notice: "For six years, the Liberals and Conservatives have had Canada involved in a counter-insurgency combat mission in southern Afghanistan." It wasn't even close to being true. In early 2002, a Canadian battle group of about 750 soldiers took on a combat role with American troops in the Afghan south, but by July of that year, Canada's battle group came home. After NATO took the helm of the UN's International Security Assistance Force in 2003, about 700 Canadian soldiers returned to Afghanistan to assume a fairly conventional "peacekeeping" role in and around Kabul, in northern Afghanistan. In October 2005, Canadian troops handed off the assignment to Turkish soldiers, and nearly all Canadian Forces personnel in Afghanistan were brought home for a second time. It wasn't until early 2006, after Canada answered the call from the UN to set up a provincial reconstruction team in Kandahar, that a Canadian battle group was deployed to southern Afghanistan.

In these ways, the Afghanistan that has insinuated itself into the attentions of the English-speaking world since September 11 is a lot like Absurdistan, which is what the dissidents of Czechoslovakia, East Germany and Hungary called the world they read about in their East bloc newspapers before the Berlin Wall came down. In its post-9/11 iteration in the West, Absurdistan is a world that replaces Afghanistan with an apparatus sustained only by the suspension of disbelief, a contrivance wholly impervious to the objective realities of the world in which Afghanistan actually exists.

If that seems a bold claim, let's try a little thought experiment. It will take the form of an account of Afghanistan's story that situates September 11, 2001, at its heart. It will take up only two paragraphs. You could quibble with it according to your political sensibilities, but you won't be presented with the lunatic belief that September 11 was an inside job, or that it's all about oil, or that we're all engaged in an illegal and imperialist war in that country. No Zionists enter into it, either. It may even be the least contentious way of talking about Afghanistan. It goes like this:

After Soviet troops poured into Afghanistan in the late 1970s, the United States opened up a decisive front in the Cold War by arming and training anti-Soviet mujahideen in order to overthrow Afghanistan's communist government and drive out the Russians. U.S. president Ronald Reagan's mujahideen forces were victorious, but they then turned on one another in a long and horrific civil war that ended only in 1996, when the Islamic fundamentalist Taliban seized control of the country. At first welcomed by war-weary Afghans, the Taliban soon imposed an oppressive and brutal order derived from a strict interpretation of the Quran. The Taliban ended the anarchy of the warlord years, halted opium production and tackled corruption, but in a classic case of foreign-policy "blowback," America's former anti-Soviet allies became America's sworn enemies. Owing to the strict Afghan tribal code of Pashtunwali, which demands that Afghans protect their guests, the Taliban continued to provide shelter to Osama bin Laden, whose al-Qaida terrorist network had targeted the United States.

In response to the catastrophe of September 11, the White House rallied America's NATO partners to a "war on terror" coalition that invaded Afghanistan and overthrew the Taliban government. But it wasn't long before the NATO coalition was sinking into a quagmire of Afghan hostility. Resentment of the U.S. occupation soon evolved into defiance of Hamid Karzai's corrupt government and a dramatic upsurge in popular support for the Taliban insurgency. The ambitions of the U.S.-led mission failed to take into account the deeply rooted religious traditions the Taliban represented in Afghan culture. While they are Muslim extremists, the Taliban have no ambitions for global terrorism, and Afghanistan is chronically plagued by insurgencies. Afghan society is conservative and profoundly misogynistic, and Afghans are fiercely independent and quick to take up arms against any foreign intervention. This is why the West has failed in its efforts to impose democracy on Afghanistan at the point of a gun.

There.

You could tell that story just about anywhere. You could tell it during Question Period in the House of Commons in Ottawa, at a union meeting in Manchester, in a *Toronto Star* column, or in a lecture at a university symposium in California. Nevertheless, each sentence in those two paragraphs contains an outright falsehood. Most contain at least two. What is at work here is not merely a matter of differing opinions, either.

Opinions are fine things to have, and none of us are without our biases. I have mine. We're all "embedded" in something, somehow, and while I make no grand claims upon the truth in these pages, I have written this book from the standpoint that evidence should matter to what we accept as the truth, and the truth should actually matter to what we believe. What we believe about Afghanistan determines the way we talk about Afghanistan, and whether we like it or not, the way we talk about Afghanistan determines to a great extent what happens in that country. It makes a difference.

In 2009, the University of Maryland's Program on International Policy Attitudes (PIPA) carried out a massive survey of public opinion in twenty countries around the world. The survey showed that most people thought Afghans wanted foreign troops out of their country—which wasn't true. But it made a world of difference: "Among those who believe that the Afghan people want NATO forces to leave, 76 percent say that NATO forces should leave," PIPA found. "Among those who believe that the Afghan people want NATO forces to stay, 83 percent say NATO forces should stay."

This book provides a glimpse of what Afghanistan has meant to Canadian soldiers engaged in the NATO effort in Afghanistan, but mainly I want to show something of what has been happening in the democratic spaces those soldiers have helped to open up. Some of the bravest people I've ever met live out there, and their courageous devotion to the values Westerners profess as their own would put most Westerners to shame. If I do my job well, you will see that Afghanistan is a country whose people are more worthy of our sacrifices and solidarity than you might have imagined. When you finish reading this book, maybe you won't think about Afghanistan in quite the same way you did when you started. Maybe you will think about some other things quite differently, too. But whatever we think or believe, to remain indifferent to objective truth is to submit to the "sealing-off of one part of the world from another" that George Orwell noticed all those years ago. It will only make it easier to cling to lunatic beliefs, and harder to know what is really happening, as the years pass.

So, to begin, I want to dispense with the Absurdistan that is set out in those two earlier paragraphs. There's some history that's important to get right, straight away, because if it's left upside down or sideways, nothing about Afghanistan will make any sense. What follows is how Absurdistan comes apart.

THERE IS NOTHING uniquely or hopelessly misogynistic about Afghan society. Afghan women have been no less enslaved than women elsewhere in the so-called Muslim world and, in the purdah tradition of the full-veil burqa, perhaps more noticeably. But by the late 1800s, Afghanistan was among the leading Muslim-majority countries in the cause of women's emancipation. By the 1920s, unveiled Afghan women were taking up posts as university professors and government ministers. By the 1970s, Afghan women were attending the theatre in Kabul and Kunduz, taking in the plays of Chekhov and Molière and Brecht, and they could look back on two generations of women who were university graduates, skilled-trades workers, judges, doctors, lawyers, teachers and senior government officials. When the Taliban swept into Kabul in 1996, 40 percent of the women there were holding down jobs; a third of the city's doctors, half of the university students and civil servants and most of the teachers were women. Afghan women have waged a valiant struggle, and their struggle continues. Their fight for equality has nothing to do with anything the West is trying to impose on them or on Afghan men.

The Taliban do not represent religious values that are deeply rooted in Afghan culture. You can inquire into their mumbo jumbo as closely as you want, and you will not find an

Islamic antecedent for it in Afghanistan. "Before the Taliban, Islamic extremism had never flourished in Afghanistan," notes Ahmed Rashid, the Pakistani journalist and author who is one of the few authorities on Taliban history. "The Taliban represented nobody but themselves and recognized no Islam except their own." In the nineteenth century, when the tyrannical amir Abdur Rahman was attempting to stoke jihadist xenophobia among Afghans, he appealed to the country's Muslim clerical council to condemn a mullah who had been preaching peaceful coexistence with Islam's Christian "brothers." The council defied the amir and refused to condemn the mullah. Twice.

It is untrue that Afghanistan is chronically plagued by insurgencies. "Afghanis do not want us in their country. They have been fighting this war or that since the beginning of time," declared a leaflet titled "Get Out of Afghanistan Now," distributed at the World Peace Forum at the University of British Columbia in 2006. The sentiment in this "left-wing" leaflet was echoed by Canada's Conservative prime minister Stephen Harper in 2009: "We are not going to ever defeat the insurgency. Afghanistan has probably had—my reading of Afghanistan history—it's probably had an insurgency forever, of some kind." But as Boston University anthropologist Thomas Barfield, author of *Afghanistan: A Cultural and Political History*, observes, if a bit too generally: "From 1929 to 1978, the country was completely at peace."

As for the origins of Afghanistan's most recent agonies, it is important to know that the United States was already funding Islamist forces in Afghanistan before the Soviet period, during the time of the mildly Moscow-friendly Daoud government. Further, in his 1996 memoir, former Central Intelligence Agency director Robert M. Gates disclosed that the American president who first armed Afghan Islamist groups against the communist regime that overthrew Daoud in 1978 was not Ronald Reagan, but Jimmy Carter, the peace-loving southerner. Carter's interventions began a full six months before Soviets soldiers poured across the border and a year and a half before Reagan's election.

The United States was by no means alone in funding anti-Soviet fighters in Afghanistan. Iran, China, Saudi Arabia, Pakistan's Inter-Services Intelligence (ISI) agency and uncounted numbers of oil-rich Arab privateers spent billions of dollars funding Afghan mujahideen armies through the 1980s. Still, for all the money they cost and the trouble they caused, the mujahideen never did manage to chase out the Russians. The Soviets' 1989 pullout was the culmination of a carefully planned, three-year phased withdrawal based on diplomatic, economic and military terms guaranteed by the White House. The withdrawal had little to do with Ronald Reagan's geostrategic genius, and nothing to do with the Afghans' legendary ferocity and cunning in warfare.

The U.S.-funded anti-Soviet mujahideen couldn't even manage to bring down the government the Soviets left behind in Kabul. By the time Soviet soldiers left Afghanistan, more than a million Afghans were dead and a third of the country's people lived in exile as refugees. The Afghan countryside was a moonscape of bomb craters. The country was littered with several million landmines. Human Rights Watch reckons that by the time of the Russian departure there were more small arms in Afghanistan than in Pakistan and India combined. Still, Mohammad Najibullah's reformist republic carried on quite competently for another three years after the Russian troops left, fending off assaults and mutinies from unreconstructed Stalinists and from mujahideen militias. Najibullah's government ended up outlasting the Soviet Union. When his regime collapsed in 1992, it was mainly because it ran out of gas. With Washington's quiet blessing, Moscow's proto-capitalist Russian Federation cut off all fuel shipments to Afghanistan and scuppered a UN-brokered transition plan Najibullah was in the middle of implementing, which was to have opened the way for a new multi-party Afghan state.

The long Afghan civil war that followed was mostly a bloody campaign of bombardment and massacre that Iran, Pakistan and Saudi Arabia waged by proxy armies almost wholly upon Kabul and its civilian population. Enflamed by the prospect of a sovereign Muslim democracy emerging in Afghanistan, each Islamist bloc competed with the other to be the first to capture the Afghan capital and sabotage the Peshawar Accord, the successor to Najibullah's aborted UN-brokered transition plan. The accord contained a two-year roadmap to the new Islamic State of Afghanistan and national elections, which were to be held in 1994. While incoming U.S. president Bill Clinton was famously playing his saxophone on the *Arsenio Hall Show,* Kabul was being turned into a human abattoir. The massacres that began in 1992 left three-quarters of Kabul's two million people dead, missing or wandering the roads as half-mad refugees.

The sociopathology of Talibanism is not attributable to a too-strict interpretation of the Quran. The Taliban arose in the 1990s from lowbrow madrassas in Pakistan where poor hill-country Pashtun boys were indoctrinated into a cargo-cult perversion of a debased form of Deobandism, which originated in India in the nineteenth century. (These same Pakistani madrassas were still churning out roughly 250,000 fanatics every year, ten years after September 11). The Deobandi-inspired doctrine the Taliban adopted was itself a corruption of an eighteenth-century Arab-supremacist Salafism, which asserts that Islam's glory days were in the ninth-century Arabian deserts, and it has all been downhill ever since.

Apart from the fighters in the Taliban ranks whose illiteracy rendered them incapable of reading the Quran in the first place, literate Taliban commanders would indeed resort to a Quranic lexicon when they issued death-by-stoning verdicts. The Quran was likely the only book they'd ever read. But nowhere does the Quran stipulate death by stoning as the punishment for any crime, and all that mattered in Taliban discipline was what the supreme leader Mullah Omar said. Omar was the Taliban führer-figure, the Amir al-Mu'minin, Commander of the Faithful. Omar's word was religious law, and for his followers, a proper Muslim was burdened by a religious duty to murder anyone who disobeyed Omar. The only consistency in the purportedly Islamic order Omar imposed on Afghanistan during the Taliban years was the cruelty of his rules and the sadism of the prescribed punishments for breaking them.

Despite their own boasts, the Taliban are not owed any credit for having been anti-Soviet holy warriors. Mullah Omar was once employed by a third-tier anti-Soviet mujahideen groupuscule, and any number of ageing Taliban soldiers-for-hire may once have been retained by the Pakistani ISI and paid with American money to fight the Soviets. But among the mercenary Taliban generals in bin Laden's circle were cold-eyed men who had been senior Afghan army officers in the Stalinist coup that took over Afghanistan in 1978. Some had served the Soviet-backed Afghan police state at the highest levels of command.

To trust the Taliban claim that they have no global ambitions, you'd have to forget that they were claiming the same back in the late 1990s. It's true that the Taliban have had a lot of the stuffing knocked out of them since September 11, 2001. But it was only about six years before September 11 that the Taliban began as a Pakistan-financed project to hijack Afghan sovereignty, and it quickly leveraged itself into a multinational joint venture and crime syndicate involving several foreign jihadist organizations, only one of which was al-Qaida. By the early months of 2001, China, Russia and all the Central Asian states were girding themselves for a renewed wave of terrorist attacks launched from Taliban-held Afghanistan. In the days leading up to September 11, Pakistan was still sending convoys of free supplies and armaments to camps in Taliban-controlled districts where thousands of Algerians, Yemenis, Turks, Palestinians, Lebanese, Filipinos, Jordanians, Uzbeks, Chechens and others were studying, training and preparing for their assignments in the Maghreb, the Levant, the Philippines, the Caucasus, Kashmir and beyond.

Afghanistan's so-called civil war did not come to an end because war-weary Afghans welcomed the Taliban. Most of the country was stable and at peace by the time the Taliban began their reign of terror in 1994. By then, the Saudi, Pakistani and Iranian proxy armies had fought each other to a standstill and had been collectively fought to a draw by the Northern Alliance forces of Ahmad Shah Massoud, who had remained loyal to the embryonic Islamic State of Afghanistan. Kandahar was a free-for-all of Pashtun gangsterism and internecine warlord feuding, but life in most of the tentatively constituted Islamic State of Afghanistan—Herat, Mazar-e Sharif, Hazarajat, Kunduz, the Shomali Plains, the Panjshir Valley and so on—was trundling along in a fairly orderly fashion before the Taliban showed up. The Taliban had to bomb, bribe and bully their way across Afghanistan. Christian Bleuer, a leading Afghanistan analyst with the Australian National University's Centre for Arab and Islamic Studies, has looked long and hard for evidence to support the fable of war-weary Afghans welcoming the Taliban. He hasn't found any, outside parts of the Pashtun belt, and neither has anyone else. "I call it a ridiculous lie," says Bleuer, "because the 'pre-Taliban chaos' myth is basically Pakistani ISI and Taliban propaganda."

The fiction that the Taliban eliminated opium production also originates in propaganda. The Taliban first claimed to have banned opium farming in 1997, but the UN Office on Drugs and Crime database shows an upward trend in Afghan opium production straight through the Taliban years. The Taliban ran profitable protection rackets in the transport and export of opium and heroin, and brought in more cash through their 10 percent *zakat* tax on farmers. The Taliban's July 2000 *fatwa* against opium farming accrued a measurable propaganda value; U.S. Drug Enforcement Administration data show an immediate surge in the price of stockpiled Afghan opium that year, from $44 a kilo to $350, and on a good day, $700. Whether that benefit was intentionally gained or not, the *fatwa* was especially cunning in the way it opened up a speculative stream of revenue from U.S. drug war coffers and lucrative UN Drug Control Program disbursements. The only year Afghan opium production actually fell was 2001, which was a rather busy year for the Taliban, as things turned out. But they were soon back in the drug trade. The Taliban subsidized their post-2001 mayhem not just with racketeering and strong-arm taxation but through the direct ownership and operation of heroin refineries.

Nor did the Taliban tackle corruption. They just monopolized it in the areas they controlled. Pashtun Taliban commanders stole thousands of non-Pashtun farms for themselves and their cronies. For the crime of not being Pashtun, tens of thousands of Afghans were robbed, dispossessed of their homes or simply put to death. The Taliban murdered aid workers, extorted enormous sums of money from international aid agencies and murdered and robbed each other. A bag of cash and the wink of an eye could often get you anything you wanted. You could buy a woman from the Taliban for as little as $100, but the price might depend on who you were. A wealthy Arab jihadist in Khost was reported to have paid $10,000 for a slave girl. In Parwan province alone, the Taliban captured hundreds of women to sell into the slave markets that supply Pakistani brothels.

As for the code of Pashtunwali that is so strict it binds Afghans to protect even guests like bin Laden (as its name suggests, this code applies to Afghanistan's minority Pashtuns, when it applies at all), it is a fiction that the Taliban were prepared to hand him over after September 11 if only evidence against him had been produced. Osama bin Laden had been Mullah Omar's most-valued partner in crime since 1996. By September 11, the Taliban had already laughed off numerous and elaborately detailed international warrants for bin Laden's arrest, not least an October 1999 demand from the UN Security Council. In the three years leading up to September 11, U.S. officials met with Omar's envoys and intermediaries more than twenty times in Bonn, Islamabad, Kandahar, New York, Tashkent and Washington.

The Taliban persisted in their refusal to give up bin Laden, but less than two weeks after al-Qaida had so dangerously enraged the Americans on September 11, the pantomime of Pashtunwali was dropped. The Pashtun-dominated religious council ruled: If the Americans want Osama, they can have Osama. The High Council of the Honourable Ulema met in

Kabul, uttered the usual high-pitched threats of jihad against any crusaders or infidels who were thinking about attacking Afghanistan and rendered their decision: Osama, please go; Mullah Omar, please make him go away. Mullah Omar said no.

It isn't true, in any conventional meaning of the term, that the United States or its NATO partners "invaded" Afghanistan. By September 11, there was no sovereign country left to invade. At the time, while the multinational jihadist joint venture known as the Taliban did control most of Afghanistan, Pakistan was the only country that formally recognized the regime. The only other countries that had ever recognized the Taliban as Afghanistan's government were the United Arab Emirates and Saudi Arabia, but they'd bailed long before September 11. Afghanistan's seat at the UN in New York was occupied by the Islamic State of Afghanistan, led by the Northern Alliance chief Berhanuddin Rabbani and the charismatic Ahmad Shah Massoud. They'd been pleading for military help for years. Immediately after September 11, even Pakistan was scrambling to give the appearance of disowning its Taliban progeny, and Rabbani's government was loudly reiterating its long-standing invitation to the Americans to help chase the Taliban out.

Strictly speaking, it isn't even true that the Taliban were overthrown by the United States, or by the United States and its NATO allies. The Northern Alliance would have remained dug in up in the mountains had it not been for a U.S. bombing campaign, American arms and supplies drops and all the Special Forces soldiers skulking around. But the Taliban, al-Qaida and their sundry jihadist brothers-in-arms had been driven out of Kabul by a ragtag assemblage of Afghans before any regular American troops arrived. The Taliban were even chased out of their legendary heartland of Kandahar by the locals before any U.S. combat troops showed up.

Neither is it true that the White House rallied NATO to America's side in Afghanistan. Immediately after September 11, the NATO countries invoked the all-for-one clause in the NATO charter. Washington only begrudgingly acknowledged the move and made it plain that NATO's help wasn't particularly wanted. As late as 2005, the United States was still only lukewarm to the idea of an expansion of the international military and reconstruction effort in the country.

The NATO coalition did not quickly sink into a quagmire of Afghan hostility. That happened neither quickly nor slowly, because it didn't happen at all. At least fourteen major national opinion polls and focus group surveys were undertaken by various independent agencies across Afghanistan in the decade following 2001. All the available data show unambiguous Afghan support for the so-called U.S. occupation of their country and for the military intervention overseen by the UN's poorly resourced, forty-three-nation NATO-led International Security Assistance Force (ISAF). The polls do show Afghans to be impatient about the paucity and ineffectiveness of American and NATO troops, however. The United States deployed a mere 7,000 troops to Afghanistan during the first two years after September 11—this was before the White House could use Iraq as an excuse—and almost all the U.S. troops in Afghanistan were dispatched in a "war on terror" exercise known as Operation Enduring Freedom, mostly in the country's remote southeastern borderlands. As late as the autumn of 2005, ISAF had extended its reach to only half of Afghanistan's 34 provinces, and there were only about 40,000 ISAF troops in the whole country. It took until 2009 for the combined ISAF troop strength to reach roughly 150,000.

Paul D. Miller, who served as Afghanistan director for the U.S. National Security Council from 2007 to 2009, put it this way: "The insurgency did not pick up steam until late 2005, and ISAF, which started changing its posture and strategy in late 2006, arguably did not implement a coherent counter-insurgency campaign until 2009. It would be myopic and irresponsible to conclude that the international community should walk away from the mission due to a lack of adequate progress. The greatest threat to long-term success in Afghanistan is not the Taliban, who are fairly weak compared to other insurgent movements around the world. It is the Afghan government's endemic weakness and the international community's failure to address it."

For all the persistent stories about rising Taliban popularity, by 2009 opinion surveys were finding no more than 4 percent of the Afghan people expressing support for the Taliban. Despite his weakness, his cronyism, the ballot stuffing that tainted his 2009 re-election and the corruption that undermined his government, President Hamid Karzai consistently enjoyed approval ratings that would cause any Western politician to writhe with envy. As late as 2009, 90 percent of Afghans reckoned Karzai's performance was excellent, good or fair. Afghan polling also showed consistent country-wide support for democracy, the right of girls to go to school and the rights of women to get an education, to work outside the home and to run for political office. Eighty-six percent of Afghans opposed polygamy. Eight years after September 11, 2001, in a poll conducted for the BBC and ABC News, the Afghan Center for Socio-Economic Research found that in spite of the great failures of the UN mission and the ISAF-led foreign forces in their country, only 2 percent of Afghans listed "foreign influence" as Afghanistan's biggest problem.

Seventy percent of respondents reckoned their country was still headed in the right direction.

It wasn't the West that was trying to impose anything on Afghanistan after September 11. The Americans took years to rethink the ruinous "we don't do nation-building" approach counselled by Secretary of State Donald Rumsfeld. Although American and NATO troops figured disproportionately in it, the UN's ISAF alliance included soldiers from Singapore, Malaysia, the United Arab Emirates, Jordan, Bosnia-Herzegovina, Georgia and Azerbaijan. By 2006, ISAF's marching orders were set out in the UN-backed Afghanistan Compact, authored by more than sixty countries, among them Bahrain, Brunei, Kuwait, Kyrgyzstan, Kazakhstan, Iran and quite a few others that don't show up in the usual rogues' gallery of Western imperialist puppet states.

There.

Subject Absurdistan's claims to scrutiny, and what you find is the opposite of evidence for a quagmire of hostile, irredeemably xenophobic and crazy misogynists chafing against attempts by the West to impose democracy on them at the point of a gun. You might also notice that Absurdistan invites a racist view of the Afghan people and absolves the rest of us from the responsibility of seeing in Afghans the fundamental human rights we ordinarily claim to recognize in one another. Absurdistan flatters the postures of the Western liberal nomenklatura and generally affirms the prejudices of conservatives. It says a lot more about "us" than it does about "them." The story Absurdistan presents might be powerful and seductive. But that still won't make it true.

ABDULRAHIM PARWANI, WHO visited Marefat High School with me in the spring of 2010, is someone from whom I've learned a lot. When we met back in 2006, he was a wiry, goateed and cerebral forty-two-year-old journalist working for free with a seat-of-the-pants outfit called Ariana TV, a program with Vancouver's M Channel that served the city's Afghan community. He was also a frequent contributor to a variety of Afghan- and Farsi-language journals, and was well known in Afghan, Iranian and Pakistani émigré circles. His wage work was a job with the federal government at Vancouver International Airport, helping newly arrived immigrants and refugees get themselves sorted out. On weekends, he was a pizza delivery driver. He'd settled in Canada only six years before we met, and he lived with his wife, Sima, and their daughters, Soraya, Maryam and Asma, on the outskirts of Vancouver in the neighbourhood where I'd grown up in my own immigrant family.

We'd both cut our teeth as journalists, Abdulrahim in Afghanistan and me in Canada, and by 2006 we'd both begun to question why the loudest Canadian debates about Afghanistan involved fairytales about Third World resistance to hegemonic American imperialism and the crimes of the Zionists. If we held anything in common to guide us in our inquiries, it was only a kind of a compass bearing, a way of knowing magnetic north. We were both "embedded" in the old-fashioned conviction that objective truth should matter to the way we make sense of the world around us. You could say we hit it off straight away. Abdulrahim had a knack of finding things to laugh about in the most melancholy circumstances, which also helped.

In some of the circles I moved in, it had become perfectly acceptable to refer to Canada's UN-mandated engagement in Afghanistan as complicity in an illegal war in aid of covertly helping American neoconservatives do the devil's work in

Fallujah. But the Afghan immigrants I knew were fully supportive of Canada's military engagement in Afghanistan. They had no time for the Islamists—the "political Islam" zealots who were always barking about Israel. They were all "progressive" Muslims, and they were proud Canadians, like Abdulrahim. To varying degrees, they were all perplexed by the masses of white people staging demonstrations to demand that Canada pull its soldiers from Afghanistan.

Abdulrahim and I ended up with a cross-section of Canadians in forming the Canada-Afghanistan Solidarity Committee. The group came together around the starting position that the UN wanted Canadians in Afghanistan, the Afghan people wanted us there and Canadian soldiers were necessary to the work required of us. It was going to be an uphill slog. In 2007, Canada came close to becoming the only NATO country to defy a UN-brokered Afghanistan consensus of more than sixty nations and bolt from what was then a thirty-nine-nation ISAF alliance. While Canadians boasted that unlike the Yanks, we were for "multilateralism," the House of Commons came a mere handful of votes from snubbing its nose at the UN Security Council and pulling Canadian troops from Afghanistan entirely.

That's how close Canada was to plunging headlong into what the otherwise scrupulously taciturn UN Secretary-General Ban Ki-Moon called "a misjudgement of historic proportions." It was dismaying enough that the rich world's disorientation had allowed the Taliban to regroup and relaunch a crusade of drug running, suicide bombing, aid-convoy hijacking, kidnapping and murder. "Almost more dismaying is the response of some outside Afghanistan," the UN secretary-general wrote, "who react by calling for a disengagement or the full withdrawal of international forces."

It was especially dismaying to Afghanistan's democrats, reformers and women's rights leaders. They had been counting on Canada, a wealthy liberal democracy with no history of overseas imperialist adventures and no hand in any of the invasions, betrayals and sabotage to which Afghanistan had been so cruelly subjected during the final decades of the twentieth century. And Canada was letting them down. It was in the effort to make sense of all this that Abdulrahim and I ended up in Afghanistan together.

One thing that took me a while to figure out—Abdulrahim isn't exactly the boastful type—was that he'd been something of a big deal in Afghanistan, back before the Taliban came. Having trained as an engineer in Moscow and graduated with a degree in ideological issues from the University of Marxism-Leninism at Volgograd, Abdulrahim was a devoted liberal democrat. He'd stuck it out in Afghanistan right up until the Taliban seized Kabul in 1996. Over the years, through all the sorrow he'd endured, Abdulrahim remained a loyal partisan of the great Ahmad Shah Massoud, scourge of the Red Army, the Taliban's worst nightmare, the "Lion of Panjshir," who was assassinated by an al-Qaida suicide bomb squad only two days before something came out of the sky above Manhattan on September 11, 2001. That's what you could call Abdulrahim's bias. I've written this book as a partisan in the cause of Afghanistan's democrats. That's my bias.

There may be readers of this book who will remain unshaken in a conviction that Western countries should not "interfere" in Afghanistan, and it's all too expensive anyway. Some readers may cleave to the wishful hope that the jihadists will confine their depravities and torments to the people of Afghanistan and leave the rest of us out of it. Some who do this may even be morally untroubled to find solace in such a wish. There may also be readers who will make it to the very last page and still prefer readings from Absurdistan, as though it were all just a matter of choosing one's favourite version from the competing hermeneutics and narratives within the discourse.

Everyone's entitled to their opinions, but if Abdulrahim and I ended up taking the delirium about Afghanistan a bit personally, we did so because the implications involved not just some unreal place that was a mere function of various and conflicting narratives. There is also a real country called Afghanistan, with real, living, breathing human beings, for whom the debates in Western countries could mean the difference between freedom and slavery, life and death. For me, it was also because the "misjudgment of historic proportions" involved the clamour for troop withdrawal.

What Irish historian Fred Halliday had to say about that aspect of things is especially unsettling to people who think of themselves as of "the Left," which is how I've always situated myself. Halliday's insight happens to have an overwhelming body of evidence in its favour, which is why it's all the more disturbing.

A keen observer of Afghan history, Halliday, who died on April 26, 2010, was a professor of international relations at the London School of Economics. He was competent in a dozen languages and the author of more than twenty books, most of them concerning political history in Muslim countries. Halliday paid close attention to the broad arcs of history, and he insisted that the so-called war in Afghanistan is properly situated in a direct line that originates in the anti-fascist struggles of the 1930s: "To my mind, Afghanistan is central to the history of the Left and to the history of the world since the 1980s. It is to the early 21st century, to the years we're now living through, what the Spanish Civil War was to Europe in the mid and late 20th century." One thing I hope to show in this book is that Halliday was, if anything, more right than he knew. If I've done my job properly, the evidence will speak for itself.

Another thing I hope to show is that the way we in the West talk about Afghanistan has meant more to the course of events in that country than all the soldiers and guns and money we've sent there since September 11. What we say matters. It will continue to matter for some long while. It determines what Afghans hear from us, how much they allow themselves to hope for a peaceful and democratic future and how far they're prepared to come from the shadows, out into the light.

two

THE CHILDREN OF SETH

CAIN SLEW ABEL. On that much the Torah and the Bible and the Quran agree, though in the Quran, these first sons of Adam and Eve are called Qabeel and Habeel. Qabeel wandered eastwards from Eden to the Land of Nod with a mark of some kind on him, a curse. His lineage came to nought, so it fell to his younger brother Shiith, known in the Bible as Seth, to be the settler, the farmer, the builder. Allah bestowed psalms upon Shiith, and Adam taught him the hours of prayer, bequeathed to him the duties of prophethood and further burdened him with the knowledge of the Great Flood that was to come. It is from Shiith Ibn Adam that all humankind today is said to descend. It is also said that Balkh, the "Mother of All Cities," as the first Arabs called it, a city once greater than Babylon and lovelier than Nineveh, is where Shiith died and was buried.

Balkh is now little more than a sleepy northern Afghan town of overgrown ruins, forgotten by the world. On market day, down lanes that wind through apple orchards and cherry orchards, merchants slowly make their way to the central bazaar, their wares teetering on donkey carts. The alleyways they follow traverse vine-covered tombs and shrines and zigzag across a series of mysterious, concentric roads that radiate outwards from the centre of town, just as much of the long, joyful and sorrowful story of human civilization radiates outwards from Balkh. It is a story sometimes celebrated and sometimes mourned, but always contested. It is not at that tomb near Babylon but here in Balkh that the prophet Ezekiel was buried, the locals will tell you. There are also Islamic scholars who insist that it was to Balkh, and not to Egypt, that the prophet Jeremiah fled.

What is without controversy is that the metropolis, which once sprawled across a fertile floodplain of the Oxus River, was one of the world's first cities. About 3,500 years ago, when a patriarch called Moses is said to have led a tribe of Seth's descendants out of the deserts of the Sinai Peninsula, another tribe of shepherds and pastoralists had already established a small kingdom at Balkh. We know that this tribe had crossed the Oxus River—the Amu Darya—from the north, centuries before. We know the language they spoke bloomed into dozens of languages from the Ganges to the Danube. About a billion people speak those tongues today, in an orchestral echo of Scythians, Hittites, Persians and scores of empires and dynasties forged down through time. Among these were the Timurids, the Mughals who ruled India before the British came, and the Achaemenid Empire of Cyrus the Great.

The hybrid Greco-Bactrian Kingdom that arose from the death of Alexander, the conquering Macedonian, was called the Kingdom of a Thousand Cities. Its capital was the city of Bactrus, also called Paktria, also called Balkh. The world's first emperor to be called sultan was Mahmud of Ghazni, grandson of a slave keeper from Balkh, conqueror of all of

what is now Afghanistan and Pakistan, most of Iran and
great swathes of northwestern India. It was here in Balkh in
1370 that Tamerlane crowned himself before setting off as
the Sword of Islam to slaughter and conquer from the Tigris
to the Volga. It was in Balkh that Aurangzeb, Conqueror of
the World, first held court. "In its heyday, Balkh was larger
than Paris, Rome, Beijing, or Delhi," says S. Frederick Starr,
a research professor with Johns Hopkins University's School
of Advanced International Studies. "Like all the great regional
centers, it had running water, baths, and majestic palaces."

The heart of Balkh nowadays is a jumble of pleasantly
unkempt gardens where old men sit on park benches or lounge
under trees on ratty blankets playing chess. Women haggle
with spice vendors in the shadow of the towering, blue-domed
mausoleum of the Sufi philosopher-prince Khwaja Abu Nasr
Parsa, whose shrine was built in the late fifteenth century by
the sultan Husayn Bayqarah, Tamerlane's great-great-grand-
son. But there is nothing of Tamerlane's bloody glory here
now. Balkh is one of the world's great cradles of empire, but
there are no interpretive centres, no splendid museums and no
fleets of tour buses. There aren't even any stores that sell gar-
ish souvenirs.

In the older Persian epics, the first man was not Adam, but
Kayumars, who built his kingdom at Bakhdhi, which is the
name for Balkh in the *Hymns of Zarathustra*. It was in Balkh,
they say, that Zarathustra, the Zoroastrian Moses, first
preached his revelations. It was here that some say he died,
about 2,700 years ago. Seven centuries later, during the reign
of the Kushan kings, Balkh was second only to Rajagriha
as Buddhism's most holy place on earth. Monks from as far
away as Ceylon made pilgrimages here. Sombre historians and
Muslim scholars still quarrel about the dynastic Barmakids

of Balkh, who went on to become courtiers, viziers and warriors for the Abbasid caliphs of Baghdad. Khalid ibn Barmak even ended up as the governor of Mesopotamia. But were the Barmakids Muslim converts from Zoroastrianism or from Buddhism? It's hard to say.

Within the remnants of an old ring of walls that encloses Balkh and its surroundings to a length of about ten kilometres, the scatterings of Zoroastrian fire temples clutter gardens and pastures amid the detritus of Buddhist stupas, convents and monasteries. The townspeople sometimes engage in spirited quarrels over tea at the bazaar about which ruin is Zoroastrian and which is Buddhist, and in those debates, both sides can be right. Down through time, Zoroastrians and Buddhists took converts from each other and stole or traded temples and shrines. When Islam came along, the custom carried on. It's rare to come across a Muslim shrine here that cannot claim a pedigree dating back to some earlier holy site.

From the seventh to the thirteenth centuries, Balkh was also an epicentre of the Nestorian Church. Its schismatics had been driven east after Rome declared them heretics at the Council of Ephesus in 431. Nestorian missionaries from Balkh travelled far and wide, and it was the Nestorian Church that introduced Christianity to China during the enlightened years of the Tang Dynasty. Their churches flourished as far east as Canton until the fourteenth century, when the Ming Dynasty chose to purge "foreign influences" and even to erase their legacy from China's memory. But history is not so easily disappeared. The story of how the Chinese Nestorian Church was founded is inscribed upon a massive eighth-century stone tablet that was buried near the Chongren Buddhist monastery at the Silk Road's eastern terminus at what is now Xi'an, the resting place of the famous Terracotta Army. The tablet was

lost to the world until the seventeenth century. At the base of
the monument, the identity of the man who commissioned
the work in 781 is revealed, in Syriac script: "The Lord Jazed-
buzid, Priest and Vicar-episcopal of Cumdan, the royal city,
son of the enlightened Mailas, Priest of Balkh."

Long before the European Enlightenment, there was Hiwi
al-Balkhi, also known as Hiwi the Heretic. He was a ninth-
century Jewish contrarian who busied himself composing
more than two hundred rationalist objections to the miracles
of Hebrew scripture. Little remains of his effort except some
fragments of text and the rousing controversies he set off in
the writings of Jewish scholars from Babylon to Andalusia.
Hiwi was also a poet—Balkh is renowned for its poets—and
his work may have been the first to employ Hebrew verse for
purposes beyond its sacred function in the synagogue. Balkh's
Jewish quarter persisted for ten centuries after Hiwi. The people were weavers, gardeners and merchants. After the Arabs
came, the Jews were obliged to pay a special tax, like all non-
Muslims, but they were outwardly much like everybody else,
except that they were wine-drinking monogamists who liked
to wear conical fur hats. The Jews were gone by the 1930s, but
the Jewish quarter is still remembered in Balkh by the name
of the neighbourhood Jehodanak: the Town of the Jews.

A century after Hiwi there was Ibn Sina, the Prince of
Physicians. A polymathic genius from a Balkh Ismaili family, Ibn Sina was known to medieval Europe as Avicenna, and
is still known to modern scientists as "the father of modern
medicine." Among Roman Catholic historians, Ibn Sina is
known for his profound influence on Catholicism's founda-
tional theologian, Thomas Aquinas. Among philosophers,
Ibn Sina is perhaps best remembered for his critique of Aris-
totelian metaphysics. Otherwise forgotten are Ibn Sina's

numerous pioneering texts on geology, paleontology, astronomy and physics.

A century after Ibn Sina, Balkh was a teeming city of perhaps 200,000 people when the eleventh-century poet Omar Khayyam was a schoolboy here. His classic *Rubaiyat* was unknown to the English-speaking world until the 1800s. In Khayyam's day, Balkh was still a city of Persians, Turks and Chinese, who practised Hinduism, Christianity, Buddhism, Judaism, Islam and Zoroastrianism. Their leavings are a muddle, and it doesn't help that no one has ever undertaken a systematic archaeological survey of the place. UNESCO scientists have placed Balkh on their wish list of world heritage sites. It easily ranks with Angkor Wat or Tenochtitlán or Petra. You've probably heard of those places. Chances are you've never heard of Balkh. Don't be hard on yourself.

In the frightening country called Afghanistan that we hear about in the West, Balkh cannot exist. That country is the "graveyard of empires." The real Afghanistan is the womb of empires. Even in its blighted twenty-first-century form, Afghanistan is a concoction of at least a half-dozen major ethnic groups and more than thirty languages from long-lost civilizations loosely contained within the shrivelled remnant of the Durrani Empire, the eighteenth-century Pashtun imperialism that supplanted the ancient Turk, Mongol and Persian dynasties. The Durrani Pashtuns came from Kandahar, and it was they who first imposed "Afghanistan" upon the maps of the world. The Durrani Empire once covered a vast realm, from the Amu Darya to the Arabian Sea, and from the Iranian Khorasan to Delhi. In the upheavals of the Durranis' long and grisly history of conquest, the child's-play imperialism of the nineteenth-century Anglo-Afghan wars barely rates as a footnote.

But Balkh does exist. It is situated in the real country of Afghanistan. It is a small town in a big province that is also called Balkh, and in the summer of 2010, in the place where the Taliban throat slitters are supposed to be, children lead flocks of goats through groves of pistachio. Instead of the vast plantations of opium we always hear about, there's wheat, barley, flax and cow pasture, though here and there, you might notice a plot of cannabis. Eccentric, long-haired malangs, decked out in garlands of plastic flowers, amuse passersby with their poems and their hashish-induced visions of Islam's elysian afterlife. Stroll through Balkh around noon, and you come upon families gathered in copses of mulberry and Oriental plane trees for their midday meals of cherries and naan and melons. They will notice straight away that you are some sort of *kafir* from a faraway country. They smile and wave hello. *Salaam.* The word does not mean "war."

For some reason, there is neither a tomb of Zarathustra in Balkh, nor a grand shrine of Kayumars, the Persian Adam, but there is a particular tumulus that everyone swears is the tomb of Seth, Shiith Ibn Adam. It is situated on the outskirts of town, embedded within a strange outcropping of clay and surrounded by a cheek-by-jowl amalgam of derelict mud-walled huts. The little tomb complex is painted sky blue and adorned with tattered green flags that flutter in the breeze. The crypt itself is open to the heavens, but it is covered by an unlikely shroud of green tarpaulin. Under a thatched roof at the entrance, an old man with a long white beard sits cross-legged behind a low bench, and he will take coins in exchange for holy cards, mementos and verses from the Quran written on little scraps of paper. Saddled horses doze in a grove of great-crowned chenar trees nearby.

Across an open field, arising from a hardscrabble plain, there is what appears to be a long ridge of steep cliffs climbing to a plateau. But once you've made your way through a ravine, you see that you've come through one of the ancient gates of the old city's fortress, the Bala Hissar, and the cliffs are in fact the old fortress walls. Inside the fortress, a hollow expanse of goat pasture forms a nearly perfect circle more than a kilometre across. The Bala Hissar was sacked and ruined by Genghis Khan in 1220. The walls were built up again by the Timurids, who also built a grand citadel and a splendid mosque within. But there's nothing left now except scattered shards of pottery and the sad little tomb of some long-forgotten warrior where a family of nomadic Kuchis has made a home, with a small garden, in the shade of some scrubby trees around a burbling spring.

From atop the Bala Hissar's northern walls, six storeys high, you can look out on a prairie that fades into the horizon. A chaotic eruption of ragged clay hills in the middle distance is all that remains of the Buddhist monastery and university of Nava Vihara. It had been flourishing for dozens of generations by the time the Henan scholar and traveller Xuanzang visited in the seventh century. He arrived in Balkh at the close of an epoch, just a few short years before the Arab conquest brought Bactria within the Muslim orbit of the Umayyad caliphate of Damascus. Centuries before the Arabs came, camel trains were making their way to and from Balkh carrying furs and silks and precious gems from China, spices and perfumes from India, curiosities from Byzantium, frankincense and silver from Persia and wine from the Roman Empire. Down through the years, the Silk Road also brought ideas, slaves, arguments, discoveries and pilgrims from Isfahan and Lhasa, Samarkand and Athens, Xinjiang and Persepolis. Xuanzang found Nava Vihara teeming with scholars and pilgrims, its grand statues of the Buddha glittering with jewels. A dome-topped stupa stood twenty storeys high. Centuries after Islam laid its late-seventh-century foundations in Balkh, Nava Vihara was still thriving as Navbahar, a place of Buddhist worship and study.

That summer of 2010, I was standing on the Bala Hissar's crumbling walls with Abdulrahim Parwani. We were looking out on the sad remnants of Navbahar, when he turned to me with a melancholy look. "There was even a barbershop," he said. I noticed a bit of a gleam in his eye. Earlier, back in the town, Abdulrahim had been fondly remembering a barbershop from his boyhood days here. He couldn't seem to recall where it was exactly, no matter how much he racked his brains. "I guess it's gone, too," he said sadly. Then he laughed out loud.

One of the most important things Abdulrahim taught me about Afghanistan is that it helps to keep your sense of humour. When I stepped into a slurry-filled ditch one day in Kabul after I mistook its dust-thick surface for the hard ground of a footpath, I was left with septic goo up to my knees. He laughed. Then he somehow got me to laugh along with him. The next day, it was my turn. A bright blue bruise had erupted right in the middle of his forehead. He'd been kneeling and bowing in the Muslim way of praying, except his head had missed the prayer mat and hit the cement floor a few times. I laughed at him, and he laughed with me.

We'd come to Balkh together almost as an afterthought, and mostly by luck. It had been three years since the two of us had signed on as founding members of the Canada-Afghanistan Solidarity Committee, and Canada was still showing every willingness to wash its hands of Afghanistan.

We'd been invited to Mazar-e Sharif, the boisterous capital of Balkh province, to look into an idea that had been making the rounds of Toronto's Afghan-Canadian community. Babur Mawladin, the Solidarity Committee's Toronto president, was especially enlivened by it. He'd already talked about it with Balkh's no-nonsense governor, Mohammad Atta Noor, who was just as enthusiastic.

The idea was fairly straightforward. After the parliamentary paralysis that brought Canada within a few votes of entirely withdrawing its troops from the UN's ISAF coalition in Afghanistan in 2007, Canada's minority Conservative government handed off the file to an independent panel headed up by former Liberal foreign minister John Manley. The Manley panel recommended extending the Canadian Forces' battle group duties in Kandahar to the summer of 2011, after which the soldiers were to be pulled from Kandahar. The Solidarity Committee had few objections to that. Barack Obama had ascended to the White House partly on his pledge to take Afghanistan seriously, and he'd promised a major troop "surge" in the south. He'd come through. Canadian soldiers had spent four years doing brave work rousting brigands in Kandahar's treacherous Taliban strongholds. We could let the Americans worry about that now. Maybe Canada could set up a new provincial reconstruction team in Balkh instead. The Canadian Forces could make use of itself, too, training up the local military and police.

Go north. It was a faint hope, all things considered, but worth looking into. Abdulrahim and I had arranged to meet various provincial officials, academics, human rights activists and journalists in Mazar-e Sharif. We were curious to hear what they had to say.

I'd told Abdulrahim that if we had a bit of spare time, I

wanted to see something of the fabled city of Balkh. It was the hometown of the great Mawlana Jalaluddin Balkhi, the thirteenth-century Sufi mystic and poet known to the English-speaking world as Rumi and commonly described as the greatest poet Islam has ever produced. I'd heard that the school Rumi first attended was still standing. Balkh was only a short drive from Mazar, the roads were mostly paved and we could hire a rattletrap cab for the morning. We really should see the place, I'd said. It was only then that I learned Abdulrahim had spent some of his early childhood in Balkh. He remembered playing in the shadow of the ancient walls. When the rains came, the children of Balkh would carefully reconnoitre the ground along the base of the walls, because a good downpour would sometimes dislodge old coins from some ancient realm. A handful had come into Abdulrahim's possession this way. So yes, of course, we must try to get to Balkh, he'd said.

We'd intended to meet Governor Noor, but he'd been called away on some last-minute emergency shortly before we arrived at Mazar's desolate and decrepit airport. So we had an opening in our schedule, and instead of having to hire a motor rickshaw or something to take us out to the fabled capital of the Kingdom of a Thousand Cities, we ended up travelling in the company of Colonel Asif Brumand, a bald, stocky and always beaming professor of medicine, a confidant of the governor. The colonel greeted us in Mazar in camouflage fatigues, packing a heavy sidearm. He introduced us to his friend Farid Ahmad, a tall and somewhat distracted mujahideen veteran who appeared to have been conscripted to our service because he owned a functioning Toyota Land Cruiser. Colonel Brumand informed us that the district police chief in Balkh happened to be an old acquaintance, who would be pleased to have us in for tea at the Balkh police station.

We piled into Farid's Land Cruiser and headed out of town escorted by two Ford Rangers, one carrying four heavily armed members of the Afghan National Police (ANP) and the other carrying an equal number of similarly equipped members of the Afghan National Army (ANA). Farid himself sported a brace of pistols underneath his loose-fitting kameez. This was not the way that Abdulrahim and I usually got around, and it certainly wasn't necessary for our security, but the governor's office apparently considered it necessary to Afghan hospitality. The young police officers and soldiers in our escort seemed perfectly happy to have the lark of a morning out in the country, besides. "They are good men," Farid confided on the drive out to Balkh, "but if the people around here see any Taliban, they will just attack them and kill them themselves."

When we got to Balkh, Police Chief Wahdood treated us to the customary and affectionately solicitous Afghan ritual of tea, almonds, apples, melons and toffees. Actually, there is not always much police work to do, Wahdood confessed. With a staff of 90 and a sprawling district of only 150,000 people, his biggest headaches were disputes over title deeds, water rights, property lines and all the other minor tumults you'd expect from the steady trickle of families returning after long years of exile in Iran and Pakistan. I mentioned that the bucolic scenery on the road to Balkh seemed punctuated by an exceptional quantity of the rusting hulks of broken Russian tanks that you see elsewhere in Afghanistan. This caused Colonel Brumand and Chief Wahdood to fall into reveries about the old times. As the conversation turned to politics and pleasant gossip about provincial affairs, Abdulrahim and I wandered off in the company of Sali Mohammad, chief of the Balkh District Criminal Investigations Division, who seemed to have some time on his hands.

A smiling and slightly built man in civilian clothes, Sali ambled along with us through Balkh's central gardens until we came to a nondescript rectangular stone edifice, a shrine of some kind. "Yes, this is Rabi'a Balkhi," Abdulrahim said happily. The locals say this is the very place where the ninth-century princess-poet was cruelly imprisoned and died, Abdulrahim explained. The poems attributed to Rabi'a are of a distinctly erotic tone, inspired by her lovemaking with a palace slave named Baktash. As the story goes, when Rabi'a's courtings came to light, her enraged brother imprisoned her in this dungeon. Heartbroken but defiant, she slashed her wrists and wrote poems to her beloved Baktash in her own blood, and thus the dungeon became her tomb. For more than a thousand years, the lovestruck young women of Bactria, Persia, Khorasan and all the other empires and nation-states that have come and gone in their places have offered up their devotions to Rabi'a, entrusting her with their sighs and their longings.

Sali took a key from a caretaker and unlocked a low barred window that opened into a subterranean crypt. We peered inside a dark chamber containing a grand blue-tiled sarcophagus covered in a tattered green blanket. After Abdulrahim and I had squeezed through the window's narrow opening and stepped down into the tomb, two young women descended into the darkness, paid their whispered respects to Rabi'a, covered their shy smiles behind their veils and climbed quickly back out into the light. "There was a tunnel," Abdulrahim said, dimly remembering a story from his childhood about a tunnel that led from the tomb to the Bala Hissar, two kilometres distant. He shrugged and laughed.

We were soon on our rounds of Balkh in Farid's white Land Cruiser, with the ANA and the ANP in their green Ford

Rangers and children running along the dusty roads behind us. After only a few minutes, we were winding our way through a hive of narrow orchard lanes, and then there it was, like some giant, forlorn sandcastle, abandoned to the tides and falling apart: the *khanaqa* where the young Rumi had studied as a boy. It was the same Sufi madrassa where Rumi's renowned father, Baha al-Din Walad, had taught, eight centuries ago, in the last days before the Mongol armies swept through and the shadows fell again.

The original structure was still evident in some high arches and collapsed domes, but other than that, it was just a mound. There was some evidence of a recent and rudimentary archaeological inventory. Kabul had little enthusiasm and less in the way of resources to take care of the place. Ankara and Tehran were squabbling over the rights to restore, protect and interpret Rumi's ruin, but because of some arcane disagreement, work had stalled. It was probably just as well.

Some boys were tending a herd of goats nearby, and we managed to coax one of the boys to approach us. From Farid, I learned that his name was Sher Khan and he was seven years old. He was shy at first, but then he took me by a sleeve and guided me up into the mound, instructing me with words and gesticulations I couldn't comprehend. Some of the other boys joined us. They scrambled up and down through collapsed passageways and alcoves and then stood silently with me, gazing up at the gently curved and half-vanished arches as though they were as astonished by the marvel of the place as I was.

As the story goes, the splendid Sufi boys' school of Rumi's childhood was destroyed by Genghis Khan. At that moment in history, the splendour of Balkh is said to have begun its long eclipse. A malaria epidemic that swept through the countryside and a flood that caused the Amu Darya to change its course away from Balkh are said to account for the city's final withering at the close of the nineteenth century. By then, Mazar-e Sharif had displaced Balkh as the provincial administrative centre and locus of commerce and livelihood. But there was more to Balkh's death than that.

There is also much more to the burial of Balkh's great palaces and the forgetting of certain ancient Persian shrines. That story, too, involves an empire, one that was supposed to last a thousand years. It's what those concentric rings of roadwork radiating outwards from the centre of town were all about. They weren't ancient at all.

Go grubbing around in Quranic texts or CIA plots for the origins of Talibanism, and you come up empty. Look to the evidence of history, and you come across a network of wellworn roads that run back through time. Most of them peter out in the deserts and the mountains, but one of them forms a straight line back to a virulent Pashtun chauvinism that erupted in the years when the Pashtun royalty was propping itself up with military, financial, cultural and ideological support from the Third Reich. The lash of ethnic cleansing and cultural obliteration that the Taliban wielded to scourge Afghans in the 1990s was first put to the backs of the people of Balkh sixty years before, with Nazi Germany providing the guns, money, technical wherewithal and revisionist propaganda that Pakistan's ISI would so generously provide the Taliban all those years later.

For the past 175 years or so, Afghanistan's emirs, kings, shahs, mullahs and presidents have always had to rely on foreign stipends, subsidies, tributes or other such financial life supports from some foreign power, somewhere. By the early 1930s, the German colony in Kabul was the largest foreign enclave in Afghanistan, and German master-race theorists had convinced themselves and their Afghan hosts that they had discovered in Balkh the ancient Germanic "cradle of Aryanism." The Afghan government's *Almanac of Kabul* of 1933 begins with an essay entitled "The Race of the Afghans," which claims Balkh as "the cradle where our nation was nurtured, even more, of the Aryan race." The ring roads radiating from the city were laid down according to Nazi inspiration and an imagined Aryan history that required Balkh province to be cleansed of its Jews by an edict of the kingdom and the ancient city of Balkh to be emptied of its non-Pashtun inhabitants by decree of the king's interior minister, Mohammad Gul Khan Momand. The young British art critic and historian Robert Byron happened to have lunch with Momand during a visit to Balkh in 1934. Although he did not know it at the time, Byron had already encountered Momand's handiwork, several days earlier. On the road to Balkh, Byron had seen a caravan of hundreds of Balkhi Jews, travelling in the opposite direction, fleeing to Herat.

The ring roadwork, the purgings and the deportations began in earnest that year. The destruction did not require obliteration on the scale of the Taliban bombing of the ancient Bamiyan Buddhas during the late 1990s. But anything in Balkh that stood too obviously as a rebuke to the new Aryan version of ancient Afghan history was bulldozed or reinvented to represent the ruins of something else.

During the 1930s, Momand was known to British intelligence as a fanatical devotee of "Pashtunization"—the imposition of the Pashto language in all government transactions, the erasure of non-Pashtun cultural influences from the affairs of state, the marginalization of non-Pashtun Afghans and the mass resettlement of Pashtuns in the Tajik, Hazara, Uzbek and Turkmen regions of the country's north. To the people of Balkh, Momand was known as "the second Geng-his Khan." According to Tajik historian Akhror Mukhtarov, author of *Balkh in the Late Middle Ages*, "The last significant changes in the fortunes of the city were tied to the uproot-ing of the indigenous inhabitants of Balkh and the influx of a Pashto-speaking population ... simultaneously, he [Momand] took steps to ensure that existing monuments and grave mark-ers provided no reminder that anyone other than Pashtuns had ever lived in the city."

Historian Robert D. McChesney of New York Universi-ty's Department of Middle Eastern and Islamic Studies has paid close attention to "the susceptibility of monumental com-memorative structures to reinterpretation and consequent renovation." The stories accounting for the origins of Balkh's monuments proved acutely vulnerable to revisionism during the tenure of Momand, McChesney observes. Momand was a principal figure among the Pashtun elite, with whom the notion of a German-Pashtun kinship arising from a shared, imaginary Aryan origin found a particularly "warm recep-tion." Their affections did not go unrequited. "In those years, the idea of a superior Aryan race was growing out of the anti-semitism at the heart of the National-Socialist movement in post-war Germany, and because of it, German diplomats and scholars had come to see a kinship between themselves and the Afghans as Aryans," McChesney writes. "Promoting Ary-anism literally took a more concrete form in the decision to build a new Balkh."

The Abu Nasr Parsa shrine and its surrounding gardens were to form the epicentre of a grand new city, with straight roads leading from its heart and circular roads emanating out-wards as well, reminiscent of Washington, D.C., or Paris. The Abu Nasr Parsa shrine had served generations of Balkhis as a necropolis, surrounded by the precincts of a lively and welcoming Sufi madrassa. Momand obliterated everything but the shrine's core and re-imagined it as an exemplary artifact of Aryan architecture, "the focal point of Aryan dreams," as McChesney puts it.

The Afghan-Nazi relationship was sufficiently cozy that by 1936, the Reich had agreed to provide Afghanistan's twenty-two-year-old Pashtun king, Zahir Shah, with military supplies worth 15 million deutsche marks. German military specialists took on a mentoring role for the Afghan army. By 1937, Lufthansa was running regular flights between Berlin and Kabul, and it wasn't just Afghanistan that got swept up in the Nazi orbit. In February 1941, the German consulate in Tehran was pleased to report: "Throughout the country spiritual leaders are coming out and saying that 'the twelfth imam [akin to the Judeo-Christian notion of the messiah] has been sent into the world by God in the form of Adolf Hitler'. . . One way to promote this trend is sharply to emphasize Muhammed's struggle against the Jews in the olden days and that of the Führer today."

The Second World War brought an end to direct Nazi influence in Afghanistan and to Balkh's reinvention as the birthplace of the Aryan race. At least two thousand Afghan Jews had managed to evade the deportations of 1934, and many of Balkh's original families eventually managed to return to their homes and their farms. Still, the 1930s-era effort to manufacture an Aryan Absurdistan can explain why the people of Balkh differ among themselves about the provenance of so many of the ruins, shrines and tombs that distinguish their little town.

Interior Minister Mohammad Gul Khan Momand is still remembered in some Afghan circles as a great statesman and

Afghan patriot. The Pashtun chauvinism he nurtured during his tenure has unambiguously lived on. It is impossible to be certain in the absence of a proper census, but Pashtuns appear to make up somewhere between a third and a half of the Afghan population. Even so, Pashtun master-race delusions persist in the commonplace, reactionary notion that the Pashtuns are the only "pure" Afghans and are consequently entitled by their ethnicity to govern the country. Pashtun chauvinists educated in Nazi universities remained in the most intimate corridors of power in Afghanistan well into the 1960s. Afghan journalist Soraab Balkhi takes the point further, pointing to the "crypto-fascist" Afghan Mellat Party, which purports to be a kind of Afghan social-democratic party. The Afghan Mellat, founded in 1966 by the Nazi-educated Pashtun chauvinist Ghulam Farhad, persisted into the twenty-first century as a force in President Hamid Karzai's Pashtun-dominated inner circle. "The party itself had gone through many changes, but has always kept the same imperious, self-serving goals," Balkhi writes.

The Taliban are a Pashtun phenomenon, though to leave it at that would be woefully imprecise and invite slander against the Pashtun people. Neither are the Taliban merely a function of the Pashtun elite's encounters with the Nazis—Talibanism is sufficiently grotesque without having to bring European fascists into it. But it does warrant attention that the Taliban and their Islamist contemporaries—Hamas, the Muslim Brotherhood, the Iranian Khomeinists and so on—have antecedents distinguished by an admiration for and often open collaboration with European fascism. North Americans may recoil from "clerical fascists" as a descriptive term for the Taliban. For many Afghans, however, it is completely without controversy that the Taliban years resembled nothing so much as the state-sanctioned purges, pogroms and expulsions visited upon Afghanistan's Shia Muslims, Hazaras, Tajiks and Jews during the 1930s.

When the Taliban swept through Balkh in the 1990s, it was as though Mohammad Gul Khan Momand had returned a second time and Genghis Khan a third time. As always with the bloodletting Afghanistan's various late-twentieth-century militias and armed groups exacted from each other, it is worthwhile noting that "atrocities were committed on all sides." The Northern Alliance carried out at least one mass execution of captured Taliban soldiers. But nothing was equivalent to the genocidal bloodshed the Taliban visited upon the non-Pashtun civilians of the country's north during the years and months leading up to September 11, 2001.

One bloodbath, the subject of a Human Rights Watch investigation, was the August 1998 Taliban takeover of Mazar-e Sharif. The Human Rights Watch preliminary report, gleaned from the accounts of witnesses who fled the slaughter, describes a "killing frenzy" that began with the Taliban (comprising Pashtun, Arab, Pakistani and Chechen fighters) shooting "anything that moved." The Taliban next turned their attention to the city's Shia Muslims; men who could not recite Sunni prayers on demand were either shot or rounded up for transportation to concentration camps. Taliban commander Maulawi Hanif then declared that the time had come to "exterminate" the city's Hazaras. "During the house-to-house searches, scores and perhaps hundreds of Hazara men and boys were summarily executed," the initial report found. A later UN investigation estimated that eight thousand people were murdered in this way over a two-month period. The Hazaras tried to flee the city, but thousands were caught. Men and boys had their throats slit like sheep in front of their families. The Hazara women and girls who were allowed to live were raped and enslaved.

Just as Momand had set about the work of obliterating Balkh's rich cultural legacy and replacing it with an invented history, the Taliban banned the ancient Nowruz celebrations that had made Mazar famous throughout the former Persian realms. The same obscene "peace" that prevailed under Taliban rule elsewhere in Afghanistan fell like a dark shadow upon Mazar. Ride a bicycle with your husband or wife: a beating. If you're a woman, and your footsteps can be heard when you walk down the street: a beating. If your husband says you are an adulteress: burial up to the waist, stoning to death by a crowd. You are said to be a homosexual: death by having a wall toppled over on you. The keeping of caged birds is against Islam because a bird might sing. No television sets allowed, no photography allowed, no card games, no chess playing, no music, no kite flying, no movies. Beards must be regulation length. No Western-style trousers permitted. If a woman lives in your house, you must paint over your windows. Shia Islam is apostasy. Debate is heresy. Doubt is sin.

History was repeating itself, and while it is sometimes said that history's tragedies are repeated as farce, they do recur now and again as tragedy. But history is shadows and light, too. Sometimes its course is determined by dreams, and it is a dream that explains the breathtaking, heart-stopping beauty of the Shrine of Hezrat Ali in Mazar-e Sharif. The dream came to a Balkhi imam in the twelfth century, during the time of the Seljuk Empire, a Europe-sized Sunni domain that reached at its apogee from the Persian Gulf to the Caspian Sea and from the Aral Sea to the Aegean Sea. There was a legend that the body of Hezrat Ali, son-in-law of the Prophet Mohammed, did not lie in glorious repose at Najaf, near

Baghdad, but rather in some distant place. As the story went, Ali's corpse had been spirited away from Najaf by his followers, who were concerned that it would be desecrated there. Ali's remains were carried for weeks on the back of a white camel until the beast came to rest. The Balkhi imam dreamed that an old crypt on the plains to the east of Balkh was not a Zoroastrian tomb at all—and so not merely a fitting place for pre-Islamic Nowruz rituals—but rather the final resting place of Ali himself.

The Seljuk sultan Sanjar took the dream as divine direction and built a grand shrine around the crypt. The shrine was destroyed by Genghis Khan, but three centuries later, the Timurids restored it in the most extravagant style. That's how it came to pass that Mazar is now Afghanistan's third-largest city, a pilgrimage place for Sunni and Shia Muslims during the annual Nowruz festival. The city's heart is a splendid blue-tiled, twin-domed mosque, the Tomb of the Exalted, enlivened by the flurries of hundreds of white doves.

It was only a few blocks from the Shrine of Hezrat Ali that Abdulrahim Parwani and I ended up meeting with several "civil society" leaders from Balkh. We wanted to know what they thought about the talk of shifting Canada's efforts in Afghanistan from Kandahar province to Balkh province and its capital city. We heard from Nasima Azkiwa of the Balkh Civil Society and Human Rights Network; Ayatollah Jawed of the Afghanistan Independent Human Rights Commission; Rajab Ibrahimi of the Afghanistan Civil Society Organization; Arzoo Aby, the coordinator of the Mazar-e Sharif Youth Cultural Network; and some Mazar journalists. It was as though the question didn't even need to be asked. Of course Canada should come north, everyone said.

The Swedes were running the Balkh Provincial

Reconstruction Team, and while they were appreciated, they were regarded as parsimonious, timid and bureaucratic. The Germans were handling most of Balkh's International Security Assistance Force duties, and they were all right. But Canada was seen as a particularly significant and aggressive ISAF contributor. Unlike the Germans or the British, Canada had no imperialist history. Unlike the United States, Canada didn't carry all that Pakistan-ally baggage around. We didn't bring any baggage at all. It was Canadians who would have to be convinced of the idea's merits, everyone said, not the people or the government of Balkh.

In the cool of an evening, our hosts joined Abdulrahim and me on a stroll around the grand plaza of the Shrine of Hezrat Ali. Accompanying us was a young journalist who asked that I not mention his name. "There are still Zoroastrian families here, you know," he said. "They changed their names to Muslim names a long time ago. I have been to their ceremonies, and they are very beautiful." In the first years after the Taliban were driven from Mazar, the Zoroastrian families had thought about coming out into the light. "But not anymore, not now, anyway," the young journalist said. "I can't write this for the newspapers here. I can't write about religious things."

The subject had come up as we were talking about Mazar's strengths and its vulnerabilities. Both the government and the people were committed to social and economic progress. The city's Shia and Sunni Muslims coexisted and prayed together in traditions inflected by Sufism, Islam's mystical cosmopolitanism. Women were not expected to closet themselves away in kitchens or hide themselves underneath burqas. But by standing out as a rebuke to the religious fanaticism that had for so long stultified civilized life from Persepolis to Peshawar, Mazar was being targeted for jihadist subversion. Among the radical mullahs who were quickly growing in influence in the city was the Sunni reactionary Mawlawi Abdul Qahir Zadran. He'd spent time in Pakistan, he was a powerful orator and he seemed to have a lot of money. You could buy his CDS and tapes in the markets. In Zadran's sermons, Muslims who failed to cleave to Deobandist discipline were apostates. Americans were invaders and crusaders. Schoolgirls were prostitutes.

The young journalist and I talked about Iran, about the colleges the Tehran regime was opening on the outskirts of Mazar and the propaganda the Khomeinists were finding ways to get into the Afghan news media. As the "war-weary" Western world was losing interest in the cause of Afghan democracy, Iran's shadow was looming over everything. Khomeinist Iran was the empire to contend with now.

At the entrance to Mazar's grand Blue Mosque, the shrine guard took me accurately to be a *kafir*. He gently refused me entry, with obvious embarrassment to himself and to my hosts. The new rules say *kafirs* can't come in, he said. I wandered around outside and mingled with the pilgrims happily enough, but the guard noticed me later and called me over to have tea with him, as a gesture of cordiality. He told me he was sorry. But the insult had been given. He knew it. I'd seen that it had offended him more than me, and he seemed to know that, too.

As it happens, I'd discreetly slipped into the mosque anyway, or at least into a chamber accessed by a back entrance, where the Sufis still had a secure place for themselves. I joined them for a few moments as they engaged in their euphoric and hypnotic ritual chantings. In the song they were singing, the refrain was from a poem by Rumi: "My life is going to end, but I hope to join with God."

Afterwards, my hosts told me that the way things were going, even the Sufis' days of liberty at the mosque were rumoured to be numbered. The Iranian-influenced Shia imams considered the Sufis dangerously unorthodox. The Deobandi-influenced Sunni imams had started calling them heretics.

Only the day before, on the plaza where we were walking, Mazar's Khomeinists had gathered in an angry demonstration. "Death to America," they chanted. "Death to Israel. Death to the Jews."

three

A TALE OF TWO CITIES

AMONG THE MANY things that came as a surprise when I first visited Kabul in the autumn of 2008 was the Dari version of Marilyn Manson's "Personal Jesus" playing on the radio. There was also the astonishing courtesy, solicitousness and exuberant friendliness of the people. The view from the mausoleum of King Zahir Shah at the top of landmine-pocked Maranjan Hill, where the kids come to fly their kites on weekends, revealed a city of perhaps four million people, ten times the population of thirty years before. Kabul's motor registry department was adding eight thousand new vehicles to its rolls every month, and the roads were choked with traffic. Down in the gritty backstreets, uproars of laughter erupted from men sitting around TV sets watching Afghan talk shows. The bazaars were bursting with life and commerce. Even in the dingiest parts of the bomb-blasted metropolis, down among the rickety vendors' stalls that sell cow heads and sheep guts, there was always a newly opened computer school or a long line of unveiled women waiting for their literacy or accountancy classes to open for the day. Every morning, the streets were filled with schoolchildren.

It was as though there were two completely different cities in the world called Kabul.

The city that routinely showed up in English-language television reports and daily newspapers was a Central Asian version of Stalingrad during the siege, or Phnom Penh just before the Khmer Rouge rolled in. Shortly after I arrived, Britain's *Sunday Telegraph* judged Kabul to be "as dangerous as Baghdad at its worst"—the Taliban were at the gates. But the Taliban were not at the gates, and the city I came to know—making my appointments, buying naan and bananas at the bazaars, popping into bookstores, drinking tea in mud houses and half-collapsed buildings, sitting at tables in pleasant offices and coffee shops—was not the city the world was being told about. The Kabul that trundled along before my eyes was a thriving, heartbreakingly poor but hopeful and splendid place.

Over the years, I'd made Afghanistan a bit of a personal study, and I could count Kabuli émigrés among my friends. Still, nothing had quite prepared me for certain things. The prompt pizza delivery service, for one. For another, the fact that you could take a handgun to the bank with you, leave it with the guard and pick it up on the way out. Perhaps most surprising was the spectacular contrast between the cosseted little universe inhabited by Kabul's "international community" overclass and the raucous reality of everyday life among Kabul's rambunctious masses.

Kabul, the capital of Absurdistan, is the city you see at sunrise over the shoulder of the television reporter, the city that crackles at twilight from the verandas of jittery foreign diplomats, aid-agency bureaucrats and journalists. It's the city with helicopters always flying overhead and rapid-fire text messages on everyone's cell phones relaying intelligence bulletins about the latest assassination attempts and kidnappings.

The real Kabul can be a perilous place, true enough. As in almost every big city between Amman and Calcutta, something horrible happens almost every day. The day before I arrived, Gayle Williams, a British aid worker, had been shot dead by two Taliban thugs on a motorcycle outside the gates to Kabul University. Humayun Shah Asefi, a prince from the old royal family, had just been kidnapped along with his son. The Canadian Broadcasting Corporation's Melissa Fung hadn't been heard from for weeks—she'd been kidnapped by bandits. A French aid worker was snatched just a few blocks from the guest house where I'd settled in. Notably, an Afghan who lived on the street where the incident occurred died in his attempt to prevent the Frenchman's abduction. He grabbed a kidnapper's machine gun by the barrel and was shot in the chest.

A few days after I got to Kabul, while I was interviewing Fatana Gilani, head of the Afghan Women's Council, one of her staff ran in with a cell phone. Gilani took the call and gasped. The young man she'd just sent to pick up some office supplies had been caught in the blast from a suicide bombing at the Ministry of Information building over on Feroshgah Street. Five people were killed. The council's young employee was okay, though. Just a bit shaken up.

But the real Kabul was not a dreary, white-knuckle-dangerous place where the crazy locals are just itching to slit foreigners' throats. It was a city that got knocked around, picked itself up, dusted itself off and carried on with its business. This was the city I came to know, a city of polio victims, almond sellers, seamstresses, football players and anti-poverty activists. A city of cab drivers, teachers, money changers and beggars. It wasn't especially difficult to get to know the place. The trick, I learned, was to run with savvy Kabulis. Don't keep routines. Don't make ransom bait of yourself. I found I could pass as an Afghan easily enough, shambling down the street or wandering the markets on some errand. But up close, even with my Afghan shawl and Panjshiri hat, I wasn't fooling anyone. All the better, too. Get noticed as someone from away, and people are likely to watch your back or invite you in for tea.

In this other Kabul there is a sprawling sub-metropolis, where life unfolds in dramas and excitements all its own, in the hordes of kite-flying children on the city's flat roofs. At least seventy thousand of these Kabulis are more or less orphans. They descend into the streets every day to hawk maps, magazines and packages of chewing gum, sometimes resorting to begging and ragpicking or the refined art of pickpocketing. In this vast rooftop district, the talk was not about kidnappings or a looming Taliban takeover. It was about President Karzai's decree outlawing begging. Karzai had instructed the Interior Ministry to clear the streets of panhandling ragamuffins by trundling them off to orphanages and to the network of Dickensian "care homes" run by the Afghan Red Crescent Society. Nothing came of it, though, which was not a great surprise. It was just another thing to laugh about. Kabulis like a good laugh. And they like to tell jokes.

Two country bumpkins visit Kabul and decide to take in a movie. A cow appears on the screen, and one of the hillbillies gasps, "Watch out, everyone; there's a cow in the theatre!" The other guy says, "Don't be silly; it's just a movie." Then the first guy says, "Sure, but the cow doesn't know that." A mullah is making a spectacle of himself by crying and moaning at the funeral of a rich man. Nobody recognizes the mullah, so somebody asks him, "Were you a close relative?" The mullah says, "No, I'm crying because he was so rich, and I didn't know him when he was alive."

There are vast fleets of armour-plated Toyota suvs ferrying nervous European bureaucrats around Kabul's rubble-strewn streets, but instead of being pelted with bricks, they're made the butt of jokes. Aid workers are generally regarded with affection by Kabulis, but the urbane expatriate community they represent is known as "the cow that drinks its own milk," and well put, too. By 2008, the world had pledged roughly $25 billion to Afghanistan, but the Agency Coordinating Body for Afghan Relief reckoned that only $15 billion had made it to the country, and half of that was going to expat salaries, consultants' fees and country-of-origin subcontracts. Another joke: The un tells Karzai the world has had enough of the corruption in his government, and he has to act, once and for all. Karzai responds: "Of course!" Then he whispers: "How much will you pay me to fix it?"

Kabul is a city of hovels and wedding-cake palaces, armed compounds and shell-pocked ruins, sidewalk shawarma stands and crumbling fortresses, razor wire, blast walls, traffic circles and ambitious boulevards. Tracts of newly built, ancient-style mud houses creep up the ramparts of steep-cliffed, flat-topped mountains that rise from the Kabul plain, with ruined castles at their summits. Ford Rangers carrying heavily armed soldiers are as ubiquitous as donkey carts and bicycles. A stadium here, a glass hotel there, minarets and mosques, collapsed factories—it's urban bedlam. To get at the heart of Kabul, you make your way down some of the more ancient and narrow alleys in the centre of the old city. Eventually, you will find the place, hidden away in a hive of narrow streets and alleys bustling with fruit and vegetable sellers, blacksmiths and silversmiths. Jewellers call out to you, holding aloft glistening strands of lapis lazuli. There are naan bakers and gem cutters, potters and leatherworkers, seamstresses, tailors, raisin hawkers and spice merchants. There's one winding alleyway taken up entirely by peddlers selling caged songbirds.

There are seven gates that lead inside the busy passageways of the Murad Khane, the eighteenth-century walled quarter of the old city of Kabul. Along its passages you will still find old, richly filigreed window frames, door screens and façades in the Nuristani and Kabuli styles. There are still *hammams*, the old dome-roofed bathhouses, and relics of ornate Simgili plasterwork in walls that surround cool, quiet courtyards. Some of the old houses tilt and groan against elaborately carved Kandankari veranda posts, and there are faint echoes of the grand Mughal style in the great *serai*, the central gathering place.

Through winding corridors and up-and-down staircases I was led by Zabi Majidi, a thirty-year-old Afghan architect raised and schooled in Germany and Britain. Zabi is the youngest of the Afghan journalist Mohammad Shah Majidi's five children. Kabul's old city was Mohammad Shah's boyhood neighbourhood, and Zabi grew up on its stories— not for nothing was Kabul once called the Paris of the East. When Mohammad Shah came back to the city shortly after the rout of the Taliban in 2001, he brought Zabi with him. The old man wept, because everything from his childhood was gone. "It was terrible for him," Zabi remembered.

Zabi worked for a while as a project architect in London and Shanghai; then he went back to school to finish his thesis on urban redevelopment. In 2007, he took a job with the Turquoise Mountain Foundation in Kabul, becoming part of a bold vision to restore and rebuild the Murad Khane. This is why he was so happy to show me around and explain what

I was seeing. There, the grand home of a long-forgotten khan. Here, the remains of several buildings demolished by bombs, their ancient timbers plundered for firewood during the muja-hideen wars. There, at least twenty structures that collapsed during an earthquake in 2006. And here, from this rooftop, look, you can see the old king's place and the famous brick bridge across the Kabul River.

From just about any of the flat roofs of the Murad Khane you can also see the ugly concrete office and apartment blocks that steadily encroached upon the neighbourhood during the Soviet era. Over here, this will be a teahouse once again, Zabi went on. And there, that will be a gallery. When Zabi came here to work with Turquoise Mountain, it was still the offi-cial intention of the municipal authority to demolish the whole place. This remained the municipal plan long after the Murad Khane project was well underway. That's not the plan anymore. "I love this place," Zabi said. "I love the work. I love it here."

The Turquoise Mountain Foundation is the brainchild of the eccentric British soldier-diplomat Rory Stewart, author of *The Places in Between,* a chronicle of his journey across Afghani-stan on foot in 2002. The foundation's big idea is that Afghan civilization, long buried in the ruins and the rubble of sav-agery, must be allowed to re-emerge from its hiding places. Rebuild its wellspring, and civilization will flourish and tri-umph across the land. By 2008, the Murad Khane, a place that had been a decrepit slum, was emerging as a centre of art and learning and commerce.

The place was alive with seasoned artisans and young apprentices, carpenters, ceramicists, calligraphers, sculp-tors, plasterers and jewellers. There were literacy courses and embroidery classes and the clattering and clunking of ham-mers and chisels in the work of rebuilding old guest houses for visiting scholars. All of this was unfolding in the alley-ways around the Abul Fazl minaret, a defiant testament to everything that for so long had been forced to hide there from the angry world outside. In the local vernacular, these hidden places are known as *taqunya*, places only the local people know, where neighbourliness, tolerance and everyday decency can persist without hindrance, no matter the regime in power. At the Abul Fazl mosque, everyone, Sunni and Shia, prays together. Among the Murad Khane's hidden places are small courtyards where Shia imams have gone about their devotions for generations, ministering to Hazaras and Farsiwans in the same neighbourhoods that have long been home to Sunni Pashtuns and Tajiks, Sikhs, Ahmadiyyas and the descendants of the Qizilbash.

The Qizilbash, who show up in the Kabuli dialect as Qili-bash, were warrior-noblemen, mostly Azerbaijani Shias from Anatolia and Turkey who followed the great Nadir Shah, the Persian Napoleon, in his conquests. The Murad Khane goes back to the first Qizilbash who settled in Kabul in the late 1700s. The Persian-speaking Qizilbash "redheads" managed to survive, in remnants, through the terror of the ruthless late-nineteenth-century "Iron Amir," Abdur Rahman Khan, and also through the Taliban years, when even a hint of het-erodoxy would invite the most macabre punishments and repression. In the Murad Khane, the old Afghan civility qui-etly carried on. Many of the old families were bombed out or fled during the mujahideen wars, but the descendants of the Qizilbash walk the streets of Murad Khane to this day. You will find them among the young girls in their school uniforms and among the wizened old men in the late-autumn sun in the grand *serai,* the ones with the look of Old Testament prophets about them.

Zabi continued with his enumerations. Of the 600 residents in the Murad Khane, about one-third are from the old families who have been here for generations. There are roughly 120 children in the neighbourhood school. Average depth of the garbage and detritus removed to excavate the courtyards and passageways down to street level: 2 metres. Number of dump truck loads it took to haul it all away: 12,000. Number of buildings identified for special protection or restoration: 65. Carpenters and other tradesmen were busy working on 22 of them. The restoration project's largest backer: the Canadian International Development Agency, with $3 million over four years—I'd had to come all the way to Kabul to find that out.

It dawned on me, as one day bled into the next, that the whole city of Kabul was *taqunya* to the outside world, hidden between the lines of frightening stories in English-language dailies. The realization prompted me to move out of my comfortable low-rent guest-house compound in the Shar-e Naw district by the Dutch embassy. The compound was a delightful place to retreat at the end of the day, a pleasant hive of leafy passageways and corridors with a shop, a restaurant and even a barber. Surrounded by high blast walls and razor wire, I took comfort in the knowledge that I was guarded while I slept by polite but serious-looking lads with AK47s. But it felt a bit too much like hiding, so I moved into a plain house down a dirt backstreet in the Taimani neighbourhood, with no phalanx of guards, just a woman named Vic from Idaho, who was helping organize the upcoming elections, and Gerry, a Kiwi with a rockabilly haircut and sideburns who specialized in small-scale, rural electrical-generation projects. At the time, there was electricity for only two or three hours a day in Kabul, mostly in the evenings. When it gave up its last, you'd go straight to bed. In the mornings, you'd begin at the first hint of sunrise when the muezzins began singing their sad supplications, their prayers bleeding out of loudspeakers from the minarets into a glorious dawn. The skies above Kabul are already filling with kites. At night, it was Gerry's habit to play the Pogues full blast from the veranda whenever the electricity came on. This was not what you could call hiding, and the neighbours didn't seem to mind at all.

Something else dawned on me around the same time. I was in Kabul to do some freelance journalism, but also to work on a joint project of the Canada-Afghanistan Solidarity Committee and the Funders' Network for Afghan Women. The plan was to produce words-and-pictures profiles of Afghans who were rebuilding their shattered country and trying to make a functioning democracy from its ruins. The working title for the project was Unsung Heroes. It ended up doing quite well and was presented as an exhibition at the Canadian High Commission in London. But a problem I had to grapple with was the people I'd encounter everywhere in Kabul. The one-legged man in the kiosk on the corner selling vegetables, the kids selling maps and chewing gum at the intersections, the exhausted traffic cops, the schoolteachers—who among them was not a hero?

One afternoon, I happened to meet Sharifa Ahmadzai, a seventy-five-year-old dressmaker from Baghlan who was visiting with relatives in Kabul. In an astonishing accomplishment for an Afghan woman, Sharifa had managed to raise four children on her own—her husband had left her when she was still a young mother. Her brothers had taught her to read as a child, and although she'd never set foot in a formal school, Sharifa had spent her life teaching women how to read and how to sew well enough to earn a small income as seamstresses. Over the years, hundreds of Baghlani women had enrolled in the makeshift courses Sharifa offered in her tiny house, and she carried on straight through the Taliban years. Even after the Taliban were gone, misogynist lunatics at the mosque around the corner were tacking up bulletins calling for her murder. Still she kept teaching.

Then there was Nasir Ahmed. He lived in a squatters' camp in a row of tumbledown horse stables a short walk from a famous Kabul landmark, the bombed-out shell of King Amanullah's 1920s-era palace. About a dozen families made their homes in the stables, and I'd been invited in for tea. In the manger where Nasir spent his days, light streamed through a hole in the ceiling. Nasir had the face of an old man and a body the size of a six-year-old's. By his own reckoning, he was sixteen, but he was dying of tuberculosis and polio. At least one of those easily treatable afflictions was also bleeding the life from Ramin, his younger brother. Ramin could no longer stand up because his legs had stopped working. They shared with me a meal of apples.

There were even heroes among the expats. Zachary Warren, an American divinity student I met at a bar, had come to Afghanistan to tell stories and perform magic tricks for kids to cheer them up. Four years later, he was still there, managing a touring circus. Once upon a time, he was kidnapped, but he managed to escape from his abductors by reducing them to fits of laughter with a fart joke. Zachary thought nothing of roaring around Kabul at night on his beat-up old motorcycle. He'd settled into a life of teaching aspiring Afghan sideshow artists how to juggle and ride unicycles. He loved the people. He loved his work.

The Afghans you're least likely to hear about from foreign journalists, oddly, are the fixers, drivers and translators without whom journalists here could not function. The fixer I'd had the good fortune to fall in with was a muscle-building Afghanistan Iron Man contestant who went by the name Shuja, which means "brave." It was Shuja who showed me around the real Kabul, the dirt-poor, beautiful shambles of a city that seethes with millions of hopeful, helpful, warm and utterly ordinary people. Shuja was only twenty-eight when I met him, but he'd already survived four deaths.

The first was when he was a kid, during the "Hekmatyar Time," when Pakistan's Gulbuddin Hekmatyar was raining bombs and mortars on the people of Kabul from the hilltop necropolis of Shahada during the so-called civil war. One of Hekmatyar's rockets landed, without exploding, in Shuja's courtyard. The second near-miss was a couple of years later, near the Iranian embassy, when another Hekmatyar missile landed near Shuja's feet. This one exploded, killing about one hundred people, but Shuja was left with only faint scars around his eyes. The third time was in July 2004, in Ghazni, when Shuja was working as a driver for an NGO. He drove over a landmine. The car immediately behind him was turned into a compacted chunk of metal with a dead man inside it. Shuja was uninjured, and the car he was driving sustained only two flat tires. Shuja fixed the tires and drove on. His last close call occurred near Massoud Square in Kabul, in September 2006, during an attack on a military convoy. At least sixteen people were killed. "It was a suicide bomber," he told me. "He drove right past me in their car, around me. And it went into the convoy. There were shrapnels coming down everywhere, but it did not break my car. It was such a huge blast. The whole plaza. Even the trees were on fire."

Shuja is highly skilled in the art of orienteering, and he's a master navigator, which is to say he can get you around Kabul with ease, owing to his intimate familiarity with the city's hidden terrain of back-alley shortcuts, must-avoid traffic circles, troop-convoy dynamics and herds of goats. But even with a journeyman like Shuja at the wheel, it's a rare day that you'll make it across town without getting banjaxed by ISAF caravans of scary-looking, armour-plated troop carriers sporting flags you don't recognize. Get pulled over by nervous young men with AK47s at the Afghan National Police checkpoints, and they usually just smile and say hello and wave you on your way.

But there were also the dodgy private-security outfits staffed almost entirely by demobilized hard boys from any of several half-forgotten militias. The Uzbek warlord Abdul Rashid Dostum had his own informal regiment of these mercenaries. Dostum lived in an absurdly opulent, heavily guarded pink and purple mansion on a street in the posh Wazir Akbar Khan district. All his cronies lived in the same neighbourhood, in similarly ridiculous though slightly less enormous wedding-cake houses, plucked straight from the style of the nouveau-riche districts of Islamabad. In the grocery store around the corner from Dostum's place, you can buy fancy smoked salmon and frozen lobsters. Just two blocks away, you're back in the seventh century, with people trundling around in donkey carts.

On an errand one day, Shuja came upon an old Hazara man. The man's fruit cart had toppled, and he couldn't right it, so Shuja pulled out of traffic to help him pull his cart home. It turned out the man was desperately ill and the only breadwinner in a large family, so Shuja started giving the family $25 a month from his own meagre earnings. That was the kind of generosity that animated Shuja, but he took a dim view of the nervous, high-powered foreigners in Kabul with their phalanxes of armed guards. Ask him whether a particular errand is safe, or about the security in a particular place, and his answer is always the same. "Everywhere is dangerous. Everywhere is safe. This is Afghanistan."

Although Shuja was a perfectly competent translator, he recommended a young friend of his, Baktash Muqim, for the more high-brow conversations I'd sometimes find myself having to engage in. Baktash ended up being a welcome third wheel on our rounds. He was only twenty-one, but he could speak Dari, Pashto, Urdu and English. Baktash hadn't worked much since graduating from high school, but he had taken some English and computer courses. He wanted to be a journalist, too. He was constantly peppering me with questions, but I didn't have much useful career advice to give. Being a journalist in Afghanistan is not quite the cozy vocation it is in Canada. There were certainly job opportunities—within five years of the Taliban's 2001 rout, there were dozens of radio stations operating across the country, alongside seventeen television stations and scores of newspapers and magazines. In Kabul, the award-winning and wildly popular Tolo TV has been at the forefront of building a new national conversation among Afghans. There was work to be had. But it came with certain occupational hazards.

The Afghan news media that emerged after 2001 was more diverse, more lively and in the main more quick to comfort the afflicted and afflict the comfortable than the Canadian news media tends to be. This meant Afghan journalists had come to be seen as a menace, not just to the Taliban but also to the political and religious factions that controlled much of the Afghan economy and influenced the Afghan government. Newspapers, magazines and radio stations connected to Tehran and Islamabad, former warlords and powerful clerics had begun to edge out independent journalism. Professional journalists were under constant threat. In 2005, Tolo TV's Shiama

Reziaee was murdered for "un-Islamic" behaviour. In 2006, radio station Istiqlal was firebombed. In 2007, the pioneering radio journalist Zakia Zaki was assassinated in Parwan, and television news presenter Shokiba Amaaj was murdered in Kabul. In a case that drew international condemnation, student journalist Sayed Parvez Kambaksh was arrested in 2008 for allegedly distributing what was claimed to be blasphemous material that raised questions about the rights of women in Islam. Kambaksh was sentenced to twenty years in jail, and it was only after a wave of international protests that he was pardoned and spirited out of the country.

Baktash knew the risks. After working with him for a while, I discovered that he was intimately acquainted with the dangers Afghan journalists faced. It was because of what had happened to his cousin, Ajmal Naqeshbandi, whose story is summed up on a plaque in the cemetery of one of the poorer sections of Kabul. The cemetery is just off the high street in Barakey, which had been renamed Ajmal Naqeshbandi Road, with a whirling and chaotic traffic circle called Ajmal Naqeshbandi Square. In the cemetery, the most prominent shrine is devoted to the same Ajmal Naqeshbandi, who was executed by the Taliban in the spring of 2007. He was twenty-six years old. The inscription above his raised stone coffin reads, in Dari: "He was kind to his people, and was intolerable to the enemies of Afghanistan. Ajmal Naqeshbandi will always be remembered with honour by the people of Afghanistan."

On March 5, 2007, Ajmal was kidnapped with the Italian journalist with whom he was working—Daniele Mastrogiacomo of La Repubblica—along with Mastrogiacomo's driver, Sayed Agha, in Helmand. A few days later, the Talibs murdered Agha on the charge of "spying for foreign troops." To ransom Mastrogiacomo, President Hamid Karzai agreed to release five of the highest-ranking Taliban prisoners in custody, one of whom was Mansur Dadullah, brother of the notorious Mullah Dadullah Akhund, the Taliban's senior military chief. Shortly after Mansur's release, Mullah Dadullah was killed in an airstrike, and Mansur took over his brother's job as commander of Taliban forces. He ran several suicide-bombing operations from his base in Pakistan and was also well known, ironically, for courting Western journalists. In a candid interview with the Swiss weekly newspaper *Die Weltwoche*, Mansur vowed: "Ours is a global struggle, and I have promised Allah that I will spread it across the world until the end of my days." Mansur was also open to power-sharing negotiations with Karzai. After a dangerous falling out with Taliban supremo Mullah Omar, Mansur was back in custody in 2008 following a much-disputed operation carried out by the Pakistani ISI. Much wild speculation ensued about a Karzai-sanctioned backroom deal. There's no intrigue like Kabuli intrigue.

But Karzai refused to ransom Ajmal. Ajmal was beheaded on April 8, 2007. There was an uproar. The Naqeshbandi family says the Afghan government, trying to calm things down, ended up paying a ransom of $30,000 and a Toyota Land Cruiser for Ajmal's remains, which had been left in the desert for three days. The body was returned to the family in Kabul with its head sewn back on. When Baktash and I visited Ajmal's shrine with Shuja, Baktash told me, "I want to be a journalist like Ajmal. I am a good storyteller. I trust myself that I can do this. The most important thing is to trust in yourself, and so I do trust."

Trust.

During each of my visits in Afghanistan, trust was the thing brought to my attention time and again. In conversations and interviews with everyone from the lowliest workers through the busiest activists to the most exalted politicians, it kept coming up, illuminating the confounding twists and turns of more than a generation of Afghan hopes for peace and freedom. Back home, it usually came up in questions like this one: Does the West have a partner it can trust in the Afghan presidential palace, in Hamid Karzai? In Afghanistan, it would come up in questions like this: Can we trust the West to stick with us, or is everyone going to sell us out again? The way Afghans answered that question for themselves depended on what they'd hear from the world's democracies. It determined the risks they were prepared to take for a democracy of their own. What they heard from us, I came to see, mattered more than all the military force and the financial support the world had pledged to Afghanistan since September 11.

In the days and weeks following that September morning, trust was the thing that made the difference. Until September 11, the Islamic State of Afghanistan was stuck up in the mountains. It had hardened into the Northern Alliance, a government without a country in a country without a government. Afghanistan bled and writhed in a Taliban-terrorized, failed-state limbo. On September 9, 2001, an al-Qaida suicide squad assassinated Ahmad Shah Massoud, the beloved Lion of Panjshir, scourge of the Red Army, champion of the Peshawar Accord and Northern Alliance leader Berhanuddin Rabbani's right-hand man. But two days later, the shadows that had darkened Afghanistan for so long suddenly lifted. September 11 came to mean a lot of things to a lot of people, but to Afghans, it meant one thing and one thing only. At last, the outside world could be trusted to put its back in the fight against the Taliban. Massoud was dead, but his promise was alive. People started pouring out into the light, and within weeks, the Northern Alliance had gathered its ragged partisans together. They roared down from the mountains.

Before any American combat troops had entered the fight, Afghan partisans were throwing themselves into the massed forces of sixty thousand Taliban fighters that had formed defensive rings around Kabul, Kandahar, Takhar and Herat. The Northern Alliance was up against another nine thousand recent Taliban recruits from Pakistan's madrassas, three thousand hardened fighters mustered by al-Qaida from a dozen Arab countries, and at least another three thousand Chechen, Uzbek, Filipino and Uighur jihadists. The Afghans fought because they trusted that this was one time America could be trusted not to run away.

During the autumn days of my first visit to Kabul in 2008, what was haunting everyone's dreams was not the spectre of Taliban militias encircling Kabul, creeping inexorably towards the city gates from their redoubts in Kandahar, Ghazni, Helmand and the tribal borderlands in Pakistan. That's just what rich white people were reading about in their newspapers. Among Kabulis, the larger threat was coming from the great cities of Europe and North America, where a defeatist resignation was setting in. From Berlin to Vancouver, whenever the subject of Afghanistan came up, the conversation was usually about how foreign powers should cut some behind-closed-doors deal with the Taliban and just get out.

Kabulis had been betrayed before. They can smell betrayal a mile away. The more talk there was about brokering an exit-strategy deal, the less Afghans trusted the West, and a fatal feedback loop went to work. The louder the clamour for a negotiated exit strategy, the less ordinary Afghans were inclined to stick their necks out in the long war for democracy, human rights and the rule of law. That's how the "spiral of doom" Westerners read about in their newspapers was actually working in Afghanistan. The louder the troops-out crescendo grew, the quieter progressive Afghan voices became. It was even exacerbating the corruption that had come to characterize the Karzai regime. If this isn't going to last, the thinking went, we might as well get it while the getting's good. In a rare glimpse into the way the spiral worked, Mohammed Anas, a bureaucrat in the Kandahar governor's office, told a magazine writer, "Nowadays, everyone is trying to get rich. They think, 'I'm only here for a short time—I've got to take the money that I can.'" The day the suicide bombers on Feroshgah Street nearly killed one of her office staff, that's precisely how Fatana Gilani of the Afghanistan Women's Council put it to me. We'd been talking about the diplomatic back-channel work underway for a deal with the Taliban. "We do not trust these things that are happening behind closed doors. It is coming from outside the country," she said. "Anybody who does this is not a friend of Afghanistan."

During the bloody Russian occupation, the way ahead had been clear. "I was for jihad," Gilani told me. During the Taliban tyranny, things were similarly straightforward. "It was a jail." By 2008, Kabul had become a city of foreign intrigues, espionage and innumerable agendas. While Gilani spoke kindly about Canada, with its focus on security, building up the Afghan National Army and backing only Afghan-led reconciliation efforts, her misgivings were clear: "There are forty countries in Afghanistan now. It is very difficult to know which country is our friend."

Sometimes, it was just as difficult to know whether the Afghan government was Afghanistan's friend. When Karzai was first elected in 2004, he was saddled with jihadists and warlords who had to be drawn close to the centres of power to keep them from pulling the country back into the politics of the rocket and the gun. Competing and conflicting agendas routinely converged, split and merged again with the back-channel strategies of Kabul's diplomats and spies, greased along with Iranian bribes that bought favours deep within the Afghan parliament and the presidential palace. There was Abdul Rashid Dostum in his fancy house in Wazir Akbar Khan—he'd been given a ceremonial "commander in chief" role in the Afghan National Army. There was the hugely influential and extremely slippery MP Abdul Sayyaf, a Saudi proxy, an old friend of Osama bin Laden and a Muslim Brotherhood alumnus with a Filipino terrorist group named after him. The pudgy little mullah Abdul "Rocketi" Salam, a high-ranking MP, a proud Pashtun chauvinist and a former Taliban commander, was one of the most enthusiastic members in the pro-negotiations camp. In Karzai's inner circle, the finance minister was another Pashtun chauvinist, Anwar ul-Haq Ahady, leader of the crypto-fascist Afghan Mellat, the relic of the pro-Nazi Pashtun elites from the 1930s. You could get dizzy trying to keep up with all their shadowy comings and goings.

Even before he was formally elected, Karzai was promising Afghanistan's remaining gangsters and outlanders that he'd embrace them, too, if only they'd pledge to honour the Afghan constitution and respect the rule of law. Immediately after his 2004 election, he'd started up with the peace offers again. In return, the Taliban had consistently thumbed their noses at Karzai. By the autumn of 2008, Karzai's entreaties were going into overdrive. With ambassadors from Europe and the Islamic bloc egging him on and stumbling over themselves to offer him their services, Karzai achieved little except to alienate the pro-democracy camp in his own government. After the Saudis quietly brought together some Taliban-connected characters in Mecca with Qayyum Karzai, the president's businessman brother, even Afghan foreign minister Rangeen Spanta couldn't bear it anymore. Spanta uttered a blistering rebuke to what he called the "so-called peace-makers," warning that their shady peace-talk gambits would "surrender this land to the enemy."

It wasn't obvious then, but the patterns that caused such disorientation and distrust among progressive Afghans in the final months of 2008 would determine everything to come. If it wasn't the rumours of a reconciliation with the Taliban, it was the talk about postponing or even cancelling elections—even though the promise of a sovereign Afghan democracy was keeping most Afghans onside. If it wasn't talk about ditching elections, it was news about another "anti-war" demonstration in Toronto or London on the front page of the *Kabul Weekly*.

To people like Mahboob Shah, a tireless, thirty-eight-year-old Kabuli who spent his days driving around the city in a rickety old Korean bucket of bolts, visiting squatters' camps and writing down the particulars in a little green notebook, it was more than just a bit distressing. Mahboob had pretty well invented his own job. He'd visit Kabul's homeless in their encampments, determine their most pressing needs and try to hook them up with help from his contacts in Kabul's anti-poverty agencies and international charities. He'd found a small NGO willing to pay him a modest salary to do his work. He asked me to withhold its name to protect it from reprisals from the Taliban. It was a job he did in order to cope with the uncertainty and the rumours, the grinding poverty and his frustration about the untapped potential of his beloved city.

"It only feels better if I am finding something to do for these people," he told me. "If I can't, I always wake up in the middle of the night. It is like they are my own children, my own brothers and sisters. All the refugees in Kabul know me, I think." Then he laughs at himself, pointing out that this could not be, because you could say that as many as half the people of Kabul were homeless refugees. They were living in cellars, alleys, tent encampments, hastily built mud houses and bombed-out buildings. "I become sad, yes. But when I find someone who is very poor, I feel very happy to help them stand on their own feet. So I just stop thinking about these things. I just do what I can do."

On our rambles through Kabul, Mahboob Shah pointed out some of his haunts. Here, a complex of half-collapsed buildings left over from the mujahideen wars, behind the Russian embassy. Maybe fifty families. There, near the opulent mosque-and-madrassa complex run by the sinister and wealthy Tehran-backed ayatollah Mohammad Asif Mohseni, another encampment about the same size. "And there." Shah pointed to a warren of canvas hovels along a busy thoroughfare. "That is a new one."

Every day he would rise at dawn, say goodbye to his wife, Waghma, and his infant sons, Sharem and Pashan, and go for a long run. Then he'd begin his working day with his notebook and his rickety Kia, "the dustiest car in Kabul." He was making a difference, too, and it was because he'd figured out that it's actually the small stuff that works best. For $1,000 you can run a tent school for two hundred kids for a whole year. One hot water bottle can keep a child from dying in the winter. Give an unemployed man $5 worth of fruit, vegetables and hand-me-down clothes in a pushcart, and from that he can build his own enterprise. From the cast-off intravenous bags and tubes from local hospitals, he'd helped a small, independent charity develop a hydroponic gardening system for a destitute neighbourhood on a hardscrabble city hillside. The leftover shipping pallets from the sprawling U.S. base at Camp Eggers provided a fortune in construction material.

The improvisational genius of Kabul's anti-poverty activists was a thing to behold.

Like Mahboob Shah, forty-year-old Mohammed Yousef confronted his own despair at the brutalization of his country by trying to alleviate some of the despair around him. "It is not easy, but you want to do something. You have to do something," he told me. Yousef had been a radio engineer before the Taliban came. There wasn't much work in radio stations when Hekmatyar and the others were reducing Kabul to rubble, and when the Taliban came, they banned radio stations altogether. Yousef spent a brief spell in a Taliban prison for the crime of teaching girls how to read, and he worked in a refugee camp in Pakistan for a while. After the Taliban were chased out of Kabul in 2001, Yousef started looking for ways to make himself useful.

Yousef, like Mahboob Shah, was a canny innovator. He'd decided to focus on the city's roughly seventy thousand street urchins—the runaways, bubble-gum hawkers, shoeshine boys, porters, scrap-metal collectors and trinket sellers. Straight out of the pages of *Oliver Twist,* they'd be up at first light, carrying heavy water jugs up the mountainsides to the growing slum settlements to sell water for the equivalent of pennies per jug. During the day, they'd be begging or running errands for spare change, and at dusk they raced around the choked intersections trying to sell their trinkets, matches and cigarettes to people stuck in traffic. By his own efforts at begging and scratching up donations from foreign NGOs,

Yousef established Aschiana, in the heart of Kabul. It's part elementary school, part emergency shelter and part outreach program, as well as the head office of the student-run *Voice of Afghan Children* newspaper, a vocational training centre and a hub for political advocacy. Aschiana's services ended up reaching nearly one in seven of Kabul's ragamuffins every year.

Wander through Aschiana's complex, and you'd find children tending gardens, playing on a basketball court or working hard in literacy, photography, calligraphy and computer classes. There were sewing, embroidery and tailoring programs, karate classes, a traditional music program and an artists' workshop. But Yousef's pride and joy was the Children's Development Bank he'd set up. It was less a bank than a member-run credit union, owned by the kids themselves. The point was to teach street kids about taking control of their own lives and managing their money. By the time I visited with Yousef at Aschiana in 2008, the bank's membership had swelled to more than one thousand street kids, mostly girls. An initial deposit of 20 afghanis—about 40 cents—got the kids a passbook, a safe place to keep their meagre street earnings and the right to apply for loans. The kids elected their own loan committees. Children over fifteen who applied for small business loans had to make their case to an elected committee of children under fifteen, and vice versa. The loans were awarded on merit—applicants had to find backers and guarantors and show that they'd developed sensible business plans. "They are also motivated to bring some extra money for their savings. For every 10 afghanis you borrow, you should save 2 afghanis in the bank," Yousef explained. "At the end, when their loan is finished, then they have some savings, too."

Mohammed Yousef and Mahboob Shah had figured out ways to create an economy from cast-off shipping pallets, intravenous tubes, art workshops and self-employed street kids. What they could not figure out was how anyone in the rich countries of the world could seriously think they were helping Afghans by marching in rallies demanding a withdrawal of troops from Afghanistan. "People who say the foreign soldiers should go away, they do not know what they are saying," Maboob Shah reckoned. "Yes, it should be Afghans who decide, but we have decided that the world should come to us, as a brother."

Shamsia Sharifi was just as mystified. When I first met her, Shamsia was running a formerly clandestine operation called the Hope for Poor Women Organization, known as Negeen ("the gem") for short, from a ramshackle house with a half-collapsed roof down a dusty side street in Kabul's down-at-heels Khair Khana district. A woman of broad smiles and bright grey eyes, at ease yet all business in a smart blue-grey suit and black silk shawl, Sharifi likes a good laugh. When she put together the troops-out clamour so fashionable in the West with the peace-talk delusion that usually accompanies it, all she could do was laugh out loud. She found it especially amusing that in countries like Canada there were people who considered themselves feminists who would talk like this. "Maybe your country should make a visa for me," she joked. "We need to have the troops in Afghanistan. If the Taliban come back, the target will be us again."

To listen to her laugh, you'd never know what she'd been through. Sharifi was taken out of school when she was twelve. She'd had all the education a woman should need, her parents felt, so it was against their wishes when she enrolled at the Sayed Jamaluddin Afghani School in Kabul. During the Taliban years, with no husband or children, Sharifi worked as a home-school kindergarten teacher, supporting herself partly by selling eggs from her small flock of chickens. But on the quiet, she was involved with a group of educated women, teaching poor women how to read. "For my own pain, for my heart, I wanted to help women to be educated, and to earn some money for herself [sic]. I opposed those difficulties from the Taliban. I wanted to decrease the cruelties suffered by Afghan women." Sharifi's students relied mainly on the Quran, one of the only books people could own that did not invite Taliban inquiries and persecution. Two of the teachers Sharifi worked with were caught. They were arrested and imprisoned, and the small, secret school in Khair Khana was abandoned. "I saw the deaths," Sharifi said. "I saw the cruelties."

After the Taliban were chased out of Kabul in 2001, Negeen got underway. It started as a women's garbage-collection collective and offered only a few literacy classes—a small operation with modest expectations. But Negeen quickly became an important oasis for poor Kabuli women. Sharifi was soon overseeing a workshop producing textiles, classes in gemstone polishing and adult literacy and rights-education programs. By 2008, Sharifi could count four thousand women among Negeen's graduates. Sharifi also distributes micro-loans for women's businesses and manages the marketing end of Negeen's clothing, jewellery and handicraft production. She's particularly proud of Negeen's shawls and dresses and its line of elegant chapan-style coats of the sort popularized by President Karzai. She'd recently signed a small contract with a firm in Thailand to supply jewellery made by Negeen's artisans.

"It is very hard, even now," she said, referring to the reactionary Islamists who still wield such influence throughout Afghan society. "It is a risk for us to do this, what we do, teaching women about their rights. But we are very scared of the Taliban coming back. And the Taliban is also always attacking NGO persons. So we are very scared that they might come back, and we pray to God that they don't come back. We know that Canada is for peace. Canadian soldiers should be in Afghanistan. We need to have these troops in Afghanistan."

But against this backdrop of fear and disquiet, and in spite of the rumours of retreat and abandonment, there was still a great deal of optimism in Kabul in the autumn of 2008, for two main reasons.

First, something was happening on the Jalalabad Road at an unlikely, desolate place on the outskirts of the city, just beyond the Hodkheal district, a slum notorious for its gangs of murderers and thieves. From the outside, the headquarters of Afghanistan's Independent Elections Commission (IEC) looked like a maximum-security prison. Inside, a grim collection of Quonset huts housed the command centre of Afghanistan's embryonic democracy, planning for the 2009 presidential and provincial elections, and the parliamentary and district elections in 2010. The intertwined forces hoping to scuttle it all were not confined to the illiterate jihadists terrorizing the Afghan countryside and the warlord parliamentarians lounging on their cushions in Kabul. Western diplomats had been busy, too, whispering to Western journalists about why it would be best for the elections to be cancelled or postponed. Afghanistan could be further destabilized. Better the devil you know. The security challenges were too daunting. But voter registration was roaring ahead anyway. Things were looking up.

"Yes, we have had some logistical problems," Marzia Siddiqi, the IEC's harried external relations officer, told me, with no intended understatement. Voter registration workers had been kidnapped in Wardak. Stacks of registration forms had been set ablaze in bonfires. A registration office in Nuristan was hit by a Taliban rocket, and in Faryab, women working for the IEC were getting death threats. There were only about 12 million eligible voters in 2004, when Hamid Karzai was elected president in Afghanistan's first direct polls. By early November 2008, registered voters had exceeded the 17-million mark. More than twelve thousand temporary IEC workers were fanning out across the country, and after only a few weeks in operation the IEC had opened registration offices in fourteen of Afghanistan's thirty-four provinces. More than one hundred political parties were registered, too, reflecting the broadest spectrum, from ultra-conservative Islamist groupings to liberal, secular and leftist coalitions.

It was a bit much for Afghans to be told that "security concerns" should shutter the country's emerging institutions of democracy. A massive Asia Foundation opinion poll showed "security" was by far the key concern among Afghans, even in Kabul. It was security that foreign powers had pledged to bring to Afghanistan. The NATO countries were getting all skittish about the elections owing to security problems? The NATO countries had helped midwife democracy in Afghanistan and made huge promises in the Taliban's wake. Even in the presidential palace, it was hard to stomach.

"There is no reason to postpone the elections, and no reason to cancel," Jafar Rasouli, a prominent Afghan journalist and one of Karzai's more eloquent defenders at the time, told me over lunch one day. Rasouli was Karzai's speechwriter and an international affairs analyst Karzai had handpicked for his credentials as a Hazara intellectual. He was a necessary voice among Karzai's Pashtun-dominated advisers, and he'd emerged as one of the loudest and most articulate voices among Afghanistan's democrats. "We must have the elections.

This is what we must do, as people who believe in civilization."
Facing an upwelling of public indignation, Karzai himself had
started to make noises about being unhappy with the election-
snuffing talk.

So that was one reason to be optimistic, in spite of
everything.

The other great cause for hope was felt perhaps most
acutely among the roughly one thousand American aid-agency
staff, private-foundation consultants and second-tier human
rights workers who worked outside of Kabul's cloistered military and diplomatic enclaves. Out of this little community
sprang Americans Abroad for Obama, the largest pro-Obama
group among American expats anywhere in the world. In the
middle of it was Susan Marx, a thirty-one-year-old human
rights worker, born in South Africa, a Californian by way of
Connecticut. In August, when Obama squared off against
Hillary Clinton during the Democratic Party primaries, Marx
had organized a pro-Obama rally in downtown Kabul, in a
tent. About ninety Americans showed up. Kabul's Obama
supporters gathered at Marx's house—by then known as
Casa Obama—to watch the Democratic Party convention in
Denver live on television. Then came the morning of November 4, 2008. It was crisp and cold under a deep blue sky.

On Kabul's street corners, radios were blaring from the
shops, with reports from the American elections announced
every few minutes. At dawn, I'd made my way to the Hare
and Hounds, a pub in the cellar of the Gandamack Lodge, a
converted 1930s-era British villa straight out of the days of the
Raj up in the Simla Hills. Its name is intended to be ironic,
since the 1842 Gandamack massacre was Britain's most
humiliating military defeat in Afghanistan. You check your
guns at the desk on the way in.

The place was packed with Americans, drinking coffee and kibitzing. They'd all come to watch the election results on the Hare and Hound's big-screen television. Only minutes after I arrived, everybody started screaming and cheering. The CNN's Wolf Blitzer had just said something on the television, but from where I was sitting under a display case of antique Lee-Enfield rifles and Bren Guns, I couldn't tell what was going on. Then there were boos. Apparently the Republican candidate John McCain had just said something nice about his running mate, Sarah Palin. Then everything went quiet. There was Barack Obama's handsome face, filling the screen. He'd won. The place erupted.

"This is just so great," John Denoso said, raising his voice over the cheers. "It is just so great." Denoso, a fresh-faced young worker from Bellingham, Washington, was in Afghanistan to help the Afghan government build its IT capacity and infrastructure. For him, an Obama win would mean "a return to competence" in American policy on Afghanistan and greater attention to the more problematic players in region, not least Iran. An Obama win was a slam dunk from the beginning, Denoso reckoned. "The only question was how far to the left we could push it."

John Schroder, also from Washington State, thought so, too. He was a tough-looking guy with a black baseball cap and a reluctance to talk about what kind of work he was doing in Afghanistan. "I just hope Obama can dedicate as much attention to Afghanistan as he dedicated to his campaign," he said. "But I gotta go." He was taking a call on his cell phone. "It's my mom calling from Seattle."

I bumped into Susan Marx as Obama's "Yes We Can" campaign song started pounding out of the loudspeakers. She could barely contain herself. She was in tears. "It's just so exciting. Oh my God! I can't tell you . . . what can I say? I am so thrilled. I haven't been so thrilled, so happy, since the election of Nelson Mandela." It wasn't just Susan. Almost everyone in the room was in tears, all those young American faces, all shapes and colours, from Oklahoma, Florida, from Virginia, Washington, California. Everybody was hugging everybody, chattering away about how Obama's win would mean a return to American competence in Afghanistan. Obama's win would mean a military strategy at last properly integrated with the forty-one other International Security Assistance Force countries. It would mean a seamless military and development approach that would finally pay proper attention to the important work being undertaken by NGOs and aid agencies. It would mean that, at long last, the Afghan people, and the country's democrats and reformers, would finally have a partner in the White House.

It was hard not to get caught up in the moment and its historic resonance. America had just elected its first Black president in the largest Democratic Party landslide since the 1964 triumph of Lyndon Johnson, the year of the bloody voter registration drive in Mississippi. Thousands of young Afghan voter registration workers were at that moment starting their day, fanning out across the provinces of Kunduz, Faryab, Balkh and Baghlan, in one more small movement forward for Afghanistan's embryonic democracy. Soon, America would assert some credible leadership in helping to build a healthy Afghan democracy.

It was nice to savour the moment while it lasted.

But as the euphoria of that morning subsided, it was still obvious that Afghanistan was nowhere near the hopeless basket case so much of the Western world seemed to think it was. Kabul wasn't even close to being "as dangerous as Baghdad at

its worst." You might not have known it from reading, say, the
Toronto Star, but for all its sorrows, Kabul was the capital of a
country fast becoming the bright spot of Central Asia. Millions of refugees had returned to Afghanistan, and in Kabul,
work was underway on twenty thousand new homes. While
Iran was sliding further into police-state thuggery, and Pakistan's frail democracy was sinking deeper into the anarchic
abyss of Islamist violence and lunacy, Afghanistan was getting better. A lot better. Afghanistan could boast one of the
fastest-growing economies in the world. The country's gross
domestic product was growing by more than 12 percent a
year. Government revenues were growing, too. During the five
years before Obama's election, per capita income in Afghanistan had nearly doubled, to $355.

In the year before Obama would order his massive "troop
surge" and push a half-hearted American rededication to the
Afghan state-building project, 400,000 girls started school
for the first time in their lives, joining more than seven million young Afghans in school or attending one of the country's
ten new or newly reopened universities. More than 100,000
women were benefiting from micro-finance loans to help them
set up their own businesses, and one in four MPs in the half-
baked Afghan parliament, the Wolesi Jirga, were women.
Public opinion polls found that Afghans were troubled by the
slow pace of the country's institutional development, but more
than three-quarters of Afghans were happy with democracy.

More than four thousand medical facilities had opened
since 2004, and eight of ten Afghans had at least some access
to basic medical facilities, up from one in ten in 2004. Three
out of every four Afghan children under the age of five had
been immunized against childhood diseases. Since the rout

of the Taliban, more than six hundred midwives had been trained and deployed to every province of Afghanistan.

Since September 11, 2001, more than 4,000 kilometres of roads had been built or paved. More than a billion square metres of mine-contaminated land had been cleared, and roughly 17,000 communities had benefited from development initiatives in the form of wells, schools and hospitals built under the auspices of the Afghan government's National Solidarity Program. One in ten Afghans owned a mobile phone, up from two telephone lines for every 1,000 Afghans in 2001. Across the country, 150 cities and towns had access to Internet service and to seven national television stations, and more than 100 radio stations were up and running, along with dozens of newspapers and magazines. To the great delight of Afghans, Bollywood was back.

When the Taliban ruled the streets of Kabul, the city was nearly empty of cars. Now, one of Kabul's biggest problems was its nightmarish traffic jams.

You couldn't call things rosy, but it simply could not be said that the NATO intervention was making things worse. Afghans certainly didn't think so, and a 2006 PIPA poll revealed Afghans to be among the most optimistic people in the world. Only five years before, Afghanistan had nothing that even looked like a functioning government; it had had no currency or professional army or police force, and five million of its people were refugees. By the time the Taliban got through with them, the Afghan people were living on the equivalent of about 48 cents a day, which is as poor as a people can get without being among the poorest people of sub-Saharan Africa. Only one in five Afghans had access to clean water. Afghans had the shortest life expectancy and the highest infant mortality rates of any people on earth. "They had Somalian anarchy, Haitian poverty, Congolese institutions, Balkan fractiousness, and a North Korean–style government" is the way Paul D. Miller, the Afghanistan director for the U.S. National Security Council, succinctly put it.

For all the complaints in Canada about the time and effort Afghanistan was taking up, in 2011, Canadian soldiers were just wrapping up a nineteen-year sojourn in the Balkans. At times, there were more Canadian soldiers stationed in the Balkans than the top-end 2,800 troop limit in Afghanistan. Canada still had soldiers in Cyprus forty-six years after they first went in. And the NATO effort in Afghanistan was downright measly compared to that in the Balkans. In Afghanistan, by late 2007, there were four soldiers in the country, including Afghan soldiers, for every 1,000 Afghans. At the same time, there were 20 NATO soldiers per 1,000 Kosovars and 19 NATO soldiers for every 1,000 Bosnians. The total NATO commitments in Afghanistan added up to only $57 per Afghan per year, as Anita Inder Singh with the Centre for Peace and Conflict Resolution in New Delhi pointed out. By comparison, the contribution to Kosovo was $526 per capita, and in Bosnia $679.

Despite the inexcusable post-9/11 disasters of America's so-called light footprint Afghan policy, its "we don't do nation-building" idiocy and the opportunities that had been heartlessly squandered by U.S. secretary of state Donald Rumsfeld, you certainly could not say that the "war in Afghanistan" had been a bad thing for most Afghans. It was the best thing that had happened to the country in at least a quarter of a century. For most Afghans, it was the best thing that had happened in their whole lives.

Afghans had no shortage of rage about what the rest of the world had done to their country. They could dish out astute and furious criticisms of the way the UN, the ISAF and perhaps especially the Americans were conducting themselves in Afghanistan. But the least likely thing you'd hear from Afghans was "troops out." Least of all from the women.

four

WOMEN'S WORK

"IT IS SO very wrong to talk of postponing or cancelling. I am for the elections. We cannot cancel and do this to my country." Sohaila Alekosai, a forty-eight-year-old lawyer and social worker who runs a women's refuge in downtown Kabul, spoke with particular passion on the subject of Afghanistan's upcoming presidential election. "And we cannot postpone, because we don't know if it will be better at some later time." The edge in Alekosai's voice came from her experience during the 2005 Wolesi Jirga election. As one of 260 candidates who ran for the 29 parliamentary seats set aside for Kabul province under Afghanistan's bizarre single-non-transferable-ballot voting system, she'd been bullied and harassed by a belligerent "warlord" candidate. Those memories were still fresh.

When I met up with Alekosai at a cheap-eats restaurant just off Flower Street in Kabul in the autum of 2008, it wasn't to talk about Afghan politics. She'd wanted to talk about the madness of the country. But madness, politics and war are often parts of the same conversation. In Afghanistan, it had been all three, all the time, since the late 1970s.

After the rout of the Taliban in 2001, a World Health Organization survey concluded that about five million Afghans, roughly a fifth of the country's population, had been driven mad, or close to it, by nearly a quarter of a century of bloodletting. In 2002, a Centres for Disease Control study painted an even darker picture—more than a third of the Afghan people were suffering from post-traumatic stress disorder. A Healthnet International assessment found the country was suffering "a huge morbidity of mental disorders," not least of which was clinical depression. Even by 2008, there was only one small mental hospital in Kabul, a handful of mental health hospital wards elsewhere in the country and perhaps a total of two dozen properly trained mental health professionals to care for all the sick.

"It is all because of the wars," Alekosai told me. "So many people, they have lost their minds." With nowhere else to turn, people often medicated themselves. In a sampling of pharmacies in Kabul and Jalalabad, Healthnet discovered huge stocks of debilitating and highly addictive over-the-counter benzodiazepenes. Just as often, the poor would resort to opium, folk cures or pilgrimages to shrines. Across Afghanistan, the mentally ill are often believed to be possessed by jinns. The cure is exorcism. Sufferers are chained to trees for weeks at a time on a strict diet of bread, pepper, water and readings from the Quran. "It is not just the death and all the damage you can see around the city of Kabul," said Alekosai, who is also an outspoken women's rights activist and something of a radio personality. "It is the damage to the people. And a person who is damaged like this, he causes damage to other people. This is a very big effect of war."

In keeping with the Quranic concept of *zakat*, a form of devotional charity, Alekosai ran daily therapy sessions at the

Women's Park in Kabul. Without formal resources, Alekosai would improvise. She'd try anything. Sometimes she'd resort to yoga or relaxation therapy, and she looked into Ayurvedic practices from India. Sometimes she had her clients engage in role playing, taking on characters from the poems of Rumi. Although officially a function of Afghanistan's Ministry of Labour and Social Development, Alekosai's classes weren't funded. She worked as a volunteer.

During the Taliban time, Alekosai spent several years as a refugee in Germany, but she still managed to make twenty quiet return visits to Afghanistan to check in on the network of clandestine girls' schools she'd had a hand in organizing and funding. It's one of the astonishing untold stories about Afghanistan. The number of Afghan refugee women like Alekosai who organized, funded and helped run such underground operations in Taliban-held Afghanistan from the diaspora in Europe and North America is probably in the hundreds. In 2006, Alekosai was determined to open her own above-ground girls' school in Afghanistan. Built with volunteer labour and about $60,000 Alekosai managed to raise privately in Germany, the fourteen-room school, attended by three hundred students, is located in Khakjabar. The hardscrabble district is only fifty kilometres from downtown Kabul, but because of the poor road conditions, it was a three-hour drive. Alekosai named the school Pata Khazana, from the title of a collection of verse and folktales going back more than twelve hundred years. Roughly translated as "Hidden Treasure," the volume was gathered by the renowned Afghan poet Mohammad Katak in the early eighteenth century. The book had been banned by the Taliban.

At her classes at the Women's Park in Kabul, some of Alekosai's clients were as poor as the people of the hills of

Khakjabar. But many were teachers and government bureau-crats, and some of them were drug addicts. Many were widows. Several were routinely beaten by their male relatives. Most had lost close family members to the wars. All of them had suffered deep psychological wounds of one kind or another. Alekosai worked with them for the same reasons that ani-mated Mahboob Shah and Mohammed Yousef. "It is very important for me to live and work in these kinds of situations. With my learning and my working, it is also therapy. My ideal-ism has helped me, too."

Along with Afghanistan's addicted and insane are the coun-try's legions of the blind and the lame. When I was talking with Makay Siawash, who runs the Kabul Orthopaedic Organiza-tion from a Soviet-era building in the Afghan National Army hospital compound in Kabul's Wazir Akbar Khan district, she had to stop for a moment to compose herself. "The worst is when we have someone who has lost his legs and his eyes. We have a young man right now who has this." Then she carried on with all the reasons why up to eight thousand Afghans a year turn to her agency for help. "A lot [of injuries] are from mines, rockets, bombs. But there are also traffic accidents, children who have been blinded, or they are deformed from malnutri-tion or from some trauma or malformation during pregnancy. And women, sometimes it is from hard physical activity, or they have been hit by their husbands. We have a lot of children and women. But a lot are from mines."

The young blind and legless man whose story caused Sia-wash to catch her breath had stepped on a Taliban "improvised explosive device" of precisely the kind that was so routinely killing and wounding Canadian soldiers down in Kandahar. In 2007, the Kabul Orthopaedic Organization, begun as a charity by the British journalist-turned-philanthropist Sandy

Gall in the early 1990s, signed a contract with the Afghan defence ministry. Before twelve months were up, Siawash had added more than seventeen hundred Afghan police officers and soldiers to her client list. "They have lost arms, legs, hands, eyes..." Usually, though, the organization's clients were civilians. Eight out of every ten amputees Siawash had registered were the victims of landmine blasts. As often as not, the exploding landmines are leftovers from the days of the Soviet occupation. Well into the twenty-first century's first decade there were more than sixty thousand landmine-blast survivors in Afghanistan. In the NATO countries, it was well known that improvised explosive devices (IEDs) frequently wounded and killed soldiers in Afghanistan. The Afghan civilian casualties were rarely reported. In 2008, sixty Afghans were being killed or wounded by landmines of one sort or another every month. Although it was a drop from the roughly one hundred civilian landmine casualties a month of a few years earlier, it was still a staggering number.

Makay Siawash is the only Afghan woman I've ever met who was allowed to hold down a job during the Taliban years. "I was one of the lucky ones," Siawash told me. "The women were not allowed to work at all, except in hospitals." Trained as a teacher, Siawash lost her job as the principal of Amani High School in Kabul when the Taliban ordered all schools closed. But even the Taliban usually allowed UN landmine-clearance projects to carry on. The Taliban needed someone who could read and had administrative experience to run the Kabul Orthopaedic Organization. "The Taliban needed us in those days," she said. Not anymore.

By 2006, the Taliban had begun staking out landmine-contaminated areas in order to recover old explosives for use in the manufacture of IEDs, their weapon of choice against everything from aid-agency vehicles and buses to civilian truck convoys and the military vehicles used by the Afghan National Security Forces and NATO-ISAF contingents. The Taliban treated UN de-mining workers like claim jumpers. "This is a change," Siawash said. In 2008 alone, eleven mine-clearing workers employed by the UN and its affiliated agencies were killed, and nineteen were wounded. The death toll was rising. The UN Mine Action Coordination Center already had to cope with worker deaths and injuries from the dangerous labour of extracting hair-trigger bombs from the earth. Now, worker deaths from Taliban attacks were increasingly showing up in UN Mine Action statistics, along with data on the Taliban kidnapping mine-clearing workers, stealing UN mine-detecting equipment and hijacking UN Mine Action vehicles. "This represents a major setback," said Siawash.

In the first few years following the end of Taliban rule, the UN reckoned it cleared 300,000 landmines and similar devices from about 1,000 square kilometres of Afghanistan. As the years passed, UN mine-clearing workers were slowly making a dent in the 500-plus square kilometres still riddled with bombs. Technically, Cambodia and Angola were worse off than Afghanistan. What made Afghanistan different was that landmines were almost exclusively littered in agricultural lands, grazing areas, irrigation systems, residential areas and roads.

But Afghanistan was not so different from much of the world in the fields of labour generally designated as women's work. The UN, the World Bank and almost every ISAF country involved in Afghanistan made a show of placing priority on the status of the country's women. In the aid agencies, it was not unusual for even the most formidable women's rights advocates to roll their eyes about it. It wasn't just because the high-level UN technocrats in charge were as likely as not to be

European men in nicely tailored Italian suits. It was the often-cumbersome, clodhopper effect of the approach. In much of Afghanistan, wage work is exclusively men's work. Inattention to jobless, employable males was not the best way for a NATO country to impress Afghans of either gender. And any overbearing emphasis on women's employment further reinforced the Afghan clerical-reactionary line that the assertion of women's rights was decadent Western impudence.

It is not as though well-funded, ambitious national reform measures were not critically important—Afghanistan's post-Taliban parliamentary quota for women MPs was a triumph. But perhaps the greater emancipation was occurring with the help of projects that were diffuse, small-scale and nimble, harnessing the same innovative genius that Mahboob Shah found in Kabul's homeless and that Mohammed Yousef set free in Kabul's street kids. At that level, when Afghan women were running their own show, you could pretty well sit back and watch them change the world before your eyes. That's what was happening in Parwan province, where only a few years before, the Taliban were trafficking in women for the brothel-slave markets in Pakistan.

The women of Parwan were not for turning back to days like that, and their resolve did not derive from decadent Western impudence. Mah Jan, a widow from the Parwani village of Qala-e-Kona, well remembered the Taliban time. Covetous of Parwan's rich farmlands and orchards, the Taliban arrived in the late 1990s in heavily armed armadas of Toyota SUVs. In Qala-e-Kona, "the Taliban burned our lands and tried to force people to move to Jalalabad," Mah Jan recalled. Determined to carve up the land and dole it out among their own crowd, the Taliban roared across the landscape and hunted down the men. They butchered the brave ones who stood and fought. In Qala-e-Kona, the women hid in their cellars. "The men escaped. When the Taliban came with guns, the women would come out to beat them to death with their bare hands."

The hardships of Mah Jan's life were written in the lines of her beautiful face. She was thirty-seven, but she looked about seventy. Forced to marry a deaf and mute man who died and left her alone with four children, Mah Jan had spent most of her adult life working as a washerwoman and a farm labourer, weeding fields for four hundred grams of beans per jerbil of land, about two hectares to a jerbil. She raised her children in a tent. When I spoke with her over strong cups of tea at the Kabul offices of Through the Garden Gate, a project con-ceived and funded by Canadian Mennonites, Mah Jan made it plain. All of that was behind her now. The old days were gone and done with. Now her life involved frequent business trips to Kabul to sell vegetables. She'd just bought a sheep and a goat, and she was saving money to buy a cow.

How this had come to pass is a story that began with the Mennonite Economic Development Associates, a simple idea and a careful program of strategic investments involving only small amounts of money. A few dollars in grant money here, a few more in micro-finance loans there, and the effort was soon transforming the lives of hundreds of Parwani women.

In the 1970s, the "Green Revolution" was flowering throughout the Third World, taking root even in parts of Afghanistan before the Cold War heated up and spilled over into barbarism and madness. Much of Afghanistan remained stunted by ancient farming methods. Even so, as recently as the 1970s, Afghanistan was more or less self-sufficient in food production. But three decades of war dragged every-thing backwards, and in Parwan, farming practices remained an almost wholly subsistence undertaking, nearly unchanged from the early days of the neolithic revolution. Farmers cast seed upon untilled ground. The husbands farmed the main fields. The wives were confined to household kitchen gardens—women's work.

By investing in basic literacy classes and some training in modern horticulture and standard business practices, the Mennonites helped hundreds of Parwani households increase the yields of their kitchen crops to allow for saleable surpluses. Through composting, irrigation and other basic but "modern" methods, the Parwani women extended their growing season for potatoes, beans, carrots, cucumbers, onions and tomatoes. With training in efficient storage and marketing, the women reinvested their tiny profits to package and sell their produce in Kabul at times when vegetables in the city are otherwise scarce and expensive. These extra earnings have paid the costs of teachers, and now the women of Parwan are slowly emerging into the light of literature and commerce and the life of the world. Several Parwani villages have replicated the model. In Qala-e-Kona, it was Mah Jan who'd stepped forward to serve as the village leader. At the time, it was an uncertain and contentious enterprise.

Marzia, a thirty-five-year-old mother of eight children and a "lead farmer" under Mah Jahn's guidance, is, like Mah Jan, a widow. "The Taliban killed my first husband. They just killed him without reason. He had a simple life. He was riding a horse. They took him away and they killed him," Marzia told me. She ended up living with relatives in Khomeinist Iran, working for slave wages as tens of thousands of Afghans did in those days. Marzia worked in a factory for twelve hours a day. After the fall of the Taliban, she returned home, but she was then forced to marry a brother-in-law, according to a primitive custom distilled from sharia law. In the end, her second husband abandoned her and her children. On her own again, she survived as best she could as a seamstress until Mah Jan's Garden Gate project started taking root in the village. "We are doing our housework, and at the same time we are out working in the kitchen gardens. Now we have a savings box, and we are hopeful," she said. Marzia was investing her small profits in a shop for her sons and intended to expand her small farming business. Opportunities like that were opening up for women all across Parwan, and there was an interesting outcome: "Now the husbands in the villages are giving us chances to take part in decision making."

In the nearby village of Dashto Opyan, it was the same story. The project leader there, thirty-three-year-old Sharifa, said it was an uphill climb. "I had to tell the men, I am not taking your wives and daughters away, they will be with me." Before she got involved in Garden Gate, Sharifa's husband wouldn't allow her out of the house. She didn't even know where her husband's farm fields were. After Garden Gate's successes, her husband came around, and the formerly men-only community development council was including her in its deliberations. "I am happy, because the men listen to my suggestions now. My dreams are coming true. We are going to friends' houses and relatives' houses for a party and to tell what we are doing. We are showing that women can be independent and can have things of our own. Now I can see and I can feel that I am alive and that I have a life. We are working and we supporting our children, and also the husbands are now happy with us."

Along with kitchen gardens, cooking, clothes mending, bare-hand cleaning and all those laborious and endless chores that Afghan women do, the care and rearing of children, as in much of the world, remains almost exclusively women's work in Afghanistan. It isn't easy to deduce from statistics how much more heavily that burden falls on the shoulders of Afghan women. But some things are known about the circumstances of Afghan children.

A decade after September 11, fully half of Afghanistan's people were children, and roughly half of those children were still not in school. Schoolchildren were not safe from harm: between May 2007 and February 2008, the Taliban attacked and burned 98 schools, killing 147 teachers and students. More than two million Afghan children were orphans, enough to populate a huge city all on their own. Child labour was ubiquitous. More than a million Afghan children were their families' main breadwinners. The UN Children's Fund (UNICEF) reported that even in 2008, one in four babies born in Afghanistan wasn't expected to live to the age of five.

But for all the horrific forces haunting the sleep of Afghan children, things were getting better. Especially for girl children, there was hope now, whereas before September 11, there was none. Defying the odds were twenty-nine girls in a shambolic house behind high walls and a sturdy metal gate down a dusty backstreet in the Koshalkhan district of Kabul. The place is called the Omid-e-mirmun orphanage. To arrive there for a visit is to be ushered into a courtyard and up steps to a door where a flock of girls will greet you. I first visited them in 2008. They were bold and bright and broadly smiling, and each offered a firm and hearty handshake. Good morning. How do you do? *Salaam.*

Afza Hosa, the forty-five-year-old housemother, was quick to shoo away a few of the older girls to put on the tea and to clear a place among the toys and books in the living room. "Around Eid, it is really hard," Hosa told me as a dozen of the girls curled up in various places around the room. "They want shoes and underwear and bangles and socks. 'I need the kind of scarf that I saw at school! I want this! I want that!' They drive me crazy."

The youngest was Zarina, about eighteen months old during my first visit. She'd been a newborn abandoned at Kandahar Hospital when Hosa heard about her and arranged to take her in. The oldest was Majabeen, dark-eyed, raven-haired and seventeen. She was intent upon going to university. "I am going to school, and I need a good education. I will pass," Majabeen declared in a matter-of-fact way. "I will become a doctor." Of the forty-eight girls in her class at a school just around the corner from the orphanage, Majabeen had come in fifth in the last year-end tests. She said she was not satisfied. "I have to work harder. I am decided."

When Majabeen was small, her father died in a car accident and her mother remarried. The new husband wanted nothing to do with Majabeen or her younger sisters, Qamaria and Zamaria. So the girls were abandoned. That was how these three sisters ended up here. You would have no inkling of this sad story upon meeting Majabeen or her sisters. You would not know, either, that the two-storey brick house where the girls live is an orphanage.

There used to be a bright blue billboard outside: Omid-e-mirmun, Funded by Afghan Women's Counseling and Integration Community Support Organization. It was taken down to protect Raisa, a girl of thirteen years, with delicate features and a beaming smile. Raisa came to Omid-e-mirmun after running away from home. Her parents had decided to sell her as a bride to an old man, and if they found her here they would take her and carry out their plan. If she defied them, they might kill her. Most Afghan marriages still involve girls under the legal marriage age of sixteen. In the country's rural areas, girls are routinely married off by their parents in trade for livestock, to secure loans, to pay debts or to obtain favours of one kind or another. Girls who rebel are commonly put to death. From the time I arrived at Omid-e-mirmun to the time I left, I didn't see Raisa stop smiling, not once.

When I visited Omid-e-mirmun two years later, the girls I'd met were coming along well in their studies. They were cheerier and saucier and giving housemother Hosa more frequent backchat. Majabeen was studying furiously and so had less time for tailoring and gardening and playing volleyball at school. Raisa was still smiling and happy.

Hosa's own story is extraordinary, though quite ordinary as Afghan stories go. She met her husband at Kabul University, and with the collapse of the Najibullah regime and the mujahideen wars that followed, they fled to India, eventually ending up in the United States. They lived for eleven years in Fort Worth, Texas. Hosa and her brother ran a convenience store and a gas station. Later, in Arlington, Virginia, Hosa worked at Nordstrom. In 2004, Hosa's husband got a job as an interpreter in Kabul, and Hosa took on the job of house mother at Omid-e-mirmun. She became the mother of twenty-nine children. "I don't have children of my own," she said. "God never gave them to me, so I am happy to adopt these children for my own." During all those years away in America, Hosa and her husband were possessed of a homesickness you'll often hear Afghan émigrés talk about.

During the Taliban time, it wasn't only women in the diaspora of five million Afghan refugees who were paying attention to what had become of the country. In the American women's movement, there were senior feminists who maintained a lonely campaign to keep the Taliban isolated. They did everything they could to force the enslavement of Afghan women into the public conscience. It was a lonelier campaign than you might think.

Much is made of a 1997 visit by a Taliban delegation to Sugarland, Texas, to meet with Unocal Corporation heavyweights about the company's hopes to build a pipeline across Afghanistan. It was pressure from American feminists that forced the White House to shut down Unocal's plans. Almost forgotten is that as late as the summer before September 11, when it was no longer possible to pretend that the Taliban were some sort of Third World liberation front, there was what an early 2001 *Village Voice* investigation called "a ragtag network of amateur Taliban advocates" across the United States. They busied themselves arguing for the Taliban, making excuses for Talibanism, pleading for Americans to respect the Taliban and to try to understand where they were coming from.

University of Southern California economics professor Nake M. Kamrany figured a way around U.S. visa restrictions to get Taliban emissary Rahmatullah Hashemi into the United States. Kamrany raised money to fund a lecture tour that brought Hashemi to UCLA and even to that allegedly radical hothouse, the University of California at Berkeley. The *Village Voice* described Professor Kamrany this way: "Kamrany hardly looks the part of a foreign emissary, showing up for an interview recently in Santa Monica dressed in a Hawaiian shirt and shorts, and insisting on a tuna fish sandwich before getting down to defending the burqa." Another American Taliban apologist was Davood Davoodyar, an economics professor at California State University in San Francisco. Professor Davoodyar agreed that his preoccupation was a bit nettlesome. "If I asked my wife to wear the burqa, she'd kill me," he said. Another California Taliban admirer was Ghamar Farhad, a woman. A bank supervisor, Farhad hosted Taliban delegates during their American visits and said she thought the Taliban were okay as far as women were concerned. She'd grown disenchanted after the Taliban notoriously blew up the spectacular and ancient Buddha statues in Bamiyan, she said, but warmed up again after the Taliban told her that "satanic idols had to go."

Odder still, you could find the same apologetics and moral illiteracy years after September 11, in Canada. That never ceased to astonish Sally Armstrong, one of the bravest and brightest of the North American feminists who had stood up for Afghan women during the Taliban years. The pioneering editor of *Homemakers* magazine, Armstrong slipped into Afghanistan wearing a burqa only a year after the Taliban's 1996 capture of Kabul. She came home with a first-hand account of the depths of Taliban depravity and their brutal enslavement of Afghanistan's women. The result was a blockbuster article that prompted nine thousand furious letters and ended up mobilizing *Homemakers'* subscribers—not the sort of women who immediately spring to mind as political activists—to take up the cause of their Afghan sisters.

Armstrong had earned a formidable reputation with such breezy magazines as *Chatelaine* and *Canadian Living* by providing compelling accounts of the suffering that women and children endured in such war zones as Somalia and Rwanda. Armstrong took a keen interest in stories that the warcorrespondent fraternity tended to miss. One of her early accomplishments was an exposé of the "rape camps" of Bosnia, which housed roughly twenty thousand women, some as young as eight, some as old as eighty. Her work ended up making a key contribution to the International Criminal Court's eventual recognition of rape as a war crime. But Afghanistan kept drawing her back. She made several visits to the country after September 11 as a magazine writer, a documentary film-maker, an author and a human rights activist. Her book *Veiled Threat* bears witness to the courageous struggles Afghan women waged during the Taliban era, an epoch that surely ranks among the most malevolent eruptions of misogyny in human history.

Armstrong sometimes encountered a strange hostility among well-heeled North Americans, as though she had no business taking up the cause of women's emancipation in faraway places. I witnessed it myself, up close, in 2007. You don't need an acutely honed sense of irony to appreciate that the incident occurred during the final forum of a human rights lecture series sponsored by the International Women's Rights Project at the University of Victoria, where Armstrong was asked to give a lecture at the conclusion of International Women's Week.

Armstrong presented a fairly upbeat view of Afghanistan. The good news was that, all over the country, women were insisting on their basic rights to justice, education and equal-ity, and they were actually getting somewhere. "The seed of human rights has been planted in Afghanistan, and I believe it has taken root," Armstrong said. "If I was a betting woman, I'd say we're turning a corner." The bad news was coming from the confused political debates in Western countries. Arm-strong urged Canadian women to keep the debates focused on Afghan girls and women and to resist the isolationist demand that Afghans be left to try and sort out their problems by themselves. Armstrong was more than willing to agree that military means alone should not be expected to defeat the Taliban. But if military means was all that was on offer, keep-ing the Taliban pinned down might just have to do: "We just have to beat them back and keep them in their caves."

Armstrong wrapped up her speech by pointing out the predicament of "blameless women and girls who continue to pay the price of the opportunism of angry men." Among her closing comments were these: "They say, 'You have no business writing about our women. You're not part of our culture; you're not part of our religion.' There's a taboo about talking about it. People play it like a cultural trump card to silence women like me." The UVic auditorium was filled with about two hundred women. Straight away, four men, as if on cue, rose to confront Armstrong with the misogynist litany she had just enumerated, inflected with the same menace, but in a vaguely leftish tone. They were among only a handful of men in the hall. One after the other, before any woman in the audience had managed to get a word in, the men laid into Armstrong. Canada is engaged in an imperialist occupation of Afghanistan, women like Armstrong "romanticize" Afghan suffering, Afghan women are worse off than they were under the Taliban, Canadian women should stick to matters that directly affect them—that kind of thing.

Outside the auditorium, Armstrong's detractors persisted in their hectoring, hovering around her and handing out their "anti-war" leaflets. Armstrong was clearly rattled. "I haven't had this experience to this degree before," she told me, but eruptions like that were becoming commonplace. "I can't tell you how thoroughly surprised I am at this kind of commentary," Armstrong said. "Are we going to stand back and say, 'We only do peacekeeping'? I don't know where this stuff is coming from." By 2007, it had become controversial to merely notice, as Amstrong insisted on doing, that human rights were universal, women's rights were human rights, the United Nations and the Afghan people were pleading with Canadians to help out militarily and otherwise and Canadians were obliged to do so.

Another leading North American women's rights activist who had stuck with Afghan women for the duration was Lauryn Oates. It was with Oates that I first visited the Omid-e-mirmun orphanage in Kabul. When I visited the orphanage again two years later, it was also with her. We were working together on a research assignment with the Canada-Afghanistan Solidarity Committee.

It's not every North Vancouver firefighter's kid whose story goes from being a guest of Uzbek dictator Islam Karimov to surviving a near-fatal motorcycle accident in northern Uganda to getting tossed into a Syrian prison. Or who has both funny, pedestrian episodes—like losing luggage for the umpteenth time in Dubai—and much darker moments, like taking calls in the middle of the night from BBC reporters after the bloodbath of September 11 and patiently explaining, for the umpteenth time, the nature of barbarism in Afghanistan. But that's what Oates's life had been like. When those airliners plunged into the World Trade Center towers and the world suddenly needed people to explain what the Taliban was, Oates was barely nineteen. By September 11, she had already been an anti-Taliban activist for five years.

As for the Syria story, as things turned out, Oates spent only a day in that Damascus jail cell, but she did manage to lay into a stiff gin and tonic smuggled in by a local contact. That was in 2004, when she was running a project with funds from the International Centre for Human Rights and Development involving the translation and distribution of international human rights law and literature, in Arabic and Farsi. She'd developed the program herself. Her brief incarceration arose from a misunderstanding. The 2008 Uganda motorcycle accident left Oates with a fractured skull, nasty scrapes and bruises, a bit of useful down time in hospital and some lingering memory loss. She was in East Africa for her doctoral research on the role of digital technologies in training primary school teachers.

The way Oates tells it, it all started in 1996. She was in Grade 9, quick with the attitude and utterly shiftless. One day, her mother left a clipping from the *Vancouver Sun* on her bed: an article about the rise of the Taliban and their enslavement of Afghan women. "I just couldn't believe this was happening," Oates remembers. "And the story wasn't even on the front page. How could the world let this happen?" She spent a few days in a funk, but soon enough she'd drafted a petition and collected about four hundred signatures, mostly from friends, family, her fellow students and shoppers she'd browbeaten at the local mall. She sent the petition to Ottawa, Washington and the UN. She found a fax number on a Taliban website and fired the petition off to the Islamic Emirate of Afghanistan. She hasn't slowed down since.

For two years, Oates spent every spare minute devouring everything she could find about Afghanistan, about international human rights conventions, refugees, torture, prisoners of conscience, the lot. Every weekend she'd take the bus across Burrard Inlet to Amnesty International's Vancouver offices to work as a volunteer. She did anything and everything, from sweeping floors to giving presentations at high-school assemblies. Soon she was Amnesty Canada's youngest fieldworker.

Right through high school, Oates kept at it. The main thing was Afghanistan and the way its women were being so savagely brutalized—the notorious stadium executions, the forced confinement, the slavery. It was a tough and lonely slog, but then Sally Armstrong's article from inside Afghanistan appeared in *Homemakers* magazine, and Canadian Women for Women in Afghanistan (CW4WA) was born. It was only after

Oates founded its Vancouver chapter that the CW4WA head office learned she was only sixteen.

Oates had just begun her studies in political science at McGill University (one of the first things she did upon arriving was to organize a CW4WA Montreal chapter) when the news about the World Trade Center attacks broke. "It was like the whole world had turned upside down," she remembers. Two years later, in December 2003, she was in Afghanistan for the first time. She'd come for the constitutional loya jirga, the assembly that established the current Afghan state. She'd been assigned to write a report on the proceedings for the International Centre for Human Rights and Democratic Development. "I remember stepping off the plane. It felt beautiful. It was like coming home."

By 2011, Oates's work as CW4WA's project director had taken her back to Afghanistan nineteen times, and CW4WA had raised over $3 million for Afghan women, mainly from the small-scale fundraising efforts of its chapters across Canada. The effort had put hundreds of teachers to work and tens of thousands of Afghan girls through school. Oates didn't have much patience with the comfortable habits of the aid-agency nomenklatura. She didn't have much good to say about the soft-palmed among the foreign-policy establishment, either.

In the fall of 2008, Oates was invited to Uzbekistan to attend what was billed as an international conference on elections. The gathering followed another one of the comically fraudulent polling performances that Uzbek president Islam Karimov stages from time to time. The conference quickly revealed itself to be an opportunity for Karimov, the Butcher of Tashkent, to burnish the patina of his bloody regime's legitimacy. The diplomats, NGO big shots and European pseudo-intellectuals in attendance took pains to mind their manners. Even in the low murmurs over coffee in the corridors, you couldn't get a decent disagreement going over whether Karimov boiled his enemies in oil or just plain water. This was not the sort of company Oates preferred to keep, so she took off and headed straight for the Afghan border. Uzbek guards tried to exact a fee for allowing her to leave Uzbekistan, and a noisy and protracted standoff ensued. Oates won, and when she finally trudged into her beloved Afghanistan, she was welcomed by a crowd of whooping well-wishers who'd witnessed the whole thing.

Straight away, she fell in with a boisterous Afghan family who insisted she accompany them to the wedding they were headed for in a village on a mountainside above Kabul. The long and bumpy ride over the Salang Pass was relieved by crazy Bollywood singalongs punctuated by several steam explosions and periodic pit stops to replenish the crowded van's leaking radiator. Oates ended up conscripted as a kind of honorary bridesmaid.

Forgiving as she is, Oates was early to lose patience with "anti-war" equivocations. Not once since 2001 had she flinched from her early conviction that a profound moral duty demands that Canada send soldiers to Afghanistan. First things come first. Sometimes you need soldiers. Oates's deepest convictions rest on an uncluttered bedrock. Human rights are universal, women are human beings and it is only with the emancipation of Afghan women that Afghans will free themselves from obscurantism and slavery. Universal access to a liberal education is the one certain and rocky road to lasting peace. If that meant sending soldiers to Afghanistan to fight Talibs, then that's what it meant. Her views put Oates on the militant side of aid-agency debates and foursquare within the minority, muscular position in debates on the "Left," though in Canada those debates never really got off the ground. The Canadian liberal-left shifted incoherently back and forth along the spectrum between outright capitulation, at the troops-out end, and the mewling neutrality of the peace-talks lobby. Oates had staked her ground early. Against anything that even vaguely resembled neutrality, she dug her heels in deeper as the years passed.

For one thing, Oates understood that neutrality didn't work. It was what allowed Afghan women to suffer their torments alone all those years. For aid-agency bureaucrats, neutrality could be dressed up as high-minded opposition to the "militarization of aid," but for front-line workers it was like a game of Russian roulette, except that the gun had only one empty chamber instead of only one bullet. Writing in the *Globe and Mail* from her home in Kandahar in 2008, Sarah Chayes, a journalist, author and women's rights activist, put it this way: "The only place as dangerous to be as a NATO military convoy is a clearly marked humanitarian vehicle." Chayes wrote that essay not long after what happened to Jackie Kirk of Montreal, Shirley Case of Williams Lake, B.C., Nicole Dial of Colorado and their Afghan colleague, Mohammad Aimal. The CARE Canada workers were not connected to anything military. They were travelling unarmed only a couple of hours from Kabul, near the town of Gardez, in a clearly marked humanitarian vehicle. The Taliban executed them anyway. Oates was a friend of Kirk's.

What got under Oates's skin was that the pro-neutrality arguments allowed foreign humanitarian aid officials to cop an immunity plea, a luxury unavailable to Afghan workers. Two years after Chayes's essay was published, Oates wrote: "The Taliban kill beneficiaries and aid workers anyways. Three days ago, they beheaded two Afghan women in Helmand province who ran micro-finance programs for women. On a weekly basis, Taliban kidnap Afghans who work for both national and international NGOs. They regularly assassinate nationals who run aid programs, work as drivers or guards for aid organizations." In the Afghan "expert" community, Oates had earned a well-deserved reputation as a cool-headed, formidable academic. Among NGO staff in Afghanistan, she was widely respected for her solid, authoritative and analytical research. But when she turned to the more sinister aspects of the neutrality charade, Oates could be counted on to be blunt, especially when politicians were playing the game. "When it comes to Islamo-fascist terrorism, I want to be clear with myself where I stand. There is only one side that history will forgive, and it's not the side of the Taliban, nor the side of passivity." That kind of language suited the Afghan women's leadership just fine.

Kandahar MP Malalai Ishaqzai, only thirty-eight and the mother of seven children, had many kind things to say about Canadian soldiers when I met her at her modest Kabul house in the spring of 2010. Ishaqzai did not fit the picture of a veiled and bullied Kandahari chattel-slave. A small retinue of men attended to her papers and her tea and her telephone calls. Her male relatives, like solicitous headwaiters, came and went politely from the spacious living room where we sat. Only a couple of years before, the Taliban had kidnapped Ishaqzai's twenty-one-year-old son Mustafa. She'd rallied her extended family to pitch in and help pay the $100,000 ransom. She'd been through a lot. When I met Ishaqzai, her main consternation was about Canada's plans to pull its troops from Kandahar. Ishaqzai couldn't understand it. "Canadian troops are better than the American troops or the British troops or the Dutch troops. We don't have any problems with the Canadians. Why are you leaving?"

The question came up routinely in my conversations with leading Afghan women. It was raised perhaps most poignantly by Shafiqa Habibi, one of Afghanistan's most beloved and prominent journalists. An Ahmedzai Pashtun of regal bearing who was already covering Afghan politics for television and radio in the late 1950s, Habibi was a trusted radio voice silenced during the Taliban tyranny. But after 2001, she was back as a confident and dependable television presenter. "Canada was always our friend," she told me one day in Kabul. "For these eight years, the solidarity of your soldiers, all that they have done, everyone in Afghanistan knows about the Canadian casualties. We are really sad about Canadian soldiers' casualties in Afghanistan. But this is to protect Afghan women. How would such an active partner for Afghanistan leave us?"

It wasn't an easy thing to explain. Three years earlier, the special panel chaired by John Manley had advised a Kandahar troop extension to 2011. As the deadline approached, however, Parliament was paralyzed. The right-wing Harper was by now as firmly entrenched in the troops-out camp as his most hysterical left-wing detractors were, and nobody was talking about what to do next. Canadian Forces commanders were left to scratch their heads and lay plans to simply pack up and leave. Like so many Afghans I spoke with, Malalai Ishaqzai found it a bit too culturally exotic to comprehend. But something else about Canada was an even deeper, more confounding mystery to her. "Why don't you just bomb Ahmed Wali Karzai's house?"

She was referring to the brother of Afghan president Hamid Karzai, the Popalzai tribal kingpin in Kandahar who ran the president's elaborate patronage networks, procured lucrative American contracts for himself and his cronies and drove around in an armour-plated convoy making people offers they couldn't refuse (he was assasinated on July 12, 2011). Many astute American observers regarded him as an untouchable, ballot-stuffing crime boss, a bad bastard, but their bastard. "Everybody knows that Ahmed Wali Karzai is a big mafiosi," Ishaqzai said. "Why don't you just get rid of him? Everybody knows he is a crook." That was another good question without an easy answer.

By early 2010, almost everyone in the Afghan women's leadership seemed as dispirited and confused as Ishaqzai about where things were going. The bloom had gone off Barack Obama's rose. After months of hand wringing and policy-wonk astrology, the White House went ahead with its promised troop surge, but when Obama talked about Afghanistan, the word "democracy" never even came up. The war-weary NATO capitals were sinking deeper into dementia, Karzai's entreaties to his Taliban "brothers" were becoming more torrid, and you could never really tell which of these two things was the cart and which was the horse. The whole wagon train contraption was heading off across uncharted territory towards a cliff. Foreign-policy think tanks busied themselves by formulating complicated hypothetical scenarios in the hope of discovering the route to a cheap and squalid exit-strategy peace deal with the Taliban. In January 2010, Karzai let it slip in a BBC interview that he was desperate enough to offer the Taliban "peace at any price." It looked for all the world like the schemers in Islamabad, London, Tehran and Washington were preparing to put a shiv into the ribs of Afghan democracy once and for all, and to let women's rights die along with it.

For thirty-year-old Kabul MP Sabrina Saqib, the wagon

train was headed the wrong way. Despite being well to the left of Malalai Ishaqzai, or perhaps because of it, Saqib didn't counsel neutrality either. "We have got to win the war. We have to take out the enemy side. We have to make the enemy weak," she told me. The worst things were the Americans' hamfisted use of heavy weaponry and the NATO air strikes that produced so many civilian casualties. Even so, "this is war," Saqib said bluntly. "We are losing people who are giving space to the so-called moderate Taliban? I am using joke—moderate Taliban. This is war."

I met Saqib in the Wolesi Jirga's half-built legislative precinct, an architectural potpourri that melded mid-century Central Asian modern with Brezhnev-era blockhouse and barb-wired blast wall with 1970s French polytechnic. We sat at an elegant, nicked and scratched committee table in a dimly lit room with high ceilings. A huge portrait of some long-forgotten wazir was covered with a sheet against the dust from the renovation crews causing rickety chandeliers to tinkle in the dark hall I'd been led down after several full-body security checks outside.

"You came here to help us with democracy and to help us hold elections," Saqib said. The election that Alekozai had not wanted to see cancelled had gone ahead in August 2009, and millions of Afghans had faithfully voted. But the Electoral Complaints Commission had uncovered so much backstairs work and vote rigging that the Independent Elections Commission had no choice but to order a rerun of the whole thing. When Abdullah Abdullah, Karzai's leading contender, threw in the towel on the reasonable grounds that there was no point in trying to make a haywire machine work twice, Karzai was back in office. The still-busted machine assured another debacle in the parliamentary elections that followed. "We may have to go more than ten times before people know how it works. It is the mechanism of elections. It is not just about knowing the dates," Saqib said. "The people need more chances."

Saqib then proceeded though the follies contained in the Western world's most fashionable policy prescriptions for Afghanistan's ailments. Paying farmers for their opium: "If you promise to pay for opium, then people will grow opium." Make-work programs to replace opium farming: "If you promise jobs in favour of opium, people will grow opium to get jobs." Wooing Taliban fighters with promises of land and money: "There will be thousands of people who will call themselves Talibs." Negotiate with the Taliban: "With whom are we going to negotiate? What is there to negotiate? About the women, is this factor negotiable? We, as women of this country, we are the first victims of these negotiations. We are the first victims of these processes." That was also what I'd heard from Malalai Ishaqzai, especially the part about luring Talibs with promises of cash and property. "In Kandahar, whenever I am talking to the young people, they say it is better to take a gun and be a Talib, because the government will give them money and give them land."

Then what to do? It wasn't all that complicated, Saqib explained. The rich countries of the world could start by giving Afghans some credit for once. Afghans were desperately poor, but they weren't stupid. "The people do not want to go back," Saqib said. Canada especially should stop being so prissy about intruding upon Afghan sovereignty (I heard this from all sorts of Afghans, all the time) and hold Karzai democratically accountable to the Afghan parliament and the Afghan people. "The people of Afghanistan do not want to give up. It is changing. I got most of my votes from men. Even the women who were elected from Kandahar got most of their votes from the men. They are seeing the benefit of their daughters going to school, the wives out working and bringing in bread—there are even more job opportunities for women than there are for men."

A name came up, the same name that often entered conversations with Afghan feminists, human rights lawyers, democrats and reformers about why their voices weren't being heard in the rich countries of the world. "Should you leave because Malalai Joya is asking for this?" Saqib asked. "She is not even in parliament any more. What she is saying is not only risky for herself, it is risky for us. And she is living in Canada now." When Joya's name came up in conversation with Ishaqzai, she registered it with a muted "puh." When I visited a few days later with the outspoken young Badakhshan MP Fawzia Koofi, the Wolesi Jirga's deputy speaker, Joya's name came up again unbidden.

"I don't think there is an Afghan war," Koofi said. "There is a global war. We have lots of unfinished problems with Pakistan. Even Iran is appeasing the Taliban—they don't support the Taliban, but they support Hamas. Also there are political games going on in your countries, and these games influence what happens in Afghanistan as well." I asked her what she meant. "There is a lack of proper communication in your country about Afghanistan. They don't see all the good progresses. For me, the hope is for the younger generation. Young men are voting for women. The society is under a big transformation, and there are people who don't want to see this. In Canada, the people don't see this. The problem is that they listen to Malalai Joya."

Joya was the young Afghan MP from Farah who burst onto the scene in 2006 with a fiery speech to the Afghan parliament denouncing the warlords and criminals sitting on the

Wolesi Jirga's benches. Not a few hoary old mujahideen had elevated themselves from their comfy chairs to throw plastic water bottles at her, which turned the event into a global sensation. When Joya delivered an even more high-pitched speech during an Afghan television interview, calling the Afghan parliament worse than a zoo or a stable, her fellow MPs invoked the Wolesi Jirga's notoriously strict rules against unparliamentary language to suspend her. In Western capitals, this turned Joya into a rock star, with all the globetrotting engagements and media celebrity that goes with the job. While she slowly faded from the Afghan scene, her 2009 memoir *A Woman among Warlords,* co-authored by a Canadian "anti-war" activist, was a bestseller.

In a famous photograph taken during her 2006 speech to parliament, a dark-eyed young MP is seen shielding Joya from the shower of water bottles. That young MP was Sabrina Saqib. But since then, it had become a lot more difficult for Saqib to find a reason to defend Joya. Her thoughts about the warlords differed little from Joya's, but that was about as far as it went. Besides, said Saqib, "Malalai Joya only has some repeated sentences she keeps repeating, nothing new. You can listen to Malalai Joya once and record it, and repeat it. It doesn't change." What matters is not what someone thinks, or claims to think, Saqib said, but what someone actually does. "You came to Afghanistan because of universal values, that we have right to live in peace and practise democratic values that are practised all over the world. At least we are only throwing water bottles at each other. This is a very big step for those mujahideen. They use the red and green cards for disagreement and agreement. This is something we have achieved. It is democracy."

Saqib's view of the global nature of the Afghan struggle for women's emancipation, peace and democracy affirmed Fawzia

Koofi's proposition that it wasn't just an Afghan war or even a regional problem. "It is a worldwide problem," Saqib said. "You are here to fight against worldwide terrorism, and you prefer to fight here than to fight in Toronto or Washington, D.C., or London. But it is up to you. If you don't care about Afghanistan then you can leave as soon as Malalai Joya orders you to leave."

In the meantime, Koofi, a declared presidential candidate, saw a new world being born in Afghanistan's younger generation. She saw hope for the future in the teenagers throughout most of the country who didn't even know what a real war was like. Since her husband died in 2003 from the tuberculosis he'd contracted in a Taliban prison years before, Koofi was constantly on her guard. A few weeks after I visited with her at her Kabul home, where she was proud to show me the rabbits her daughters were raising for sale at the local market, the Taliban attacked Koofi as she was travelling in Badakhshan. Her driver was injured, and two Afghan police died in the shoot-out. But this was still far from the horrors of the past. Koofi's daughters were happy and healthy, they did not live their lives imprisoned in burqas and they were doing well in school.

Saqib saw the new world being born even in the children of the war zone. She heard it in the words of seventeen-year-old Shamsia, the most seriously injured of several girls who were viciously attacked as they made their way to school in Kandahar in 2008. Shamsia wasn't wearing a burqa, and she had acid sprayed into her face. From her hospital bed, Shamsia vowed: "I'll continue my schooling even if they try to kill me. I won't stop going to school." Said Saqib, "This is what makes me happy. That is the real voice of Afghanistan. We have female boxers now in this country. We have female soccer players, too."

Two years before I met Saqib, I'd spent some time with the sisters Yasameen and Raziea Rasoul, the star forward and the team captain, respectively, of the Afghan National Women's Soccer Team. Raziea, eighteen, was the team's midfielder, and nineteen-year-old Yasameen was also the coach of the Kabul Tornadoes, a boy's team. The Rasoul sisters were playing out their parts in the democratic revolution that was quietly transforming Afghanistan: in the Parwani villages of Qala-e-Kona and Dashto Opyan, in the dangerous streets of Kandahar City, in Sohaila Alekosai's ministrations at the Women's Park, in the orphan Majabeen's studious aspirations and in the political debates underway in the Wolesi Jirga. It was all so painfully slow. But it was moving the world forward.

Briefly, the Rasoul sisters had become rock stars. They posed for the television cameras while greeting U.S. secretary of state Condoleezza Rice at the Kabul Airport; they suffered through lunches with ambassadors; they played soccer on the Pentagon lawn in Washington. The attention eventually died down, and this allowed the Rasoul sisters to get back to what they liked best, playing soccer.

Their story begins in 2002 in a bombed-out Kabul neighbourhood a short walk from the once-glorious sixteenth-century Babur Gardens, in the shadow of Sher-e Darwaza Mountain. Duane Goodno, a just-retired Peace Corps and Defence Department bureaucrat, had wandered away from a tour of the gardens and found himself invited in for tea in a collapsed two-storey house nearby, where the Rasoul family were living as squatters. Yasameen and Raziea were eleven and twelve, but they'd grown up so malnourished they could have passed for seven-year-old twins.

Goodno and his wife, Barbara, a U.S. Army major, moved to Kabul to start up a small non-governmental organization, and they set up shop in the Karte Se district, not far from the Rasouls' hovel. In 2004, the Goodnos invited Jenny McCarthy, a CW4WA volunteer from Montreal, to come and take charge of a group of girls, mostly orphans, that included the Rasoul sisters. McCarthy reckoned she'd teach them how to play soccer, and the girls took to the game straight away. Before the year was out, they were an Afghan team at the Children's Olympics in Cleveland, Ohio. President George W. Bush was there. He made fuss over the girls, which made them famous.

It was an exciting diversion, but back in Kabul the girls just kept playing soccer. When the time came to select players for Afghanistan's national women's team, five of the eight original Afghan Star team members from Karte Se entered the tryouts. Yasameen and Raziea were among them. The girls shut out the opposing teams five games in a row, four at 3–0, and one at 1–0.

In Afghanistan, if you're a girl, to play soccer is to commit a revolutionary act. It's been grand, but rough going for the Rasoul sisters. In their efforts to add girls' teams to the Afghan soccer federation, they kept getting turned down in their bids to rent fields. Or they'd find a soccer field that would allow girls to play, only to be harassed and bullied by local men. The sisters shifted tactics. If Kabulis weren't ready for local girls' soccer teams, they might be able to get their heads around a boy's team coached by Yasameen. It worked, and the Kabul Tornadoes was born. "Now there are boys who are coming to the games, and they are very happy. They are coming to be on my team. They listen to me," Yasameen had told me. "They always come to their practice, and they are actually very good." It was a start.

The Kabul soccer stadium where the Rasoul sisters and

their teammates from Karte Se formed the Afghan national team in 2007 is the same stadium where, only a few years before, the Taliban were carrying out barbaric ritual spectacles, executing burqa-shrouded "adulteresses" to the moans and wails of the crowds in the bleachers. As the girls from Karte Se were savouring their 2007 victory and planning their next, half a world away eighteen schoolgirls from the Okanagan Valley were busy with a fundraising drive. The Grade 5 girls were led by Alaina Podmorow, who had accompanied her mother the year before to hear a speech by Sally Armstrong.

Alaina was nine years old when she founded Little Women for Little Women in Afghanistan. That first fundraising drive raised $3,000, enough to pay the salaries of four Afghan schoolteachers for a year. Over the next few years, Alaina and her young comrades from the Okanagan led three marches for children's rights on Parliament Hill to protest the world's inattention to the plight of Afghan schoolchildren, Congolese child soldiers and sweatshop child-slaves in India. By the time Alaina was fourteen, she and her fellow activists had raised $300,000 for teacher-training programs and teachers' salaries in Afghanistan.

That's quite an accomplishment for a handful of schoolgirls from a valley in British Columbia's hinterland. They'd provided more material solidarity for the emancipation of Afghan women than all the trade unions, the provincial and territorial federations, the 136 district labour councils of the three-million-member Canadian Labour Congress and the half-million students and eighty student unions of the Canadian Federation of Students combined.

five

"IF EVER A COUNTRY DESERVED RAPE"

IN THE SPRING of 2009, Master Sgt. Jeffrey Bullard, a U.S soldier embedded with a platoon of Afghan National Army troops in a remote Pashtun valley a few kilometres from the Pakistan border, was surprised to discover that the locals thought American soldiers were Russians. Word of the Red Army's withdrawal from Afghanistan hadn't yet reached the people there. In a survey of one thousand men the International Council on Security and Development (ICOS) carried out in 2010 in Helmand and Kandahar provinces, the heart of the Taliban "insurgency," nine out of every ten men questioned had never even heard about what happened on September 11, 2001. They knew nothing about the spectacle of the Twin Towers falling in New York, or American Airlines Flight 77 plunging into the side of the Pentagon, in Washington, D.C. Nine years after the events of that morning, nine out of ten Kandahari and Helmandi men knew nothing about any of it.

You could say that in much of Afghanistan, illiteracy, religious obscurantism, backwardness and isolation are responsible for what Orwell called "the sealing-off of one part of the world from another." No such excuses account for the strange things people sometimes imagine in the rich countries of the world. Even the most literate and educated people should be forgiven for sometimes "swallowing lies or failing to form an opinion," as Orwell wrote. Everybody's busy. We send the kids off to school in the morning, we try to make ends meet. To one degree or another we all tend to contract out the thinking we should be doing for ourselves. But in the broad cultural and political constituencies where Absurdistan's fictions have found their most loyal adherents in the Western world, something far more sinister has been at work. Where it did not suppress, warp and filter Afghanistan's story, it drowned out the voices of the Afghan people entirely.

Orwell's "general uncertainty as to what is really happening" is insufficient to account for the astonishing number of apparently ordinary people who came to imagine, for instance, that September 11 was an "inside job." Mere uncertainty won't explain why it was so commonplace in the years following September 11 for people to regard the Taliban as some kind of indigenous national liberation movement. Neither is "general uncertainty" enough for a phenomenon that called itself an anti-war movement to be mistaken for a progressive mobilization on behalf of the Afghan people. Something else was going on.

In Canada, it was playing out on the same tectonic scale as the emergence of a distinct democratic socialism in the 1930s, the Quiet Revolution in Quebec in the 1960s and the rise of libertarian Prairie populism in the 1990s. As is fairly common at the advent of such upheavals, journalists can be among the last to notice. Nonetheless, something new was emerging in the New Democratic Party, the trade unions, the university faculties, the student movement and the national activist

organizations of "the Left." In all these places, the response to
the events of September 11 involved the deliberate construction of an imaginary "war" in Afghanistan that required the
most progressive and intelligent Afghan voices to be ignored.

You could pick up the liberal-establishment *Globe and Mail*
and read prominent "anti-war" and purportedly left-wing academic James Laxer arguing that NATO countries should pull
their troops from Afghanistan, even though the likely result
would be a civil war that ended with a "fascistic theocracy."
This would indeed be preferable, Laxer argued, owing to the
Afghans' "ornery tendency to throw out invaders." The Canadian journalist that "anti-war" polemicists cited perhaps most
frequently as an authority on Afghanistan was Eric Margolis. It didn't seem to matter that Margolis was a millionaire
"alternative medicine" magnate with a regular column in Canada's conservative-populist Sun Media newspaper chain. A
co-founder of Pat Buchanan's far-right *American Conservative*
magazine, Margolis consistently cast the opposing forces in
Afghanistan as Hamid Karzai's communist-dominated government and secret police on one side, with the Taliban, "a
religious anti-communist movement drawn from the Pashtun tribe" on the other. But Margolis was, of course, "anti-war,"
and was therefore regarded as being on the side of "progressive"
clarity and virtue.

This sort of thing wasn't happening only in Canada—not
by a long shot. And it certainly wasn't happening just because
of Malalai Joya. It wasn't Joya's fault that scores of elite journalists all over the Western establishment news media used
her to articulately express everything they needed someone to
say about Afghanistan.

The production of Absurdistan demanded much imagina-
tive stagecraft, and sustaining the fiction over time took a lot

of hard work, many hands and much money. Things can go
wrong. In the United States, Joya's most active support base
was Code Pink, which claims 250 chapters and 100,000
members and served as Joya's occasional tour host and finan-
cier. In October 2009, a reporter with the *Christian Science
Monitor* witnessed an encounter between some outspoken
Afghan women and a Code Pink propaganda-gathering delegation in Kabul. Shinkai Karokhail, a women's rights activist
and an Afghan MP, told Code Pink: "International troop presence here is a guarantee for my safety." Said Masooda Jalhal,
a former Afghan cabinet minister: "It is good for Afghanistan
to have more troops—more troops committed with the aim
of building peace and against war, terrorism, and [committed
to provide] security—along with other resources."

Code Pink returned to the United States with what
it claimed was evidence that Afghan women wanted foreign troops out of their country. It delivered its report, titled
"Troops Out," in person, to President Barack Obama. But the
controversy was short-lived and almost immediately forgotten.
The way Code Pink manipulated the testimony it took from
Afghan women was exposed in a six-part blog series written by
Sara Davidson, one of the eight delegates Code Pink brought
to Kabul. Even that didn't make any difference.

Malalai Joya plays only a bit part in a bigger drama. It
might help to see her more charitably, not so much as the
reason for the silencing of Afghan women's voices but as a
component part of something larger, like a needle placed
into the groove of a vinyl record. The loud music drowns out
everything else, but the record can only play the music that's
already on it. "You can listen to Malalai Joya once and record
it, and repeat it. It doesn't change" is how Sabrina Saqib put
it. What sustains Absurdistan is a particular sort of cultural

predisposition, a mode of thought that does not "privilege" empirical evidence and requires only a pre-existing susceptibility to a certain category of music and a tone-deafness to everything else. How did this happen?

In 2004, philosopher-journalist Andrew Potter and author-economist James Heath shed helpful light on the archaeology of Absurdistan with their excavation of Western popular culture in *Rebel Sell: Why the Culture Can't Be Jammed*. The two Canadians trace a clear path from the European Enlightenment to the radical politics of the nineteenth and early twentieth century, and what they find at the horizon of the early 1960s is a break in the strata. Before then, in its main currents, the point of radical politics had always been to mobilize the masses to their greater benefit, usually and properly at the expense of their exploiters. But shortly past the twentieth century's midway point, radical politics started staking its authenticity on a deep suspicion of the masses. "Before long, the people—that is, mainstream society— came to be seen as the problem, not the solution," Potter and Heath write.

This was not altogether unhealthy. In the United States, a deep suspicion of the core values of mainstream society may have been necessary in the early days of the civil rights movement, in the struggles of the feminist movement and in the extension of civil rights to gay people. But you don't have to buy Marxist ideas about false consciousness to be alert to the great problem of capitalism—or to capitalism's great genius, if you prefer. Capitalism's enduring capacity to absorb and capitalize on the biggest threats it faces, even in the most ghastly sorts of economic disruptions, drives serious anti-capitalists plum crazy. Ever since the days of Lenin and Trotsky, the system has leaped from crisis to crisis, defying one socialist prophecy after another about capitalism's final drama. From the merely saucy to the reformist to the outright revolutionary, capitalism can convert almost anything into something profitable. Popular culture does it best. Che Guevara looks just as good on a $25 T-shirt as Elvis Presley and Kurt Cobain do, and nothing sells the "alternative" like mainstream marketing.

Heath and Potter begin by taking their trowels to the music of post-war popular culture. They follow a clear line of rebel authenticity in counterculture genres over time. It's all about sticking it to the man. Each new form attempts to out-transgress its predecessor, from psychedelic hippie music to punk to grunge, and even to gangsta rap, with its nihilistic celebrations of gun violence and misogyny. Each is effectively absorbed by the capitalist establishment, just as the genres, styles and sensibilities that went before it were.

"This wouldn't be so important if it were confined to the world of music. Unfortunately, the idea of counterculture has become so deeply embedded in our understanding of society that it influences every aspect of social and political life," Heath and Potter write. "Most importantly, it has become the conceptual template for all contemporary leftist politics." This is their main point: "Counterculture has almost completely replaced socialism as the basis of radical political thought. So if counterculture is a myth, then it is one that has misled an enormous number of people, with untold political consequences."

Two years after *Rebel Sell*, British journalist Nick Cohen, well to the left of Potter and Heath, presented similar but more incendiary findings. Cohen's book, *What's Left? How Liberals Lost Their Way*, is a 405-page, exhaustively detailed and extensively footnoted examination of the "untold political consequences" that Heath and Potter were on about. Cohen has no regrets that something had "almost completely replaced socialism" of the Soviet kind. But after the collapse of the Berlin Wall in 1989, the twentieth century's final decade ushered in an epoch of disorientation across the political spectrum. Something else had emerged where socialism used to be.

By the decade leading up to September 11, almost all the great struggles waged by the Western world's left had been won. The old-world empires had been swept away. Diseases that had routinely burst into plagues down through time had been eliminated. Europe, the twentieth century's charnel house, was united, at peace with itself in precisely the consensual federalism that was the revolutionary dream of the nineteenth-century anarchist Mikhail Bakunin. Digital technologies, transportation systems and the post-industrial "penturbia" phenomenon were carting off into history's dustbin the "idiocy of the countryside" that Karl Marx had lamented. With only a bus pass, a library card and an Internet connection, working people had at their command cultural wealth greater than anything the most obsessively acquisitive nineteenth-century industrialist could have hoped for himself. Workers were healthier and lived longer than the richest robber barons of the Industrial Revolution. Women had the vote, their basic rights in the work force were protected and they were outnumbering men in the universities. Christianity was imploding, freedom of speech was sacrosanct, gay people were beginning to emerge as full-status citizens, primary education was free and marriage was a mere lifestyle choice.

The old democratic-socialist ideal proclaimed that what we expected for ourselves, we would demand for everyone. By the 1990s, with the Cold War over, it was at last possible to imagine that ideal carried around the world. An injury to one would be an injury to all. The workers of the world could conceivably unite, and they didn't need to rely on a Stalinist model to do so. The democratic left's great heritage was its strikes, its voter-registration drives, its willingness to make sacrifices, to take risks and, wherever possible, to fight the enemy face to face within the system. This is precisely the kind of politics embodied by Afghan feminists like Fawzia Koofi, Sabrina Saqib, Malalai Ishaqzai and the rest.

But in the developed world, progress, as the left had always measured it, had come to a standstill. The United States was the world's sole superpower. Socialism was a dead project. The strange new era enlivened free-market neoconservative utopians and reduced their adversaries to the self-indulgence of a hopeless, losing, rearguard "resistance" to globalization. For the left, it was a disorienting state of affairs. Instead of picking up the mantle passed on by the heroic trade union-ists, anti-fascists and civil rights activists who had gone before them, the activists of the rich world's strangely mutated left acted more like spoiled children living off the legacy of their hard-working predecessors. Anti-Americanism became the left's substitute for internationalism. Delusional theories, with sinister forces manipulating world events, replaced clear-headed analysis. "Zionists" conveniently replaced the mythical shadowy, conniving Jews. You didn't actually have to *do* any-thing to assert a left-wing politics. It was all about being. You could be a Californian fair-trade coffee magnate with a man-sion in Bel-Air or a millionaire Vancouver marijuana-seed entrepreneur—you were still an authentic rebel. More often than not, to engage in left-wing activism was to engage in the politics of the gesture, the futile protest, the symbolic act.

Out of the ashes of the twentieth-century's great anti-fascist struggles there arose a standard: human rights are universal rights. Many peoples, one humanity. All people, one.

From the age of flags, this was the one banner still flying. But by the 1990s, in the newly comfortable districts of Europe and North America, the solemn internationalist obligations that arose from that standard had been "problematized" by identity politics, counterculture exhibitionism and post-colonial "theory." Instead of rising to the challenge of universal emancipation, the West's formerly Marxist left retreated almost wholly into the nihilistic morass that usually goes by the name "cultural relativism." Borrowed from anthropology, the politics of cultural relativism is a jumble of white guilt, identity politics and a weird insistence on a kind of equivalence among cultures and their various claims to truth.

If you can't criticize or even properly comprehend "other" cultures by applying universal criteria, you will hardly be allowed to offer so much as a low opinion of fascist cultures that celebrate the public stoning of women or religious belief systems that nurture the death cults of suicide bombers. But you don't need to trouble yourself with any of that anyway, because to qualify for membership in the latter-day left, Nick Cohen writes, it had come to this: "All you must be is against your own government and against America."

The result is a distressing spectacle. "Democrats, feminists and socialists in the poor world who are suffering at the hands of the extreme right turn for support to the home of democracy, feminism and socialism in the west," writes Cohen, "only to find that the democrats, feminists and socialists of the rich world won't help them or acknowledge their existence." With the bedrock of universalism corroded, the bonds of solidarity can only break down. No one owes a solemn duty of any kind to anyone else. Writes Cohen: "You couldn't have found a more lethal way to kill left-wing politics if you tried."

Thus, by the morning of September 11, 2001, across the

liberal left, people had lost their ability to comprehend any enemy more foul than the United States. When the planes plunged into the Twin Towers, the Euro-American left, Cohen writes, simply went "berserk."

In *The Left at War*, his survey of post-9/11 liberal-left politics, the American cultural studies professor Michael Bérubé looks closely at some of the consequences of all this. Cohen's focus is mainly on Britain; much of the British left, he writes, responded to the Anglo-American overthrow of the Baathist regime in Iraq by abandoning its anti-fascist traditions for a fashionable "anti-imperialism" by way of open collusion with the Islamist far right. But Bérubé's focus is the United States. His assessment pivots around the dissimulations of the counterculture *éminence grise* Noam Chomsky.

The brilliant MIT linguist's theories about media and mainstream society are widely known. This is in itself peculiar; much of Chomsky's reputation rests on the claim that he is studiously ignored by the media that preoccupies him and celebrates him as a public intellectual. Chomsky's main claims can be understood as reiterations of the Marxist Antonio Gramsci's notions of false consciousness to account for the masses' tedious habits of eating unhealthy hamburgers, voting against their class interests and stubbornly refusing to smash the state. Most helpfully for our purposes, Bérubé follows Chomsky's pronouncements on "the war in Afghanistan." The Chomskyan line that emerged in the days and weeks after September 11 would end up setting the tone and the style of the entire "left-wing" consensus about Afghanistan in the years to come.

It is not that there is no historical precedent for sordid leftist collusion with Islamist theocrats. And it isn't as though prominent figures on "the Left" started to say crazy things about Afghanistan only after the events of September 11. Two decades earlier, Alexander Cockburn, columnist for the impeccably left-wing magazine *The Nation* and editor of the once-formidable *Counterpunch* magazine, had this to say about Afghanistan in the *Village Voice:* "An unspeakable country filled with unspeakable people, sheepshaggers and smugglers... I yield to none in my sympathy to those prostrate under the Russian jackboot, but if ever a country deserved rape, it's Afghanistan. Nothing but mountains filled with barbarous ethnics with views as medieval as their muskets, and unspeakably cruel, too. "

In the immediate aftermath of September 11, both the mainstream and the counterculture media afforded Chomsky their broadest audiences. His wilder claims were also reproduced faithfully in the state-censored Arab press, which likes to encourage crazy anti-Western prejudices in its readers as often as possible. Reading Chomsky in those first few weeks after September 11 is like watching Absurdistan being born.

The seminal source for the Chomsky "line" on Afghanistan was a public speech he delivered at the Technology and Culture Forum at the Massachusetts Institute of Technology in October 2001, before any American troops had even showed up in Afghanistan. He began his speech by parroting the Taliban claim that they would be pleased to enter into negotiations for "delivery of the alleged target, Osama bin Laden." Chomsky further rebuked "the leader of Western civilization" for failing to take up the Taliban on their offer.

Chomsky spoke as though the reduction of Afghanistan to a vast, post-apocalyptic slave camp for women and a concentration camp for starving, brutalized people was not sufficient evidence for the capitulation of the network of jihadists and gangsters in charge of the country. He spoke as though the

134 / COME FROM THE SHADOWS

Taliban were Afghanistan's recognized government. He talked about them as though the United States had not met with the Taliban's emissaries more than twenty times in the previous three years in attempts to convince them to hand over bin Laden. As for the culpability of a radical Islamist network in the September 11 atrocities, Chomsky said: "Whether they were involved or not, nobody knows. It doesn't really matter much."

It was mostly a classic Chomsky lecture, with its customary litany of American imperialist misadventures over two centuries in Hawaii, the Philippines and Latin America. He spent more time talking about Nicaragua than about Afghanistan, but the clincher involved his reference to dire aid-agency speculations that U.S. bombing runs could put Afhans at risk of starvation. Chomsky put the speculations together with a U.S. government warning to UN food-relief convoys against entering Afghanistan from Pakistan to claim that the U.S. warning amounted to a "demand to impose massive starvation on millions of people." Just to be clear, he said: "Western civilization is anticipating the slaughter of, well do the arithmetic, 3 to 4 million people or something like that."

Unsurprisingly, Chomsky's remarks were heralded as controversial. It was also not surprising that Chomsky tended to be cast in the role of courageous truth teller, with his detractors playing the part of imperialist propagandists. He would later insist that his views had been misrepresented, but his speech was filmed, and the transcript was published in Alexander Cockburn's *Counterpunch*, no less. The record shows that, among other things, Chomsky said: "Looks like what's happening is some sort of silent genocide." Further: "It indicates that whatever, what will happen we don't know, but plans are being made and programs implemented on the assumption that they may lead to the death of several million people in the next couple of weeks."

Any reasonable person would read that as an accusation by Noam Chomsky, named by *Prospect Magazine* in 2005 and 2008 as one of the world's top one hundred intellectuals, that the United States was more or less deliberately planning to commit "genocide" in Afghanistan. At the very least, Chomsky was accusing the U.S. government of proceeding with a bombing campaign that it knew could lead to the deaths of perhaps millions of people over a two-week period.

It was only October 2001, but the needle was in the groove, and the familiar music was back in the air. It suited the counterculture narrative perfectly. September 11 was really about American imperialism. It was about Third World resistance to global capitalist hegemony. It was the same old story, except that some chickens had come home to roost.

The Arab press loved it, too. In Egypt, Chomsky's version of events allowed the *Al-Ahram Weekly* to cite him approvingly and to provide an account of the war in Afghanistan not two months after September 11 that went like this: American B-52s were "bombing Afghanistan back to the stone age." The headline: "Ignored by the media and dismissed by American and British politicians, millions of impoverished Afghans are being casually starved to death."

It didn't matter that in the real world, in the days leading up to September 11, roughly six million Afghans were already on the verge of starvation. In the country's north, people had been reduced to eating rats and grass. After September 11, the Taliban ordered all international aid workers to leave Afghanistan. Some aid agencies had "cried wolf," John Fawcett, a humanitarian relief worker and an authority on the politics of aid, acknowledged. He added that he couldn't really blame them for doing so. But as Fawcett pointed out, "More aid has gone into Afghanistan in the past month than in the past year." Some agencies had warned that a bombing campaign could disrupt food deliveries and produce another 1.5 million needy refugees, but "in fact, the result of the bombing is there are 150,000 new refugees—one-tenth of what they expected, and there's been a tenfold increase of humanitarian aid getting in, because everybody's focused on the problem now," Fawcett told *Salon*. Three years later, Chomsky was defiant: he'd never warned about a genocide, he was just citing the *New York Times* and quoting aid agencies like Oxfam.

And so, within weeks of September 11, Absurdistan was on the map, situated in precisely the place where Afghanistan used to be. The U.S. intervention in Afghanistan, Fawcett noted, had exposed a deep moral confusion about what real humanitarian action is in the real world, where it matters. "The fundamental question people are not willing to look at is that this military action is humanitarian action," Fawcett said. He posed the dilemma in the form of a rhetorical but mercilessly blunt question. It was the question that would become the fork in the road for the rest of the decade: "Do you want to deliver food packets to the concentration camp, or do you want to get rid of the concentration camp?"

Fawcett's question sheds some helpful light into the depths of a political chasm a *Guardian* newspaper editorial would later call "the most serious split within the left since the Soviet invasion of Hungary in 1956." But in Canada, you mightn't have known any of it was happening. You were either "anti-war" or "pro-war," and there wasn't much else to discuss.

In *The Left at War*, Michael Bérubé clearly situates himself among those on the American left who are against concentration camps. When he begins his enumerations of the "atrocities" and "travesties" attributable to the Bush-Cheney administration, he can hardly figure out where to finish. But when he looks to the left in the rich countries of the world, the landscape he sees is similarly littered with travesties.

Looking to identify the moment things went so sideways, Bérubé cites the avant-garde post-modernist Michel Foucault's enthusiastic verdict on the Khomeinist counter-revolution in Iran and the Western left's strange quietude about—and sometimes apologetics for—the death sentence by *fatwa* ordered by the Ayatollah Khomeini against Salman Rushdie for his novel *The Satanic Verses*. By September 11, Foucault had become one of the most influential philosophers in left-wing academic circles in the West. It showed.

Like Cohen, Bérubé points to the toxic effects of cultural relativism. For all their progressive claims, cultural relativists fail to recognize in Third World and Muslim "others" the very rights and duties that they happily recognize in one another, in their own well-to-do (and often tenured) class. To follow habits of mind like that, one can only end up in a place where the prevailing narrative paradigm will be the one with the deepest pockets, the loudest voices or the shiniest boots.

Much like Potter and Heath, Bérubé attributes the degeneration of rigorous progressive analysis to a miasma of countercultural posturings. "It involves a mode of belief, a way of believing rather than a set of beliefs; it is the work of a *countercultural* left that sees politics as a game rigged by corporations and the process of winning popular consent as a form of 'selling out.'" Along with cultural relativism and counter-culture histrionics, Bérubé identifies a third strand that was lingering on the "left" long before Foucault or the hippies. It's a cold cynicism, not something that derives merely from anti-capitalist antagonism or pro-Soviet sympathies, as so many

138/ come from the shadows

conservative critics have claimed, but rather a persistent loathing for and antagonism towards the ideas of liberal democracy
itself. George Orwell observed it in his day. There was something suspicious about the avowed socialism of many of his
contemporaries, whose "real though unacknowledged motive,"
Orwell wrote, "appears to be hatred of western democracy and
admiration for totalitarianism."

A politics of this type takes no serious risks. It stands
for nothing in particular. It requires the enunciation of no
real alternative. It's especially handy in mobilizing support
for the world's most anti-liberal forces and anti-democratic
regimes. The "anti-imperialist" charade requires the role of
the aggressor to be played by either the United States or Israel,
preferably both. It is not just a politics of the "far left," and
neither is it simply a composite of the "radical left," Bérubé
writes. It is very much a product of the counterculture. On
the matter of Afghanistan, Bérubé refuses to cede ground to
the troops-out camp's claim to be "anti-imperialist." I know of
no evidence to support its claims to be anti-war, either. Some
rally goers might sincerely think they are *being* these things.
But what they're actually *doing* is neither—if anything, it's the
opposite of both.

A withdrawal of the UN's forty-three-nation ISAF alliance at any point during the decade following September 11
would have subjected Afghans to a return to the most brutal
forms of Pakistani and Iranian proxy-war imperialism. That's
if Afghans had been lucky enough to somehow evade another
swarming of attacks from the Arab-jihadist private sector.

No matter what calculus you apply in order to situate the
"anti-war" demand, there was certainly nothing "progressive"
about it with regard to Afghanistan. Bérubé considers the

terms "reactionary left" and "conservative left," then settles on a classification he calls the Manichean Left, owing to the crudely reductionist mode of thought it involves. It goes something like this: "If Israel is in the wrong then Hezbollah must be in the right." That is what "the Left's" position on Afghanistan, to the extent that there was one, had come to. If the United States was involved in it, the whole thing must be wrong.

"One strains to imagine a late-1930s 'Not In Our Name' petition dedicated to the principle that Spain and Germany must be left to determine their own destinies, free from military coercion from great powers," Bérubé writes, "or even worse, an early-1980s left devoted to the principle that El Salvador should be allowed to determine its own fate by means of civil war because the world did not have any business interfering in that sovereign state's internal affairs." It doesn't take much straining to imagine the fascist right taking those positions, because it did. What was curious about the first decade of the twenty-first century was that objectively pro-fascist formulations were being taken up by "the Left."

In the United States and Britain, the Iraq debacle overshadowed everything, to the point that Afghanistan was almost a distraction. After the bombs started falling on Baghdad, all the "bring the troops home" protests were exercises in the politics of the futile gesture. There were perfectly valid arguments against the Anglo-American military invasion of Iraq, but against the UN-authorized NATO mission in Afghanistan, none of those same arguments withstand scrutiny. That the various and shifting American and NATO military strategies in Afghanistan were so often ill-advised and wrong-headed is beside the point. The Iraqi enterprise tormented the British and the Americans, looted their treasuries and haunted their sleep. Canada sat it out, but ended up with the most berserk aspects of both worlds anyway. That's why Canada makes such a useful case study in the madness of Absurdistan.

By September 11, the Canadian "left" was in the hands of a generation that had come of age with what the historian Shulamit Volkov calls an "ideational package": a collection of cultural codes taking up the empty space where, say, a class analysis would usually go. The phenomenon can be tragi-comical. On March 15, 2008, a protest in Calgary against the Atlantic seal hunt, a sustainable tradition vital to the income of working-class Newfoundlanders, transformed itself at a pre-arranged moment into a protest against both the presence of Canadian soldiers in Afghanistan and the Israeli "siege of Gaza."

The cultural codes Volkov finds embedded in the post-1960s ideational package include anti-capitalism, anti-imperialism, anti-Americanism and an often dangerously heavy dose of anti-Zionism.

Of these, the code that blends across the broadest spectrum of Canadians is a type of anti-Americanism that is essentially a bundle of deep misgivings about the United States. It includes a healthy concern for Canadian sovereignty and an equally healthy scepticism about the brute force of American military power. Canadians have long enjoyed looking down their noses at Americans, besides. There's often the tinge of an inferiority complex at work, but it is a harmless custom. Canadians are routinely the punchline in American jokes; Americans are commonly the butt of Canadian jokes; and it's all good fun. Sometimes it's wickedly funny.

In the late 1990s, the Canadian Broadcasting Corporation's political satire program *This Hour Has 22 Minutes* began a regular segment called "Talking to Americans." Comic genius Rick Mercer travelled around the United States posing as a journalist to dupe gullible Yanks into saying outrageously stupid things in front of a television camera. With surprising ease, Mercer got former Iowa governor Tom Vilsak to congratulate Canada for adopting the twenty-four-hour day. He convinced Arkansas governor (and eventual Republican presidential candidate) Mike Huckabee that Canada had just completed a new Parliament building, built of ice. Huckabee congratulated Canada on building its new "national igloo." Mercer even persuaded faculty members and students at Harvard to sign a petition calling on Canadians to end their practice of abandoning the elderly on ice floes. A CBC television special based on the segments became the highest-rated Canadian TV special in history.

But there is a less amusing side to the Canadian attitude towards the United States, and it was commonplace following the events of September 11. There wasn't much protest when Canadian soldiers joined with NATO and American troops in the initial assault on the Taliban. But by the time of the 2003 American invasion of Iraq, the mood had soured. George W. Bush seemed to represent everything Canadians loathed about the United States, and Canada reverted to its customary disdain for its southern neighbour. Paradoxically, the anti-Americanism that was abroad in Canada at the time drew most heavily from a distinctly American sensibility. The American counterculture had eclipsed old-school left-wing politics in Canada. In the years following the Vietnam war, it was like some contagious version of narcissistic personality disorder had become deeply embedded in Canadian culture. By September 11, if an American hippie celebrity was sneezing somewhere, you could be certain that a leading Canadian social democrat would soon be coming down with a cold.

The Vietnam legacy makes a special appeal to Canadian vanity. During the late 1960s and early 1970s, tens of thousands of draft-evading middle-class American college graduates flooded north, forming the largest bloc of immigrants to Canada during those years. They were the best-educated and most advantaged immigrants Canada took in over the course of the twentieth century. They were a minority group with nothing "visible" about them. They went on to make tremendous contributions to Canadian politics and culture, and by September 11 they formed perhaps the single most influential foreign-born bloc in Canada. Their story is usually told in a way that flatters Canada by exaggerating the Canadian role in the American anti-war movement of the 1960s. It's a bit of a spin, because it requires the concurrent gratification of the American counterculture's need to exaggerate its own role in bringing the American war in Indochina to an end.

The story appropriates the credit more properly due to the tens of thousands of Vietnamese guerrillas who fought and died in the struggle to drive the United States out of Indochina. Those guerrillas were not pacifists. The paradox here is that the spoils from that appropriation get shared equally between Canada and the American counterculture in a collaborative claim upon the virtues of pacifism. Plus the good guys get Trudeau and the bad guys get Nixon. Everybody's happy, and in the bargain, the American counterculture's aversion to all things military became a "Canadian" value. The result lets Canadians look at themselves in the mirror and swell with pride to see the reflection of what is in fact a particular kind of American ideal. The arrangement allows Canadians to say: We are peacemakers; Americans are warmongers. Canadians have lots of health care; Americans have lots of guns. The story buttresses the draft dodgers' self-regard and shores up Canada's delicate self-esteem. It works very nicely.

Nowhere is this funhouse-mirror effect more evident than in the works of American filmmaker Michael Moore. A counterculture giant, Moore has something of an obsession with Canada. In his television productions and feature films, he built his career by holding a mirror up to Americans that makes properly "liberal" Americans look like idealized Canadians and "right-wing" Americans look stupid. It's fairly easy work. Being at the fringe of American-dominated popular culture, Canadians always get a kick out of it when they get noticed. Moore's documentaries break all records, the Disney empire invests millions of dollars in his work and his stock holdings are to die for (and yet somehow, he's still a rebel). Nothing flatters Canadians quite like the reflection they see in Michael Moore's mirror.

Moore's cavalier approach to facts and evidence doesn't seem to bother his admirers. Yet the journalist Jesse Larner, a liberal Democrat and the author of *Forgive Us Our Spins: Michael Moore and the Future of the Left,* is deeply concerned about what Moore represents. "The problem for Americans who are interested in politics, and who are not conservative, is that Moore has so thoroughly captured the market for symbolic rebellion. This kind of rebellion is more about the confirmation of identities taken on through assumed, highly reductionist common 'truths' (No blood for oil!) than it is about understanding what is happening and changing it for the better." It's show business, in other words.

In the weeks following the tragedies of September 11, Rick Mercer declined the nomination for a prestigious Gemini Award for *Talking to Americans* and brought to an end his brilliant send-ups of American gullibility. Mercer also went on to become one of the few CBC personalities who didn't furrow his brow about Canada's engagements in Afghanistan, and he has displayed an unapologetic affection for Canadian soldiers stationed in Kandahar. Michael Moore distinguished himself by insinuating that al-Qaida should have chosen some "red state" city to bomb instead of New York, teeming as it was with Democrats. Some people thought that was funny. Moore went on to produce the wildly popular 2004 documentary *Fahrenheit 9/11*, a brilliantly made jumble of partisan innuendo and speculation. The film's narrative resembled a comic-book version of a Chomsky lecture. Nevertheless, it won the prestigious Palme d'Or prize at the Cannes Film Festival.

Moore also became one of the loudest American voices calling for the withdrawal of U.S. troops from Afghanistan. His prescription was a caricature of the worst aspects of Donald Rumsfeld's American policy: Never mind about those Afghans; let them sort out their own problems; just focus on getting al-Qaida, and al-Qaida isn't in Afghanistan. Moore tarted up his version with a lexicon that included references to Vietnam, Richard Nixon and so on. His rages grew more shrill as the years passed. "Get out," Moore demanded. "Get out, get out and apologize to the people there." He was a superstar and exactly the kind of American celebrity that Canada's liberal intelligentsia adored. An outsider, a rebel. Somebody who speaks truth to power.

By 2006, in Canada, all was chaos. A brand new Conservative Party had come to power in a minority government. The new prime minister was Stephen Harper, who spoke a new kind of conservative dialect that rendered him incapable of defending the Afghan cause in the multilateralist, humanitarian language that Canadians had long spoken and understood. The new Conservatives did mount some refreshing challenges to the Conservative establishment's dull and dreary outlook on the world, but there were no foreign-policy wiseguys among them. Stephen Harper seemed to care about Afghanistan about as much as Michael Moore did. When it came to Afghanistan, what Harper seemed to care about most was polishing his friendship with an American president most Canadians loathed. President Bush was so reviled by Canadians that Environics pollster Michael Adams reckoned you'd have to go as far back as James Madison to find a president that Canadians similarly disfavoured. (It was President Madison who ordered American troops to invade Canada in the War of 1812.)

The best opportunity to make a sensibly progressive and distinctly Canadian contribution to the debate lay with the nominally left-wing New Democratic Party. Instead, by 2006 the NDP had adopted a sound-bite-sized policy lifted word for word from a popular American slogan crafted to fit on a protest-rally placard opposing the U.S. engagement in Iraq: "Support the Troops. Bring 'Em Home." In Afghanistan, the call for troop withdrawal and peace talks with the Taliban began as the position of the far right. In Canada, it began with the NDP.

Canada's former Liberal government had consulted closely with Afghan Canadians. Within NATO, Canada had taken up the call by the Afghan women's movement to extend ISAF's reach throughout the country, and that required Canadian soldiers to return to Afghanistan in force. But just as the troops were getting into the thick of it, the Liberal Party's old guard imploded. A serious contender to fill the vacuum was Michael Ignatieff, a glamorous human rights academic from a liberal-left tradition that wasn't nervous about applying muscular humanitarian intervention to failed-state crises.

Another bright light was Bob Rae, a former New Democrat who had thought long and hard about these things. But the Liberal helm went to Stéphane Dion, from the traditionally isolationist province of Quebec. A decent, earnest but weak leader, Dion was intent upon distancing himself from the policies of his Liberal predecessors. He hadn't much cared for the idea of Canadian soldiers being in Afghanistan in the first place. Now that they were sitting in the opposition benches, the Liberals wanted the whole Afghanistan thing to just go away, except for the bits they could try to blame on the Conservatives.

What all this meant was that just as the Canadian Forces took full command of the hellish civilian-military NATO-ISAF project in the hyper-violent, strategically critical Afghan province of Kandahar, there was no one in Ottawa to champion the Afghan cause. Canadian soldiers were soon dying in Kandahar at a higher rate than American soldiers in Iraq, which was descending into a ghastly wasteland of fanaticism and al-Qaida suicide-bomb spectacles. As if things couldn't get worse, 2006 was also the year of the frightful and heartbreaking Second Lebanon War.

That summer, the emboldened New Democratic Party set out to take over the Canadian conversation on Afghanistan. "Canadians are not warmongers," NDP leader Jack Layton declared. Across Canada there were marches and parades, die-ins and teach-ins, just like in the 1960s. The Taliban were not the Vietcong, but the familiar conception of Third World resistance to American hegemony was close at hand, and the tropes and memes of the counterculture were there for the taking. All that was required of Canadians was to succumb to the reflexive habits and the beckoning appeal of the transgressive. All that mattered was to make sense of September 11 in a way that appealed to Canadian vanity and did not disturb Canadian hierarchies of virtue or the country's accustomed postures towards the United States. Canadians are peacemakers. Americans are warmongers.

In his essay "History and Helplessness: Mass Mobilization and Contemporary Forms of Anticapitalism," University of Chicago history professor Moishe Postone points out that what made the new "anti-war" movement different from earlier mobilizations was that it "did not express any sort of movement for progressive change." By 2006, Canada had become an active proving ground for the most sordid of the collusions between the white, middle-class "left" and the Islamist far right that Nick Cohen had observed in Britain. The phenomenon that Ely Karmon of the International Institute for Counter-Terrorism has called "a growing trend of solidarity between leftist, Marxist, anti-globalization and even rightist elements with Islamists" had deeply entrenched itself in Canada's "anti-war" leadership. In the pages of New York's venerable *Dissent* magazine, Canadian linguist Shalom Lappin, a devoted social democrat, cautioned that the phenomenon was no mere strategic marriage of convenience: "For this part of the left, its peculiar notion of anti-imperialism does not so much take precedence over progressive political concerns as replace them. Anti-colonialism and anti-imperialism have exhausted its content to the point that it has become ripe for merger and acquisition by militant Islamic jihadists posing as the representatives of the third world poor struggling against Western domination." In Canada's key "anti-war" coalitions, it was merger and acquisition, root and branch. To remark on this, especially if you were on the left, was to find yourself with "smear job" and "McCarthyism" ringing in your ears. Sometimes the words were "Islamophobe" or "warmonger" or

"Zionist." This isn't how you engage in a debate. It's how you shut it down.

First cemented in the core leadership of the Toronto Stop the War Coalition, the merger was replicated at the bottom end in the Canadian War Resisters Support Campaign and at the top in the Ottawa head office of the "anti-war" movement's labour-supported national umbrella organization, the Canadian Peace Alliance. The Toronto Coalition's coordinator, James Clark, vowed that "the Canadian peace movement, inspired by the Arab resistance in Lebanon and Iraq," intended to "work with Muslims to defeat imperialism." On Canada's west coast, the most active "anti-war" organization was the Mobilization Against War and Occupation (MAWO). In Vancouver, this is what MAWO had to say for itself: "Wherever Islam is fighting against imperialism, it is a progressive force ... 'the Left' must join with Muslims in this fight."

An early and prominent Toronto Coalition spokesman, Zafar Bangash, did double duty as director of the Institute for Contemporary Islamic Thought, a Khomeinist think tank dedicated to providing ideological support for global Islamist revolution and to breaking the "stranglehold" of Western ideas among Muslims. Bangash distinguished himself during the embassy burnings, murders and riots that followed the Danish newspaper *Jyllands-Posten*'s 2005 publication of a series of "Mohammed cartoons" by declaring that, like the death-threat response to author Salman Rushdie's *The Satanic Verses* in the late 1980s, protesters sacrificing their lives in response to the cartoons was right and proper, "exactly how it should be."

Like the key leaders of the War Resisters' Support Campaign, the Toronto Coalition's James Clark came from the leadership of the formerly Trostkyist International Socialists (IS) group, a branch plant of the Socialist Workers Party

(SWP) in Britain. Shortly after September 11, the SWP's politics mutated from its early-1990s "with the state, never, with the Islamists, sometimes" strategy to a full-blown joint venture with the Islamist far right. Its Canadian IS branch quickly fell in lockstep. Breaking with left-wing traditions, in 2004 the SWP joined with the Muslim Association of Britain to fight the Labour Party with the new "Respect" Party, led by the disgraced British MP George Galloway, a celebrity presenter for Press TV, the English-language propaganda agency run by the Khomeinist regime in Tehran.

In 2005, the SWP's Canadian IS subsidiary openly waged a reactionary campaign on behalf of far-right Muslim clerics against the progressive Muslims, feminists and secularists who were fighting an Ontario government plan to incorporate sharia legal tribunals into religious-arbitration courts for family disputes. The IS accused the anti-sharia progressives of engaging in "Islamophobia." By then, the campaign coordinator staff position at the Canadian Peace Alliance in Ottawa was held by IS leader Sid Lacombe, and the CPA's steering committee included Clark and other key IS leaders. The CPA could always be counted on to serve as Galloway's Canadian venue organizer, and CPA leaders were routinely guests of honour at Iranian embassy events and celebrations.

Galloway and his "Respect" Party managed to convince most of the Canadian news media in 2009 that Ottawa had "banned" him from Canada. A subsequent court case explicitly dismissed Galloway's legal action, but most of the Canadian news media ended up reporting that Galloway had more or less won. Although not well known in the United States, Galloway became almost as much of a media darling in Canada as he was a reality TV freak-show spectacle in Britain. The *Toronto Star*'s Linda McQuaig couldn't get enough of him, calling him part Noam Chomsky and part Mick Jagger. The CBC's Heather Mallick swooned over Galloway and what she called his soothing, Shakespearean voice: "I could listen to Galloway all night." Galloway was deferentially characterized by some of Canada's most respectable newspapers as a colourful, maverick and left-wing British MP who'd been expelled from the British Labour Party in 2003 for opposing the war in Iraq. Inconveniently for his admirers, there is a lot more to Galloway than that.

For starters, Galloway was expelled from the Labour Party when he was found guilty on party charges that he had "incited Arabs to fight British troops," incited British troops to defy orders, threatened to run against Labour himself and backed an opposing candidate against the Labour government. He was suspended from the British House of Commons after parliamentary watchdogs found him guilty of not disclosing his links with Saddam Hussein's police-state regime in Baghdad. The committee cited "strong circumstantial evidence" (a court case found it not to have been proven) that Galloway's charity had connived with Iraq's Baathist dictatorship to rip off the UN's Iraqi oil-for-food program.

In 2006, right under the noses of the Ottawa press gallery, Galloway travelled to Ottawa to be the guest of honour at a publicly advertised seventy-fourth birthday party for the Syrian Social Nationalist Party, an unambiguously fascist movement with shiny boots and uniforms, its own distinctive swastika and an anthem sung to the tune of "Deutschland, Deutschland, Über Alles." Try to imagine the media uproar if some backwoods Arkansas Republican congressman in cowboy boots had shown up at a publicly advertised Nazi convention in Ottawa instead.

But that's the way things were going. Reputable journalists would regularly consult and present personalities from the "peace movement" side of Canada's Afghanistan debates who made contrary claims for themselves when the cameras weren't around. Just one thing the Canadian news media didn't notice was that for several years, these same "peaceniks" were regularly attending an annual conference in Cairo to swap notes and forge common strategies with Hamas, Hezbollah, the Muslim Brotherhood and several other antisemitic, jihadist and extreme-right Islamist groups. Among the Canadian delegates were representatives of the Canadian Peace Alliance, the Toronto Coalition, the Canadian Arab Federation, the Coalition Against Israeli Apartheid, Artists Against War, the Venezuela We Are with You Coalition and the Toronto-Haiti Action Committee. To his credit, John Rees, the Socialist Workers Party boss who served as a senior organizer of the annual Cairo conference, did not engage in any make-believe when he described what it was all for. "The Cairo conference remains a unique meeting point for those fighting imperialism in the Arab world and the rest of the international movement that acts in solidarity with them."

Among "those fighting imperialism" at the founding Cairo conference in 2002, which was jointly organized by Britain's SWP and reportedly funded by Egyptian companies with business interests in Iraq, were Nabil Negm, a political adviser to Saddam Hussein, and Saad Qassem Hammoundy, a senior Iraqi Baath Party official and Iraq's ambassador to the Arab League. The declaration the delegates crafted reads like a pre-nuptial agreement between a deranged young anti-globalization protester and a pot-bellied Islamic police-state theocrat. It identifies the Palestine issue as "integral to the internationalist struggle against neo-liberal globalization," condemns "Zionist perpetrators of genocidal crimes" and commits its adherents to organize boycotts of Israeli and American goods. In 2003 and thereafter, the Cairo conference billed itself as the International Campaign against U.S. and Zionist Occupations, conveniently conflating Zionism with global capitalism.

Back in Canada, the Cairo conventioneers dutifully carried out their annual work plans, organized "Israeli Apartheid" campaigns and engaged in elaborate circumlocutions to link protesting vegetarians at World Trade Organization summits with the glorious Hezbollah resistance. They twisted themselves into knots trying to present Canada's military contribution to the NATO-ISAF mission in Afghanistan as a roundabout support mission for Anglo-American imperialism in Iraq. Their most cunning strategy was to employ "Islamophobe" as a discussion-ending term of abuse, deliberately conflating the everyday varieties of Islam practised by pious Muslims with Islamism and its various forms of police-state theocracy. Oppose the totalitarianism of the latter and you'd be found guilty of being some kind of racist about the former. Always, everything was related back to the Israel-Palestine conflict.

Hamas cites the classic antisemitic fiction the *Protocols of the Learned Elders of Zion* in its founding charter and holds the Jews responsible for the French Revolution, the First World War, the Russian Revolution and the Second World War. In Canada, it's considered bad form to say things like that, so you just change the word "Jew" to "Zionist." That way, in the pages of the venerable socialist magazine *Canadian Dimension*, senior collective committee member and frequent contributor James Petras could blame Zionists for any rotten thing he wanted. Writing about the worldwide Mohammed cartoon riots and embassy burnings that led to the deaths of at least 139 people in 2005, Petras claimed it was all a Zionist plot and that the Israeli intelligence agency, Mossad, had planted a Ukrainian-Jewish agent working under a pseudonym at the Danish newspaper that published the cartoons. That wasn't even the half of it. Petras is an American academic and the author of such books as *The Power of Israel* and *Rulers and Ruled in the U.S. Empire: Bankers, Zionists, Militants*. It was his habit to say that a shadowy group of Jewish bankers was running American foreign policy, and they'd tricked the United States into invading Iraq.

All of this hard work did not go completely unrequited. Iranian president Mahmoud Ahmadinejad teamed up with Venezuelan president Hugo Chávez to establish a "global progressive front," but it got off to a rocky start. At a 2007 Tehran conference that purported to be a celebration of the legacy of Che Guevara, one conference speaker went too far for the Argentinean revolutionary's daughter Aleida and son Camilo, who had been flown in for the occasion. Hajj Saeed Qassemi, the Iranian regime's coordinator of the Association of Volunteers for Suicide-Martyrdom, asserted that both Che and Cuban president Fidel Castro had really been quite religious, but they had hidden their faith to keep the money coming in from atheist Moscow. The Guevaras caused a scene.

There comes a point sometimes where there's nothing to do but laugh. In Vancouver, a MAWO activist was outed after he started hanging around local mosques, pretending to be a Muslim and chatting people up. In Toronto, an IS-organized "Festival of Resistance" with the theme "Building Unity: Muslims and the Left," featured veteran Cairo conference goers, Khomeinist ideologues and leaders of the right-wing Canadian

Islamic Congress. In October 2006, the Canadian Peace Alliance joined with the Canadian Islamic Congress, the nominally left-wing Canadian Labour Congress and some of the most reactionary Muslim clerics in Canada in a nationwide protest demanding that Canada pull its troops from Afghanistan. By this time, the progressive Muslim Canadian Congress was beyond the point of being either amused or surprised. The MCC's Sohail Raza told me: "No, we would not participate in that. It is necessary for our troops to be there. You just have to look at who they are fighting against. The Taliban was the biggest setback for Muslims in our history, and if we were going to have a demonstration about Afghanistan, I would rather see a rally in support of our Canadian troops there."

Not a few Muslims were justifiably afraid of these people, perhaps especially Iranian-Canadians with families back in Iran. Young Afghan-Canadians were intimidated by the "anti-war" campus shout-fests. "A curtain of fear has descended on the intelligentsia of the West, including Canada. The fear of being misunderstood as Islamophobic has sealed their lips, dried their pens and locked their keyboards," wrote eleven Muslim-Canadian academics and community leaders in a 2006 declaration published in the *Toronto Star*. "Islamism is not the new revolutionary movement against global forces of oppression, as a section of the left in this country erroneously perceives."

But the toxin the Muslim intellectuals warned about continued to spread. So did anti-Zionist paranoia and all the other debilitating contents of the countercultural "ideational package." In 2007, Toronto feminist, writer and activist Samira Mohyeddin almost gave up trying to mobilize solidarity for Iranian democrats because of the brick wall she'd run up against in the city's "left-wing" circles, especially at the

University of Toronto. "In Canada, you can't criticize what is happening in Iran without being told you're helping the White House," she told me. "I've been called an orientalist and a neocon. Isn't that funny? Can you believe it?"

On Canada's west coast, Clement Apaak of the Canadian Students for Darfur found himself at the same dead end after more than two years of effort to mobilize support for an effective Canadian response to the "slow genocide" underway in Darfur. It wasn't just a knee-jerk antipathy to the United States that reflexively kicked in because of the hectoring tone Washington took in its statements about the Khartoum regime. It was also an irrational alarm among "left-wing activists" owing to the support the Darfur campaign found in the Canadian Jewish Congress. The Muslim Canadian Congress had also noticed the cold shoulder Darfur activists were getting, not just in left-wing circles, but also in the Toronto-area Muslim community. Writing in the *Globe and Mail*, the MCC's Tarek Fatah cited an absurd anti-Zionist paranoia as one of the main causes of a widespread abstentionism on the Darfur question among Ontario Muslims.

Samira Mohyeddin chalked it up to a 1960s-style protest culture of "placards and megaphones" that required nothing more than opposition to the United States. Its followers were content to exoticize Iranian culture and to regard the Khomeinist regime as somehow "culturally authentic." Across the liberal-left, the default stance was a servile posture that regarded human rights and freedoms as impositions of "Western" values and strengthened the hand of Islamist reactionaries in countries like Iran and Afghanistan. "I think it's also simply because so many people think that fascism is dead, that it's over with," said Mohyeddin. "But it's not. In Iran, fascism is not dead." It wasn't dead in Afghanistan, either.

At a huge demonstration in Toronto in 2006 sponsored by the Toronto Coalition, there were Hezbollah flags, young men in Hezbollah T-shirts, and placard-sized photographs of Hezbollah boss Hassan Nasrallah and Iranian president Mahmoud Ahmadinejad. In Quebec, a "peace coalition" of labour and community groups with a focus on the Israel-Palestine conflict included an openly pro-Hezbollah political front. In Montreal, some young Lebanese Canadians showed up at an "anti-war" rally with a sign that read "Peace for Lebanon and Israel." They were shouted at and pushed around, and had their sign ripped up. The parade proceeded, with groups of marchers carrying the Hezbollah flag and huge photographs of Nasrallah.

In Vancouver, at the 2006 World Peace Forum, Canadian Jewish Congress activists found themselves excluded, along with officials from other Israel-friendly Jewish groups. The CJC had spent a year preparing workshops and programs leading up to the forum. When the CJC protested its exclusion, it was told that its programs on interfaith dialogue and Israeli-Palestinian relationship building could run parallel to the conference proceedings, but only if the CJC agreed to be further singled out by its officials swearing an "oath of allegiance" to the forum and its principles.

All of this was troubling, but it was Afghanistan that got me asking questions. My questions got me into trouble with many of my erstwhile comrades on "the Left," but they also led me into the warm company of such Afghans as Abdulrahim Parwani. You won't find any wistfulness for totalitarianism in Abdulrahim. He's a democrat to his bones, and everyone I met in the Afghan-Canadian community took him seriously. Another thing I came to know about Abdulrahim back then was that the strange marks on his forearms and hands were torture scars, from being sliced with a razor blade and having salt and pepper forced into his open wounds.

Abdulrahim was taken pretty seriously back in Afghanistan, too. During one of our trips, he was helping me with a flurry of interviews in Kabul. One morning he said, you know, you really should talk to Rabbani. He meant the wisened-up and wizened Berhanuddin Rabbani, president of the Islamic State of Afghanistan, which had endured the Taliban's trussed-up Islamic Emirate of Afghanistan all those years. The next day I had an audience with Rabbani.

Abdulrahim and I were curious about the same kinds of things. Our politics were more or less aligned. We were both astonished at what was becoming of the NDP and at the gruesome "anti-war" politics that were leading a lot of left-wing figures around town to say the craziest things about Afghanistan.

One prominent speech maker for the Mobilization Against War and Occupation was Tim Louis, a lawyer and a Vancouver city councillor at the time. I asked him in 2005 if he'd thought through the implications of MAWO's demand for an immediate withdrawal of foreign troops from Afghanistan. He had, after a fashion. "The government would collapse in a matter of days," he told me. So the reasonable course should be what, exactly? "Out now." When I asked how he squared his claim that Canada was engaged in an illegal military occupation of Afghanistan with the fact that several UN resolutions had authorized the NATO-ISAF mission, Louis said, "I don't have a coherent argument against the fact that the UN has authorized it."

Around the same time, I noticed something odd about the Vancouver Coalition to Stop the War, which was staging its own demonstrations to demand an immediate troop pullout from Afghanistan. A Stop the War spokesman told me that the political parties, municipalities, labour unions and church groups in the coalition had come together originally to oppose Canadian involvement with the American war in Iraq. By 2005, several of the coalition groups didn't seem to know that they were even members of the coalition, let alone know what the coalition was demanding on their behalf. That didn't seem to worry anyone, though. Iraq, Afghanistan—what's the difference?

Inayatullah Naseri, the co-editor of *Ariana Marafat,* a monthly newspaper for Vancouver's Afghan community, told me at the time: "Most Afghans, including myself, believed that it was a big mistake for the United States to go to Iraq. But the Afghanistan situation is completely different from the Iraq issue. The Canadian troops are defending poor people who are not armed." Ferooz Sekandarpoor of the Vancouver Institute for Afghan Studies considered himself to be "anti-war," but he was surprised that the protesters were incapable of distinguishing between a necessary humanitarian intervention and a coercive military occupation. It surprised me, too. "Canada and all the other countries that are helping Afghanistan right now are not invaders. They are saviours," he told me. "I could be one of those people shouting 'no war', but we have got to help people. That is what the UN is for. Think about Rwanda. There was a terrible genocide there, and now we regret that."

Afghanistan's ambassador to Canada, Omar Samad, couldn't figure out the "anti-war" movement, either. He'd read a leaflet that claimed Afghanistan was being occupied by the United States, and that Afghan women were worse off than they'd been under the Taliban. "For God's sake, these people have no clue whatsoever about what they are talking about," he said. Samad had offered to meet with Canada's leading troops-out organizations, to ask them questions, hear their complaints and maybe have some kind of dialogue. He'd been turned down. "Maybe it's political. Or ideological. I can't explain it," he told me. "But to look at Afghanistan only through the prism of the United States is wrong." When I asked what he would have wanted to tell the "anti-war" groups, Samad came up with some questions. "Where were you when the women of Afghanistan were imprisoned? Where were you when the children of Afghanistan were denied schooling? Where were these demonstrations for human rights and dignity and honour?"

By the spring of 2006, there was an urgency in Abdulrahim Parwani's voice. "I'm very afraid that we are going to make the same mistake again, like when everyone forgot about Afghanistan until 9/11," he told me. "Now, in some areas, the security situation is already worsening, and the Taliban is reorganizing. That's what I'm afraid of, that we will do this mistake again, that we will forget. And when we have placards on the street that say, 'Troops out of Afghanistan,' then maybe one day they will have to go into the streets with placards that say, 'Terrorists out of Canada.'" It was classic Abdulrahim, always finding a way to make light of something. But he was dead serious. Afghanistan needed Canada and Canadian soldiers. "Canada is my country, too, now. Canadians have to understand that this is the better way."

The NDP's Dawn Black, newly appointed as the party's defence critic, was also trying to make sense of it all. She'd worked in democracy-training efforts in Bosnia and Cambodia and was very much in favour of a robust Canadian engagement in Afghanistan. Months before the NDP's rousing Bring 'Em Home convention, Black was canny enough to refer to her party's position on Afghanistan as "evolving." She was clear on this much: "I think there is a real role for Canada to play and that Canada is playing." Other than that, all Black could say was that "it has to be a Canadian role, and it has to reflect Canadian values."

A lot of Canadians were worried about where their prime minister was headed. In 2003, before he joined the new Conservative Party and took over as its leader, Stephen Harper had called for Canada to join up with the Americans in Iraq. He later renounced what he'd said, but his apparently intimate alignment with the Bush administration continued to aggravate Canadian anxieties.

NDP leader Jack Layton had talked a troops-out line almost from the beginning, and his caucus had already voted against an extension of the Canadian mission in Afghanistan. But Layton sometimes talked about Afghanistan in such an opaque way that what he said could mean whatever you wanted it to. There was also the NDP's interest in propping up Paul Martin's minority Liberal government to consider. But in late 2005, feeling lively from reading the public opinion polls, Layton pulled the plug on Martin's government. When Layton took over the national debates about Afghanistan under the new Harper administration, he drew deeply from the ideational package, the lexicon and the vocabulary that had come to prevail in all the places where the Left used to be.

Going into the national NDP convention in Quebec City in September 2006, Layton's own Toronto-Danforth constituency brought a resolution calling on the party to demand that Canada withdraw all its soldiers from Afghanistan, withdraw the RCMP specialists training the Haitian National Police Force, abrogate the North American Free Trade Agreement and pull out of the World Trade Organization. A troops-out resolution submitted by the Nanaimo-Cowichan New Democrats caused a national media ruckus because of its assertion that Canadian soldiers could "end up acting like terrorists, destroying communities." Toronto's Trinity-Spadina New Democrats called on the NDP to "seek redress in the appropriate court to have our illegal occupation of Afghanistan cease." Several NDP-affiliated union locals submitted a resolution that called on the NDP to adopt a policy that explicitly "rejects the use of military intervention as a tool for peace." The resolution was based on the fantasy that Canada was being drawn into an American plan to use tactical nuclear weapons to expand U.S. wars in Iraq and Afghanistan to Iran and Syria.

In one convention resolution, the UN "responsibility to protect" doctrine was blasted as a ploy to justify upcoming American oil wars against Sudan and Venezuela. The paradox there was that the UN doctrine was pioneered by Canada in response to the dysfunction of U.S. unilateralism in Iraq. Several troops-out resolutions were based on the "it's all about oil" conspiracy theory; one resolution explicitly asserted that Canadian soldiers were really in Afghanistan on behalf of Canada's oil industry. There were resolutions calling for the NDP to issue a public declaration of solidarity with Venezuela's Bolivarian Revolution, to fight for a free-trade deal with the Venezuelan government and demand that Canada "cease all liaisons or cooperation with members of the Venezuelan opposition." American military deserters should be welcomed into Canada, now and in the future. Canadian navy ships should be stopped from "policing the shipping lanes of the Persian Gulf." There was a roster of demands on the "Zionist state" of Israel that mirrored the eliminationist demands of Hamas, but they were moderated only by a plausible-deniability caveat urging the NDP to "make clear its opposition to the use of suicide bombings against civilian targets."

The NDP convention package contained fifty-three pages under the heading "Reclaiming Canada's Place in the World." Some of the resolutions were perfectly respectable socialist propositions. The final troops-out resolution was crunched into a composite calling for "the safe and immediate withdrawal of Canadian troops from Afghanistan." Compared with some other resolutions, that one sounded almost reasonable. It gave Jack Layton all the validation he needed for his claim about Afghanistan: "This is not the right mission for Canada." Afghanistan was somehow the right military mission for Switzerland, Ireland, Britain and Macedonia. It was okay for little Montenegro, plucky Tonga and even far-away Mongolia. But Canada, not so much.

The keynote address to the 2006 national NDP convention was delivered by none other than Malalai Joya. "The situation in Afghanistan and conditions of its ill-fated women will never change positively as long as the warlords are not disarmed and both the pro-U.S. and anti-U.S. terrorists are removed from the political scene of Afghanistan," Joya told the delegates. Joya did not say who would disarm the warlords if the NATO-ISAF troops were withdrawn. She did not say how the anti-U.S. terrorists or the pro-U.S. terrorists would be removed from the scene.

Joya got a standing ovation.

six

THE PARTISANS

"IT WAS HERE, on the other side of this wall. There were twenty-five rooms, isolation rooms," Abdulrahim said. "I was in one of those rooms for five months." He had just turned seventeen at the time, he explained. He'd spent ten days under interrogation at the secret police headquarters in Kabul's Shar-e Naw district, and then they'd brought him here, to Deh Mazang. During a break from our interviews in Kabul, I'd asked him to show me the place. He'd been imprisoned in the early days of the Soviet-backed military coup that had seized power in Kabul in 1978 and straight away set its agents about the work of arresting, disappearing, jailing, torturing and executing thousands of people from all over the city.

We were walking along a narrow rutted road beside the old prison's east wall. The road carried on up through the old Deh Mazang district that gave the prison its name, a forlorn Kabul neighbourhood that clings in crowded shambles to the side of Kuh-e Asmayi Mountain. "The isolation rooms were for undecided cases," Adulrahim explained. "Every morning at about 2 o'clock the guards would come and read a list, with the names of four or five people. 'You are to be released.' Then after about fifteen minutes, there was the voice of the Kalashnikov. *Guh guh guh guh.*"

There was nothing at the place in the wall where the old prison gate used to be. This wall was made of cement blocks, but the wall Abdulrahim remembered had been made of mud. The guard towers were the same, though. Abdulrahim stopped for a moment to gather his thoughts, then shook his head. "So many people were killed inside this place, Terry." He cheered up a minute later when we found a sheet-metal door with a hand-lettered sign above it and a roughly rendered sketch of a building: Map of Tailoring Workshop Building Afghan National Police. Above that was a small hand-lettered billboard: Construction of Kindergarten and Tailoring Workshop Building for Ministry of Interior Affairs Afghanistan. Above that was a hand-drawn version of the Afghan flag, the flag of the Federal Republic of Germany and the flag of the Principality of Liechtenstein. Abdulrahim found the signs hilarious. "This was not my kindergarten."

Abdulrahim banged on the door, and an ANP trooper opened it. He pointed up the road, and at the corner tower another guard directed us down the old prison's north wall. And so it went, gate after gate and door after door, until we'd circumnavigated the entire complex. After giving our explanations at the new main gate on the busy main road off the Deh Mazang traffic circle, we slumped down in the plastic chairs that had been pulled out for us so we could wait in the sunshine. Then we were summoned, and after the usual security rigmarole we were led down a sand-bagged sidewalk. At the final gate, a young man made a quick call on his cell phone. He was wearing a flashy dinner jacket and had thick gel in his black hair. "You got pistol?" Not at the moment, I said, which got a laugh out of Abdulrahim.

We were finally inside. "Wow, it is changed. It is beautiful." Then he frowned. "But this is wrong. It is our history. Everything is gone." Deh Mazang Prison had been around since at least the 1920s, and in its time it had held some of Afghanistan's most famous political prisoners. It now housed the national headquarters of the Afghanistan Border Protection Services, a regional hub of the Afghanistan National Police, some sort of military equipment depot, an army uniform shop and perhaps a kindergarten. The young man in the fancy suit accompanied us through the grounds and past a small, pleasant mosque, where some officers were at their prayers. There were rose trellises and blooming flowers. We meandered over to the place near the east wall where Abdulrahim had spent all those months.

The room had been so narrow Abdulrahim could touch the walls on both sides by stretching his arms. There'd been a small window, too high to see out. "I can't tell you exactly where it was. Probably here," he said. He motioned towards the wall. We kept wandering, and at one point Abdulrahim stood still, trying to get his bearings. "I remember that place now," he said, and pointed. "Over there; it was the polytechnic building." The crowded cell block got its name from the four hundred students who were imprisoned there. They'd been rounded up from the Kabul Polytechnic on charges of anti-Sovietism.

Our escort made another call on his cell phone, and moments later we were in a comfortable upstairs office in a red-brick administration building, one of the few structures still left from the old days. The national border police chief of staff, General Abdulhai Atrofi, had invited us up for tea. A dignified Sean Connery look-alike in crisp fatigues, General Atrofi warmed to Abdulrahim right away. For one thing, he was glad to know Abdulrahim agreed that something important about Afghanistan's heritage had been lost when the prison was gutted. The general said he'd ended up regretting that he hadn't stood firm about a proper photographic archive before everything was torn down in 2002. But more importantly, he'd known Abdulrahim's uncle, Abdul Ghafoor, who had been one of the general's teachers at military college.

Uncle Abdul was among several members of Abdulrahim's family rounded up by the secret police branch AGSA (Afghanistan da Gato da Satalo Adara, the Afghan Interests Protection Service), the same day Abdulrahim was arrested. The Parwanis were taken to the AGSA headquarters in Shar-e Naw. They were held separately and tortured for ten days. AGSA tried to extract incriminating evidence from Abdulrahim about his father, Abdul Wahed Parwani, though Abdulrahim had nothing to tell them. At the end of the ordeal, AGSA held onto Abdulrahim's father, his uncle Abdul, his cousin Muhammad Ishaq, and Abdulrahim himself. The others, including Abdulrahim's brothers Basir and Ahad, were released. Abdulrahim was transferred to Deh Mazang. His father, his uncle and his cousin were never heard from again.

The rumour was that the men had been executed at Pul-e-Charkhi, the massive prison complex east of Kabul. Nobody knew for sure. They had simply disappeared. For years, Abdulrahim's mother, Bibi Shirin, lived in hope, but hope can be a torture of its own. AGSA was more or less a branch of the Soviet KGB, and every so often people would hear stories about Afghans who had been spirited off to a labour camp in Siberia. One day, AGSA published a list of prisoners it had executed, and Abdulrahim's name was on it. When his mother later learned that Abdulrahim was still alive, she allowed herself to keep hoping that one day her husband would walk through the door.

For all its sadism, there was a reptilian logic behind the AGSA terror. Before the Islamist mujahideen factions burst onto the Afghan scene, bristling with weapons and flush with foreign cash, the Afghan resistance against the Soviet-backed PDPA regime was led by democrats. The original Afghan mujahideen included liberals, patriots, "moderate" Muslims, socialists, poets, intellectuals, journalists and free-thinking students. The Parwanis fit the profile exactly. They were the kind of people police states fear most. The Stalinist regime in Kabul was less afraid of the Islamist fronts that Washington sponsored in the usual circuitous Cold War ways; Moscow would ably meet that threat, even if it meant turning Afghanistan into a typical superpower war zone.

Abdulrahim's father was a roving district administrator from a family of respected civil servants. His work meant the Parwani family would live for a year or two in different provinces, including in Bamiyan, Farah, Ghazni and Herat. That's how Abdulrahim collected such fond memories of Balkh as a child. His dad faithfully served a succession of Afghan regimes for thirty years, making him a subject of suspicion for AGSA. Abdulrahim's uncle Abdul Ghafoor was a writer, a teacher and a sometime poet who had served as a colonel in the Afghan army. He'd written a geometry textbook, which is why he was teaching at the military college General Atrofi had attended as a young man. The new government fired Abdulrahim's father, and the day the Parwani men were rounded up was not the first time young Abdulrahim was arrested.

Abdul Wahed Parwani had encouraged the mechanical aptitude he'd noticed in his son Basir. "You will be an engineer," he used to say. It was Basir's job to keep the family car in good running order. He ended up a mechanic and car salesman. In his four daughters, Abdul Wahed saw a variety of talents. They would go on to be teachers and managers and homemakers. In Abdulrahim, he'd picked up on different inclinations. Abdulrahim loved to read, and on long car trips it was his job to read aloud from the poetry of Rustam and from the *Shah Nama*, a classic by the poet Ferdowsi, along the lines of King Arthur's tales. It was also Abdulrahim's happy duty to produce a regular family newspaper with larks and stories about everyone's comings and goings.

As a schoolboy, Abdulrahim took pride in the Afghan tradition of *sher jangi*, or "poetry fighting." You compose a line, and your opponent must respond by composing a coherent following line that begins with the last letter of your line, and back and forth it goes. Abdulrahim won competitions doing this. In his mid-teens, he was a fixture at the Khairkhana branch of the Kabul library. Leading up to the Soviet-backed coup, there were great debates among Kabul's young scholars about dialectical materialism, capitalism, class relations and the like. After the coup, there were mandatory politics classes, and students were encouraged to debate political theory. Abdulrahim chose a textbook called *The Alphabet of Struggle* and contested its assertions. It was just another kind of poetry fighting.

Abdulrahim's father, now jobless, had been ordered to report to Kabul and wait there. The weeks went by, so he set up a small stationery shop for Basir and Abdulrahim to run. The brothers operated it as a kind of lending library, a Kabuli stationery shop custom. Then the Komsomols, the party youth guards, started coming around to make demands. Mostly they wanted to see Stalinist literature and posters on display. The young Parwani brothers refused and closed up the little shop. One day, as he was walking home from Khairkhana, a white Volga pulled up at the curb in front of Abdulrahim.

"It was KGB." A white Volga always was. A man with a gun got out. "He said, 'Are you Abdulrahim Parwani? Did you just come from the library? Get in the car.'" Abdulrahim was taken to a house in Shar-e Naw near the Ministry of the Interior headquarters. His library books were seized, he was peppered with questions and he was made to wait in a room for an hour and a half. An AGSA agent then took him into the basement, where a man was lying on the floor, writhing in pain. Abdulrahim was ushered into a room where the AGSA agent produced a long list of books Abdulrahim had checked out of the library. There was nothing more overtly Islamic than some Sufi verse. The agent then showed Abdulrahim some handwritten anti-government leaflets. He asked, "Did you write these?" Although Abdulrahim said no, he was then made to write sentences on a piece of paper to compare with the leaflet. Seeing that the writing didn't match, the agent started questioning Abdulrahim about his father. At long last, the agent said, "Now you can go home. But it's not the end."

It was not the end. It was the beginning of a story that has repeated itself over and over throughout what is so often called the "Muslim world," as if Muslims lived on some faraway planet too complicated for the rest of us to comprehend. "Muslim world" almost always shows up in variations on the theme that Muslims don't want democracy; if they did they'd stick up for themselves against their lunatic tyrants. You could have said the same about Europeans in the darker days of the twentieth century. In the first few years of the twenty-first century, it was commonplace to hear a certain refrain across the political spectrum: Where are the Muslim democrats? The answer is sadly and so often: They've all been killed.

As the Red Army began its scorched-earth strategy by rolling a ceaseless thunder back and forth across the Afghan landscape, Afghanistan disgorged millions of refugees. Afghan Sunnis fled to Pakistan. Out of the Shia north, refugees trundled across the border into Iran. Whichever way they went, the Afghan democrats presented as much of a threat to militant Islamists as they'd seemed to the Stalinists in Kabul. The Sunni and Shia parties that were funded, armed, aided and abetted by Pakistan's Inter-Services Intelligence agency (ISI) and the Iranian Revolutionary Guards Corps (IRGC) quickly decapitated Afghanistan's democratic popular front and put its activists to the sword.

In Pakistan, the pro-democracy Afghan mujahideen ran humanitarian projects for the refugees. Pakistan's military intelligence establishment saw this as unacceptable impudence. The ISI was pouring everything into seven compliant Islamist parties, most of which were viciously anti-democratic. The schools the Afghan democrats had established were choking off the supply of youthful cannon fodder to the Islamist networks of jihadist madrassas. In Iran, the newly victorious Islamist regime was busy jailing, torturing and executing Iran's own democrats, socialists and feminists. Iran's Khomeinist counter-revolution had already picked out eight of its own Shia militias to wage the anti-Soviet jihad in Afghanistan. Condemned by their mere existence, the Afghan patriots in Iran found themselves guilty of the crime of *mili gara*—being nationalist—a Khomeinist heresy.

In his chronicles of the terror, the Afghan resistance veteran and historian Neamatollah Nojumi describes how the democrats were targeted.

In Pakistan, the ISI first outlawed moderate Islamic and democratic Afghan mujahideen groups. In the refugee camps, the ISI's Islamist parties were then authorized to carry out "an indiscriminate campaign of harassments, kidnappings and assassinations." In the Peshawar camps, Afghan democrats were subjected to an assassination campaign that went on for days, while "the Pakistani security forces, and particularly the ISI, turned their backs and denied them any protection," Nojumi writes. An especially tragic loss was the assassination of mujahideen leader Shamsuddin Majrooh, a professor of philosophy and literature at Kabul University. Majrooh, a former justice minister, was a co-author of the democratic articles in Afghanistan's 1964 constitution.

In Iran, Hezbollah and Hezb-e-Islami were assigned the work of hunting down and arresting suspiciously democratic Afghans for summary execution. They press-ganged thousands of Afghan refugee children into a network of Khomeinist indoctrination academies. The Khomeinists assigned Afghan Shia paramilitary groups to collaborate with their avowed enemies in the Afghan secret police agencies. Tehran repaid AGSA's courtesies in the currency of bound and gagged Afghan democrats. Islamist factions trained at the IRGC's Qods Force base were particularly ruthless in targeting harmlessly devout Afghan Shias who appeared insufficiently enfeebled by Khomeinist political orthodoxy. Nojumi writes: "These accused Afghan moderates were frequently held in jail and at the end of their terms deported directly into the hands of the pro-Soviet border forces in Afghanistan."

In the work of killing a lamb, the jackal is a friend to the
vulture. From Persepolis to Kashmir, if you were an Afghan
democrat, it didn't matter what you did. You could get picked
up and tortured or killed for what you were or for what you
were suspected of being. The thing to do was hide in the shadows, keep quiet and keep your head down. After Deh Mazang,
Abdulrahim kept his head down, but one day he was brought in
and ordered to make a choice: join the Soviet-run Afghan army
or go to Russia. Abdulrahim chose Russia. He spent much
of the 1980s there. He learned Russian and graduated with a
master's degree in engineering in Moscow. Most impressively,
he earned a diploma in ideological issues from the University of
Marxism-Leninism in Volgograd. He got top marks.

Back in Kabul, it was almost possible to remain unaware
that Soviet bombers and Red Army rampages had been
churning up the Afghan countryside and driving millions of
refugees into Pakistan and Iran. Moscow had taken pains to
leave Kabul unscathed. Before Gulbuddin Hekmatyar's bom-
bardments reduced the city to rubble, Kabul was still leafy
and green in the spring. Before the rocket wars between Iranian, Pakistani and Arab factions, the skies above Maranjan
Hill were still filled with kites. One day when Abdulrahim
and I were having lunch at the imprecisely named Perfect Restaurant, near the Cuban embassy, he heard an old love song
playing on a radio and got a bit sentimental. After we left the
restaurant, as we turned to stroll through Sarak Shar-e Naw
Park, Abdulrahim exclaimed: "This is where I first touched
Sima! I touched her on her arm. It was after we had become
engaged." His marriage had been arranged according to custom, and in keeping with custom, Sima was a cousin. But
Sima had happily consented. "Oh yes. Many girls wanted to
marry me," Abdulrahim said. "You must not write that down."

We came out of the park and turned down the old main drag through Shar-e Naw. Back in the old days, the street was called the Champs-Élysées. In the dying days of the last-gasp regime of Mohammad Najibullah, there were still night-clubs. But the Champs-Élysées time was about to give way to the Hekmatyar time, when Kabul was reduced to a corpse-littered metropolis of smoking tombs.

One of the most depraved characters to ever cast a shadow on Afghan ground, Gulbuddin Hekmatyar was the ISI's favourite mujahideen commander during the anti-Soviet jihad. Of the seven Afghan Islamist parties financed and armed by Pakistan's military-intelligence establishment, none was so generously lavished with guns and bombs and money as Hekmatyar's Hezb-e-Islami. A Pashtun-supremacist-turned-Stalinist, then drug trafficker and Islamist fanatic, Hekmatyar ran his Hezb faction in Leninist style, a habit he picked up during his student days at Kabul University, when he'd been jailed for two years for his part in the murder of a Maoist rival. Hekmatyar was also the Saudis' anointed proxy in the Afghan jihad. He was a frequent guest of Khomeinist Iran.

Pakistan's ISI knew Hekmatyar had no recognizable support base in Afghanistan that might tug at his loyalties. As an added bonus, there was no fathoming the depths to which Hekmatyar would dutifully sink. Only the Taliban would be more efficient in doing Pakistan's imperialist bidding. Hekmatyar was ruthlessly dependable. It was said he had slaughtered probably one thousand Afghan civilians for every Russian soldier he'd killed. That wasn't counting the heads he'd lopped off his fellow jihadist commanders. Hekmatyar's conscience was untroubled by his massacres of innocent Kabulis: "If they are good Muslims, God will reward them as martyrs and send them to heaven," he'd been known to say. That isn't hatred.

It's profound sociopathology. Hekmatyar reserved his hatred for the young, charismatic Afghan mujahideen commander Ahmad Shah Massoud.

Because Massoud enjoyed the widest Afghan support base of all the mujahideen leaders, he was proportionately disfavoured by Pakistan's ISI. Because he was a Sunni Tajik of mild disposition and a happily unapologetic Afghan patriot as well, Tehran considered Massoud suspiciously heretical. Because he loathed the Wahhabi cargo-cult religion that came to animate Hekmatyar and the Taliban, Massoud was similarly disfavoured by the jihad's Arab financiers. Still, during the darkest hours of the Red Army tyranny in Afghanistan, it was Massoud who could be counted on to bring the Soviets to their knees. While the Islamist party commanders in Peshawar and Tehran were slitting one another's throats in the scramble for American dollars and Saudi riyals, Massoud stayed out of it. From his redoubt in the Panjshir Mountains, he stuck with his Shura-e-Nazar united front. He was the beloved commander of 130 anti-Soviet rebel leaders from across 12 Afghan provinces who answered to no foreign powers. Afghan civilians suffered nearly ceaseless war-crime atrocities at the hands of Islamist warlords. Undoubtedly, resistance fighters affiliated with Shura-e-Nazar committed outrages. But no blood was ever found on the hands of Massoud or his commanders.

And so, the Afghan lambs would lie down with the Lion of Panjshir, and by 1994 Kabul was Massoud's town. Through the city's bombed and broken streets, Abdulrahim Parwani could be found riding on a rickety Russian bicycle with copies of the two-page Massoudist daily newspaper, *Dariz*, overflowing from its carrier. Abdulrahim was also chief of the little daily's journalists' section, assigning its correspondents and providing readers with the latest news from the front against the Taliban advance in the south. Abdulrahim was the proud editor of the Kabul literary journal *Tarjuma* as well. He kept the journal going right up until the Taliban stormed into Kabul in 1996, after Massoud withdrew his forces rather than turn the city's neighbourhoods into human abattoirs again.

Abdulrahim and Sima fled to India. While Massoud was dug in up in the Panjshir Mountains, Abdulrahim served as a cultural attaché in the Delhi embassy of Berhanuddin Rabbani's Islamic state, Afghanistan's UN-recognized government. Massoud was its defence minister. Abdulrahim created its Afghanistan Civilization and Cultural Foundation and served as editor-in-chief for the foundation's journal, *Bunyad*. While the Taliban were banning books and burning libraries, Abdulrahim worked late into the night, translating more than two dozen books into Dari and Pashto.

From the time of the white Volgas, when the Stalinists ran Kabul, there were some things Abdulrahim could remember like they happened yesterday. There were many things that remained in shadows. But that barbaric junction in Afghan history was also an important intersection in world history, and it's easy to get the story jumbled. If you lose the plot you might never get it back, and you won't understand what the Afghan struggle was really all about in the years that followed September 11.

After Afghan prime minister Mohammad Daoud overthrew the Afghan king in 1973, he declared himself president of a new republic. In the April 1978 military coup, the Pashtun chauvinist Nur Muhammad Taraki assassinated Daoud and declared himself president of a new communist republic. The following year, Taraki's co-conspirator, prime minister and long-time archrival Hafizullah Amin announced that Taraki had died of an undisclosed illness. It was later disclosed that Amin had ordered Taraki's assassination, which was carried out by Taraki being tied to a bed and suffocated with a cushion. Amin took over as president, but because Moscow considered him even crazier than Taraki, KGB agents shot Amin dead after botching numerous attempts to quietly poison him. The Soviets explained themselves by referring to the articles of the Moscow-Kabul Treaty of Friendship, Cooperation and Good Neighbourliness. After Amin, there was Babrak Karmal. And on from there.

In its standard recounting, Afghan history appears as a baffling and ghastly pageant of revolutions, counter-revolutions, smashed kingdoms and imperialist invasions—a lot like those useless old-school renderings of European history. To follow the unfolding of Afghanistan's more recent history, with its succession of regimes there one day and gone the next, its rogues' gallery of warlords and its proxy-war calamities, you need a steady horizon line to get through the turbulence. The thing to keep your eye on is that in its entire two-and-a-half-century run as an identifiable nation-state, Afghanistan has been in the hands of one small clique or another from a handful of tribes within the Pashtun elite. The racket was not interrupted by the imperialist Anglo-Afghan wars. It didn't stop when the British won, and it carried on after the British left. The tectonic events that punctuate Afghan history have arisen almost invariably from outbreaks of testosterone poisoning within the same small male caste of tribal Pashtun overlords that has been running the show from the rise of the Durrani Empire in the 1740s to Hamid Karzai's Popalzai in the twenty-first century.

There are exceptions, of course, but they prove the rule, and the Great Saur Revolution of 1978, as that tawdry little Stalinist putsch is officially remembered, was not an exception.

None of the People's Democratic Party of Afghanistan leaders of 1978 came out of Moscow's Patrice Lumumba University or any other Soviet institute devoted to the recruitment and training of Third World communist insurgents. Most of the core PDPA leaders had attended American universities, notably Columbia University in New York, in the 1950s and 1960s. It is neither unusual nor unreasonable to mark the events of 1978 as the beginning of the horrors, massacres and savageries that would devour Afghanistan in the decades to follow. To most Western eyes, the spring of 1978 was the time Afghanistan disappeared down the Soviet gullet. What is not so often noticed is that the core PDPA leaders of 1978, whether they were from the Kalkh faction or its Parcham faction vendetta rival, were almost all the spoiled children of the Pashtun tribal elite that has always called the shots.

The overwhelming majority of Afghans are not tribal, and they're not Pashtun. They're conventionally classified as ethnic Uzbeks, Tajiks, Hazaras, Turkmen, Aimaq, Baloch and what have you. Among that majority, the events that show up in conventional accounts as tectonic shifts in Afghanistan's history have often registered as little more than rumours of some grisly new power struggle in the far-off Pashtun homelands. Not infrequently, the recurring Pashtun palace coups would erupt into conflagrations. Whenever that happened, the Afghans who suffered first were the masses of Pashtuns: the country's largest ethnic minority, but a minority all the same. Whenever the conflagrations burst their firewalls, they'd rampage outwards in convulsions of fanaticism, ethnic cleansing, pogrom and genocidal massacre. It's a lot like European history, when you think about it. It might even help explain the affinities Pashtun chauvinists and the Nazis found in one another back in the 1930s. Still, it should be said that Pashtuns have also ranked among the most liberal and cosmopolitan of Afghans. Pashtun leaders pioneered Afghanistan's progressive reforms in the early twentieth century and scored some impressive liberal goals just after that century's midpoint. Pashtuns were also among the leaders of the early pro-democracy mujahideen who rose up after 1978.

There was no telling whether the Pashtun grandees in the PDPA's 1978 retinue would be any worse or better, in the long run, than the *kalan nafar* (big shots) they'd just turfed out. For most Afghans, the communist talk coming out of the presidential palace was worrisome, but it was Moscow's open hand in the coup that had people bolting upright from their sleep in a cold sweat. The last time their Pashtun overlords had put on swish Afghan army officers' uniforms and gone promenading with medal-festooned Red Army colonels was in Josef Stalin's time. Tens of thousands of people had ended up dead or in concentration camps. The lucky ones were made to watch while their daughters were raped, then had their farms appropriated and spent the rest of their lives as serfs to newly arrived Pashtun landlords. Afghanistan's Tajiks, Uzbeks and Turkmen had been crushed between the grindstones of Kabul's "Pashtunization" drive in the country's north and the Red Army's "national delimitation" campaign strategy waged against Central Asian patriots. It had been a team effort by Pashtun supremacists and Soviet expansionists. And now, in Kabul, the Bolsheviks were back.

But what was really a bad sign was that the new *kalan nafar* in Kabul were mostly from the Pashtun Ghilzai tribe. The Ghilzais had been on the outer precincts of the Pashtun palaces in Kabul and Kandahar as far back as Afghanistan's history goes. The Musahiban bunch of Muhammadzais had held the upper hand pretty well ever since the late-nineteenth-century days of the appropriately-titled Iron Amir, Abdul Rahman Khan. In the standard history, 1973 marks the overthrow of the Afghan monarchy and the creation of a new Afghan republic. All that really happened was that Zahir Shah, the Muhammadzai Musahiban king, was shoved out of his cozy chair by his cousin Mohammed Daoud, the Muhammadzai Musahiban prime minister, who then set himself up as president. The thing about 1978 was that the Ghilzais had at long last given the Muhammadzais the high jump, which meant the Ghilzais would be throwing their weight around just to show everyone who was boss.

It would be wrong to make sweeping generalizations about members of the Ghilzai tribe. But from 1978 on, as the historian and anthropologist Thomas Barfield has observed, the Ghilzais would offer up three PDPA presidents, the warlord Abdul Haq, jihadist Jalaludin Haqqani, the mass-murdering gargoyle Gulbuddin Hekmatyar, the Taliban's Mullah Omar, Commander of the Faithful and Leader of the Supreme Council of the Islamic Emirate of Afghanistan, and quite a few of the Taliban's more frightful legionnaires. Long before 1978 and long after, the Pashtun tribal hierarchy's internal power struggles and the Pashtun assertion of outward power would determine Afghanistan's history. As the anthropologist M. Nazif Shahrani explains it, "Even when dressed up with ideological justifications, whether Islamist, nationalist, secularist or democratic, these struggles have not been fought for or against any ideological or institutional causes."

The helmsmen of Afghanistan's non-tribal and non-Pashtun majority have not always presented a pretty cast of characters, either. And far too much can be made of tribe and ethnicity as a way of understanding what goes on in Afghanistan. Intermarriage complicates everything. The country is rapidly urbanizing, with all the cross-cultural pollination that city life allows. Down through the generations, old loyalties blend into multiple identities. Afghan tribalism is largely a Pashtun affair, and Talibanism is mainly a Pashtun sickness. But after a generation spent in Pakistan's refugee camps and madrassas, there's not much left of an intact tribal structure in the bone-strewn killing fields of the Pashtun southern homelands. Too much can also be made of the families of Islam that Afghans are born into—the Sunni Pashtuns, the Shia Hazaras, the mostly Sunni Tajiks and so on. Abdulrahim Parwani happens to be an Afghan of the Sunni, cheery, Tajik, intellectually curious and liberal kind. But an Afghan is an Afghan, he'll say. This did not mean he's one to shy away from unpleasant facts.

As Abdulrahim and I were wandering the shell of Deh Mazang prison that morning in 2010, the war-weariness in NATO capitals was deepening. If all you were looking for in Afghanistan was capitulation and peace talks, you probably wouldn't notice what was happening right before your eyes. If you did notice, but you were looking only for "peace and reconciliation," you probably weren't concerned that Afghanistan was mutating into a Popalzai khanate with Hamid Karzai sitting on the fancy cushion. You would be satisfied to avert your gaze and mutter something cynical about the "Muslim world."

But to Karzai's "peace at any price," Afghanistan's democratic partisans were answering "democracy is not for sale." The partisans were overwhelmingly Tajik, Hazara, Aimaq and Uzbek. By 2009, an organic alliance of mainly liberals, patriots, "moderate" Muslims, socialists, women's rights activists, cosmopolitan intellectuals, journalists and free-thinking students had bloomed again. It was coalescing around Hazara, Uzbek and Tajik "ethnic" leaders who had not forgotten that genocidal depredation was among the Taliban's war crimes. Everybody was turning for leadership to the Pashtun-Tajik Abdullah Abdullah, the leader of Afghanistan's democratic opposition and Karzai's closest contender in the sabotaged 2009 presidential elections. When I met Abdullah after the elections, this is what he told me he saw: "The international community and the people of Afghanistan are no longer on the same side."

At the time, Karzai was chirruping about newfound prospects for striking a deal with the Taliban, solicitously arranged by the Saudis, with Pakistan's military-intelligence establishment serving as the catering crew. He'd already crowed to the BBC about his willingness to buy peace at any cost before he met with Afghanistan's sixty donor-country partners in London in January 2010. Karzai swept into London in a chorus of peace-talk hosannahs and made his grand, robe-swishing exit the same way. His London performance prompted the usual hymns from the troops-out choirs in the rich NATO countries, but this time there was a wobble in the usual Afghanistan feedback loop. Events in London had only stiffened the resolve of the pro-democracy Afghan opposition. This was something new.

By the summer of 2010, Karzai had assembled a hand-picked "peace jirga" to help him mobilize support for his vague plans. There were hardly any women on the jirga. The Afghan parliament had no hand in setting it up. Not a few Afghans were resigning themselves to the idea that they might have to trade democracy for something that might resemble the "peace" they'd known in the refugee camps. Abdulrahim Parwani looked at it all and saw the peace of the tomb. When we visited in the spring of 2010 with Niamatullah Ibrahimi, research officer with the Crisis States Research Centre in

Kabul, Ibrahimi was just wrapping up a survey of the scene. He told us that "with these latest talks about negotiating with the Taliban, ethnicity is now the most divisive issue in Afghanistan."

By early 2010, this had also become the view of Berhanuddin Rabbani, the president of Afghanistan's government-in-waiting during the Islamist mujahideen proxy wars and the Taliban years of the 1990s. It mattered what Rabbani thought about these things. He'd been the nominal leader of the U.S.-backed mujahideen alliance that waged war on the Red Army and its Stalinist Afghan satrapy through the 1980s. In the weeks following September 2001, it was Rabbani's Northern Alliance that drove the Taliban out of Kabul. The seventy-year-old Tajik grandfather of the Afghan parliament's warlord bloc was not happy.

During a wide-ranging conversation at his massively fortified residence in Kabul's posh Wazir Akbar Khan district, Rabbani said Karzai was playing a Pashtun-chauvinist race card that was straight out of the 1930s, when the Third Reich had been in town. If Karzai wasn't careful, he'd bring the roof down on top of everyone. "This is possible," Rabbani told me. "As I read history, when a nation's problems become this complex and they are not solved, that could result in violence and revolutions and other unwanted things. Water is very soft, but if you put it under pressure, it will explode."

By Rabbani's recounting, a not-too-subtle pattern was emerging.

After the rout of the Taliban, the United Nations had overseen a Karzai-led demobilization, disarmament and reintegration program aimed at bringing all the militias down from the mountains. Canada was happy to help fund it. The effort was clumsy and ill-managed, but it nevertheless disarmed more than fifty thousand fighters. Almost all of them were Tajiks, Hazaras and other northerners. Out in Karzai's Pashtun country, the Taliban didn't disarm.

After September 11, the entity everybody called al-Qaida, which called itself the World Islamic Front for Jihad against the Jews and Crusaders, was broken up into pieces that formed and reformed like a brand name only loosely protected by copyright law. Al-Qaida's depraved multi-millionaire emir, Osama bin Laden, was still active and apparently tucked away in some Pashtun high-country retreat on the Pakistan side of the Durand Line. The thing everybody still called the Taliban shattered and split into several chains of command, with the buck stopping on the desk of Mullah Omar, who was apparently still ensconced in Quetta. Smashed by NATO-ISAF hammers, Omar's Talibs spread throughout the vast opium fields of the Pashtun back country in such a diffuse way that terms like "neo-Taliban" had entered the vocabulary. Drug lords and Taliban commanders came in exactly the same shape and size. This was what the Afghan "insurgency" had become. The most cunning privateer was Gulbuddin Hekmatyar, still fabulously flush with cash and ammo from the salad days before the Taliban cut into his earnings. In his private war against the Jews and Crusaders, Hekmatyar was not, strictly speaking, on the Taliban side. His loyalties were as greasy as always. He alternated between killing ISAF troops and offering to wage war on Omar's Taliban in exchange for a shot at some of Karzai's lucrative action in Kabul.

The unspeakable barbarism at work in Afghanistan was the sociopathology that had disfigured the Pashtun tribal culture Hamid Karzai depended upon for his political survival. It had vomited up the Taliban gangsters Karzai had been beseeching as his "brothers" ever since December 2001, before he'd formally taken over as the head of Afghanistan's interim government. One of his first acts as elected president in 2004 was to start up with the peace talks again. It was an early Karzai amnesty that allowed several Taliban bosses to become members of the 2005 Afghan parliament. Their votes greased the way for the National Reconciliation, General Amnesty and National Stability Law that Karzai approved in 2008.

From the outset, Karzai was quietly encouraged by both the far-right Pashtun-chauvinist elements in his circles and the far-right Republicans in U.S. secretary of state Donald Rumsfeld's circles. Despite the U.S. State Department's regular gung-ho pronouncements to comfort aggrieved Americans, Karzai's entreaties and inducements to the Taliban command were an extension of the White House policy in Afghanistan, which the International Crisis Group described as "a quick, cheap war followed by a quick, cheap peace." Many Taliban leaders who had initially fled into the hills or across the border into Pakistan were quite comfortable in their new circumstances. Rahmatullah Hashemi, the Taliban envoy who so enthralled his audience at Berkeley in the days before September 11, ended up enrolling at Yale University. In lives of semi-retirement in their fancy houses in Quetta, Taliban supremos behaved like perfect gentlemen, and it became quite respectable to talk about deal making with "moderate" Taliban elements.

One of the deepest sets of footprints on the well-worn trail between pro-appeasement Pashtun chauvinists around Karzai's presidential palace and well-connected paleoconservatives in Washington were those of Lakhdar Brahimi, a senior Arab League functionary. Brahimi's close associate Mokhtar Lamani had impressed right-wing Republicans in 2002 when he'd worked with them to clinch a "family values" pact between the Organization of the Islamic Conference and the White House. The pact banned gay rights groups from international conferences on racism and blocked birth control programs for women in poor countries.

NDP leader Jack Layton, stuck with the debt of his 2006 Bring 'Em Home convention, had to give his party's line on Afghanistan the impression of heft and substance. The NDP's most elaborate plan called for Ottawa to replace the Canadian Forces in Afghanistan with an "eminent persons" group assigned to triangulate a peace deal between Islamabad, Kabul and Riyadh. The leading eminent persons the NDP chose for the work? Lamani and Brahimi. When Brahimi talked about the art of negotiating peace, you could almost swear you were hearing an old Joan Baez record in background. Brahimi had been the UN's peace-talk wazir in Afghanistan before September 11. On Brahimi's watch, the Taliban concluded several truce pacts that they broke as soon as they'd agreed to them. Still, in Brahimi's view, the Taliban's big problem was that they got bad press: "As long as you kept your womenfolk at home, they left you alone."

By 2008, Karzai was being egged on by no less an august figure than Kai Eide, the UN viceroy in Afghanistan. Eide would go on to disgrace himself by slavishly acquiescing when the Karzai camp hijacked the 2009 elections; after he resigned, Eide admitted that he'd been personally running back-channel exploratory talks with Taliban leaders for at least a year. By 2009, with the presidential election behind him, Karzai was offering to throw not just cash, land and jobs on the Taliban table, but cabinet posts and senior provincial government offices, too.

Berhanuddin Rabbani was all in favour of a national reconciliation effort undertaken with close parliamentary scrutiny.

Like almost everyone in the Afghan democratic leadership, even the feminists, Rabbani was open to almost any negotiations approach that recognized the rank and file in what people called the Taliban insurgency for what it was—mainly a bunch of overwrought, unemployable and illiterate men who needed to be made to calm down. Talk to the Taliban high command, and you'd find yourself talking to Pakistan's ISI. The subject of negotiations would be the terms of Afghanistan's surrender as a sovereign democratic republic. But negotiating with active and committed Taliban zealots didn't have to be an elaborate, Saudi-orchestrated affair. Your opening offer could be non-negotiable: Put the gun down, or we will kill you. Then you could wait for a counter-offer and proceed accordingly. It wasn't that complicated.

Rabbani's main point was that what Karzai and his shadowy friends in high foreign places were up to did not promise peace to Afghanistan's Tajiks, Hazaras, Uzbeks or any other ethnic group in the Afghan majority. It promised war. Karzai's beloved Pashtun "sons of the soil" were still armed. Everyone else had turned in their guns. At this point in the conversation, Rabbani turned to the most explosive "ethnic" subject of the lot.

In the late 1990s, a Pashtun-chauvinist *Mein Kampf*-like tract titled *Dozema Sacqawi* was widely circulating in Taliban-held areas of Afghanistan and in the Pashtun belt of Pakistan. The title translates as The Second Water Bearer, a derisive reference to Ahmad Shah Massoud; it borrows from the nickname for Habibulla Kalakani, the Tajik exception for ten months in 1929 to the two-century rule that Afghan heads of state have to be Pashtuns. Published in Germany and believed to be the work of several authors, the book was written in

Pashto under the pseudonym Samsoor Afghan. It had come to be called the Taliban manifesto.

Rabbani did not name names in speaking with me, but he said the manifesto's co-authors could be found among Karzai's closest advisers and confidants. In 2001, French journalists had traced the manifesto to an elusive, extraordinarily camera-shy group of Afghan expatriates in Germany associated with Afghan Mellat, the crypto-fascist party founded by the Nazi-educated Ghulam Farhad. As recently as 2009, Mellat party leader Anwar ul-Haq Ahady was serving as Karzai's finance minister. The manifesto sets out an ambitious final solution of Afghan ethnic cleansing. The idea is to create a Pashtun *lebensraum* by way of massive land grants in Afghanistan's northern provinces. It calls for the mass uprooting of Tajiks and Uzbeks, the banishing of Afghanistan's long-persecuted Hazaras to the country's deserts and the strict enforcement of Taliban law.

"There is a limit to the patience of the people," Rabbani told me. "Beyond that limit, no one can be patient any more."

According to Fawzia Koofi, the deputy speaker of the Afghan parliament, the patience of the Afghan people had already run out. Afghan conversations had turned to a revival of the armed democratic resistance. It was no idle chatter. "If the Taliban are brought back, you will have people in the north and the central highlands going up into the mountains," she said.

In the early summer of 2010, I would speak about this with Muhaiyuddin Mahdi, a fifty-five-year-old MP from Baghlan, a former resistance fighter and a founding participant in the Bonn Conference that created the post-Taliban Afghan state. When Abdulrahim and I visited Mahdi, he was just finishing up his translation of Baugh and Cable's *History of the English Language* into Dari. Mahdi is no hothead. "I am sorry to say that even though I am an old person, if Karzai reaches these dreams of his, I will have to say, bring the guns back," he said. Mahdi is a leading intellectual among the Massoudists and a historian of the works of the great American humorist Mark Twain. But Mahdi wasn't joking when he told us, "I would have to start resisting again. I'd be sorry if I had to take up the gun. But I have to be honest. It is better to have democratic institutions and peaceful actions. But many people believe like me, if we are not going to be allowed to have this."

Abdullah Abdullah believed like Mahdi. He'd been a senior figure in Massoud's anti-Taliban Panjshir Resistance Front. He'd been the foreign minister for Rabbani's UN-recognized Islamic State. He'd gone on to be Hamid Karzai's foreign minister and stayed in the position until 2005. After the 2009 presidential election debacle forced a runoff, Abdullah had refused to run again; he said it wasn't worth the trouble, because the fix was still in. Karzai was back in the palace, talking like he was having fits of the raptures. After everything he'd been through, I asked him, what would he do if Afghanistan's democracy was smothered in its cradle? "Violence is the only option left if you don't have other options," he said. "If we don't have the least political assurances, the safeguards, then what is the choice for me, for example, as a person?"

These were the dark clouds that hovered over Afghanistan's prospects in the spring of 2010. But in the Panjshir Valley, the wildflowers were coming up. In the Panjshir, as you move deeper into the mountains, with snow at their distant peaks, the valley opens up around you, then closes in on you, then opens up again. You wind through ancient villages of adobe-mud flat-roofed houses where flocks of chickens scurry out of the road. You notice roses coming up out of the snowy ground, and then there are flocks of lambs. What surprised me was not that the valley is like an open-air reliquary of the Soviet war machine. It wasn't the broken artillery pieces in the canyons, the wrecks of smashed troop carriers on the hill-sides or the Red Army tanks like broken children's toys in the roaring rush of the river below. What surprised me was how sublime it was up there.

Abdulrahim was in fine humour the day we headed north. Lauryn Oates was with us. Abdulrahim found it funny when Lauryn got bossy with me up in the Salang Pass. We were strolling along the tree-lined banks of the Salang River, and I'd been a bit inattentive about my own security in wandering off to say hello to a fierce-looking bearded character in a tur-ban who was carrying a heavy long-barrelled gun. As it turned out, the man walked straight up to me, gripped my right hand in a firm handshake and a hearty *salaam*, kissed me on both cheeks and introduced himself as Assan Ullah. He was armed because he'd been out hunting birds. "I think this is funny for you," Abdulrahim said afterwards. "Now is the time everyone is hunting birds."

We doubled back down out of the Salang and turned east up the old road that bends north into the gorge of the Panj-shir River, where the current flows deep green against the black canyon walls. Duck decoys bobbed in the rapids. The road wound northwards again, and the deeper into the moun-tains we got the more the world was like a poem by Rumi or Ferdowsi. You could almost see the jinns in the mulberry trees. On we went, and that afternoon, up a winding side road to a plateau high above the river, we came to the Tomb of the Mar-tyr, Ahmad Shah Massoud, the Lion of Panjshir.

It was a grand and modest place all at once. It was unfinished, with iron rebar protruding and stone-built columns rising from the ground to support a dome the height of a ten-storey building. In the middle of the shrine's single ground-floor room, the sarcophagus was a giant's bed covered in a green blanket on a marble floor, between marble columns arranged in a circle. Massoud had turned forty-eight the week before al-Qaida assassinated him, two days before September 11. When word reached them, his partisans cried out, "Amir sahib-e shahid," our beloved, martyred commander.

The shrine was enclosed in glass to allow a commanding view of the valley below. You could see why the Russians could never take the place, and why the Taliban never ruled a single square inch of Panjshir ground. Abdulrahim whispered something to himself, took off his shoes and gingerly stepped inside. He tiptoed as he approached the foot of the sarcophagus. He stood and offered up his quiet prayers, straight-backed and standing to attention.

seven

THE INTERNATIONAL BRIGADES

WHEN I FIRST visited Kandahar in the autumn of 2008, I'd shuttled down from Kabul on a creaky Ariana Airways flight. I'd been trundled with all the Afghan passengers into the 1960s airport that U.S. Peace Corps types from the Kennedy generation had built to look like something out of *The Jetsons*. I'd been whisked off towards Kandahar City in a beat-up early-'90s Toyota Corolla with a driver-fixer I will call Max, who drove like Mario Andretti. Things got dodgy right away.

We got stuck behind an ISAF troop convoy, which is never a good place to be; worse, the convoy was blocked by a jack-knifed oil tanker truck, which made Max a bit jittery. He figured the upended tanker was maybe a trap. Slowly, and one by one, the groaning contraptions in the ISAF caravan turned down into the rocky ground beside the highway to make their way around the mess. Some civilian cars that followed ended up marooned in the sand and dust. Max considered the options. Then he grabbed the wheel firmly with both hands. Will we make it? *"Inshallah,"* he answered, God willing. Max yanked the wheel and gunned it. We roared off through the rocks and sand until we were out in front of everything. Max careened back onto the pavement. A wide open road lay before us. "It is called Baghdad Road," he said. The Kabul-Jalalabad Road was called the same. All along the Kandahar version, all the way into the city, there were craters and ripped-out sections of steel highway fence, from suicide bombers, rocket attacks and the Taliban landmines known as IEDs.

When we got stuck in a traffic jam on the main road inside town, Max got jittery again. "Very dangerous," he said. He spun the wheel, tore down a side street, switchbacked a few blocks and decided to try his luck down the old main road that winds through Kandahar's narrow backstreets. Then the traffic got blocked up again. This time, more emphatically than the last, Max said, "It is very dangerous." This time it was donkey carts and pushcarts and flocks of sheep, masses of people, bicycles and black-turbaned bearded guys on motorcycles. I took Max's word for it. "No camera," he said, unnecessarily. "Roll up window. Don't look out please." This is not Kabul. This is Crazytown.

A year later, in the winter of 2009, I was looping out of the sky above Kandahar in a Canadian Forces Hercules, strapped in a sideways row facing another sideways row, full of soldiers, all of us wearing the regulation helmet and body armour you have to put on as the plane makes its whirligig missile-avoidance-manoeuvre descent. This time I'd wanted to get glimpse of the Afghanistan that soldiers see. I'd made my way to the Canadian Forces Base in Trenton, Ontario, then hitched a ride out on a Polaris airbus headed for Camp Mirage, a Canadian staging base inside a sprawling United Arab Emirates Air Force property in the desert near Dubai. A couple of days later, I boarded the Hercules, and a few hours after that I was descending in rocket-dodging loops above the Registan Desert, the bleak fastness of drifting dunes and red sandhills that stretches south from Kandahar almost all the way to Quetta. This is the way soldiers almost always arrived in Afghanistan. Alive or dead, this is the way they almost always came home.

What had changed in the brief lapse of time since my first visit to Kandahar was that ISAF's Canadian-run military complex at the edges of the desolate little Jetsons airport had tripled in size. The day I'd roared off into town with Max, I'd hardly noticed the place.

To get a picture of what the base had become, imagine a science-fiction movie. It's the distant future, on a desolate, searing-hot, faraway planet, and thirty thousand earthlings from dozens of countries are toiling away in a vast and heavily guarded mining colony in the middle of a windswept, lifeless plain. Workers are dispatched for weeks-long shifts at remote fortified job sites. Sometimes they don't make it back alive, and sometimes they come back alive but dismembered or eviscerated from bizarre volcanic eruptions triggered by invisible aliens. Groaning vehicles lumber around dusty streets. Pilotless patrol aircraft circle overhead. The aliens routinely fire exploding missiles into the place. Plus, there are creepy poisonous spiders and weird, ferocious porcupines.

In the real world, the base population was growing constantly, headed for 45,000 people by the coming summer. To get around, you could catch one of the shuttle buses on the main thoroughfares, like Bronco Road, Chinook Road or Screaming Eagle Boulevard. But traffic moved mostly on foot between high blast walls and concertina wire, down gravel alleys and dirt back streets in a grid pattern of warehouses, two-storey double-wide ATCO-type trailers, supply depots,

cafeterias, and command-and-control centres. Shambling here
and there were Romanian infantrymen, bearded special-ops
characters, Tajik restaurant workers, bubbly Australian travel
agents, Dutch technicians and even the occasional Mongo-
lian army officer. Every so often you'd see men driving around
in beat-up little white Toyota pickup trucks with Omani
licence plates. No one seemed to know who they were or what
they did.

American soldiers had been flooding in ever since that
morning at the Hare and Hounds bar in Kabul when Barack
Obama came on the big screen. At strength, the Canadian
contingent at Kandahar Air Field was rarely more than about
2,500, much of it out in the hills at Forward Operating Bases.
But KAF was still officially a Canadian town. In Absurdistan,
this was because Canadians had been doing U.S. secretary
of state Donald Rumsfeld's dirty work. In the real world, it
was because back in 2005, Canada had joined with Europe
in the first big rebuke to Rumsfeld's "we don't do nation building" doctrine. That was when the UN-mandated ISAF alliance
started getting serious about building Afghanistan. The
Hungarians got Baghlan, the Italians got Herat, the Turks got
Wardak, the Lithuanians got Chaghchara and so on. Canada
was assigned Kandahar. The KAF base was the headquarters
of the Kandahar Joint Task Force (JTF), and in the middle
of that was the headquarters of Task Force Kandahar, the
Canadian portion of ISAF's southern Regional Command
(RC-South). That's why the Canadian district of the city was
the downtown core, with its ice-less hockey rink and Labatt
Blue beer with the alcohol magically drained out of it. The
gym offered beginner's hatha yoga. *Description: Gentle stretching. Instructor: Li.* Pizza Hut delivered, open 24/7, call DSN
841-1235. Canadians were in the middle of almost everything.

Senior Canadian Forces officers by now had more American soldiers under their command than Canadian soldiers. Kandahar province also happened to be the Taliban heartland in the meanest stretch of bandit country between Delhi and Tehran. Go Canucks.

You couldn't walk very far without getting dehydrated. There were huge stacks of boxes on every corner filled with plastic water bottles. Grab one and keep walking. A rule for soldiers: Do not toss stray ammo into the garbage. All the trash here got burned, and somebody could get killed. There were lots of rules. The cat rule: KAF had been colonized by tick-riddled, feral cats. You must not go near the cats. There were also mysterious and dangerous little arachnids—when one bit me on my left knee, I was sternly told to report immediately to the medics, who instructed me to follow the dosage and frequency rules on the prescription bottle they gave me. There were the nastiest kind of scorpions, there were those porcupines, and rabid dogs.

Sometimes you'd hear a siren that sounded like an air horn. That's the enemy-infiltration alarm. When it blasted, you stayed off the streets and waited for the all-clear signal. Sometimes you'd hear a wailing siren, followed by a robot voice: *Rocket, attack. Rocket, attack.* The drill was to throw yourself on the ground, stay down for two minutes, then hurry to the nearest bomb shelter and wait for the all-clear signal. It was my bold practice at KAF to grill soldiers at every opportunity, and my first question was usually to ask what they thought they were doing in Afghanistan. It was while I was waiting for an all-clear signal in a sand-bagged blast-wall bomb shelter that I quizzed Corporal Erik Lindholm of Victoria, twenty-five, a founding editor of *Absolute Underground*, a magazine with a focus on punk and rockabilly, tattoos and skateboards.

We'd met face down in the gravel after the siren went off. At the sound of a rocket exploding somewhere in the distance, he introduced himself by saying: "If you hear one real close, my best advice is to just stay lying down." In the bomb shelter, he answered my first question this way: "You got kids?" Three, I told him. "Daughters?" One, I said. Her name is Zoe; the boys are Eamonn and Conall. "You want your daughter to be able to go to school, right? Well, so do the people here. Some people go backpacking in Europe. I picked this."

Lindholm's duties in Kandahar involved something technical in the business of "flight-line security." All I knew about that was the constant roar of Blackhawk helicopters, pilotless aerial reconnaissance vehicles, pilotless armed drones and Harrier fighter jets. There were c-130 Transports, Phantoms, f-16s and huge flying warehouses called Globemasters that supplied KAF's small city with everything you could imagine from the contents of thousands of gigantic shipping containers. Lindholm was a marathon runner who took part in whatever runs were going at KAF, and he played with the FLS Warthogs in KAF's two-hundred-team hockey league which was dominated, naturally, by Canadians. Back home, his life was photography and zine journalism. I was surprised to learn that Lindholm was a naval seaman, but he made sense of it for me. "There's no point putting an infantryman in the kind of job I do." Lindholm's unit was the Malahat, the oldest naval reserve in Canada. The Canadian Forces is an all-volunteer military. But a reservist in Afghanistan has volunteered to be in Afghanistan.

"I know what they're saying back home," he said. "You got all these organizations, these people who say they're against war. They say they support democracy, education, education for women, health care, freedom of religion, free speech. I could go on all day listing off these things, the things people here in this country don't have a chance to do. If you don't support the war, that's fine. That's fine. But on the flip side, do you support the Taliban? That's the flip side. Canada is one of the richest countries in the world. It's not like we're going to invade a country like this just for the fun of trying to take it over."

I filled up two notebooks with these kinds of conversations. Some were with Canadian Forces lifers, for whom the military was a calling, like being a firefighter or a doctor. Some were kids who had joined the army because they wanted to shoot guns and drive big machines. But to press for an answer to my first question was to always have it answered the way Lindholm did: We do this because we can, and we're doing it here because it's the right thing to do. That was the cross-country response. Nobody said anything about oil.

Private Kyle Johnston, PPCLI tattooed on his right arm, Princess Patricia's Canadian Light Infantry, from the old British Columbia fishing town of Steveston: "That's right, Steveston and proud of it." Platoon 45, Section 12-15, six months out at a time, sleep in a hole, get up in the morning, grab some rations and go—that's the working life outside the wire. Sometimes you don't have time to brush your teeth. The platoon commanders talk with the village elders about what they need. Everybody else hangs back and plays with the kids, but you have to watch them. "Sticky fingers, let me tell you."

Johnston saw nothing ambiguous about why Canadian soldiers were here. "It's all above me, man, but I can see we're making a big difference. These people had nothing, and they're benefiting from us. Women weren't even going to school before." Private Terry Allen, twenty-one, a PPCLI reservist from the other side of Canada, the Newfoundland fishing town of Bay Roberts, had the same kinds of stories to tell about being out in the boonies. He had the same gut-level sense as his buddy Johnston: "The politics, that's all beyond us. But what disappoints me is people don't have an open perspective. We're doing the right thing here. We go to where the bad guys are until they've all fucked off."

One of the peculiarities about Canadians' understanding of Afghanistan was that few people back home seemed to be aware of the critical role Canadian soldiers played while the Americans were preoccupied with Iraq and obsessed with wrapping up a "quick, cheap war" in Afghanistan. Among other disastrous consequences, the American policy allowed the Taliban to regroup in arms and mass in Kandahar. By the time the Canadian Forces operation was up and running in 2006, Kandahar was almost lost. An important part of that story was told vividly and passionately by the reservist-journalist Chris Wattie in his book *Contact Charlie: The Canadian Army, the Taliban and the Battle that Saved Afghanistan*. You get the drift from the title. The book is a blow-by-blow account of the 2006 Battle of Panjwayi. In its own small way, Panjwayi was an Afghan Stalingrad. The battle helped to break the reorganized Taliban as a conventional fighting force. Wattie's book was well received at the time, though some of the reviews were a bit snooty. But the story faded from memory.

Between the Battle of Panjwayi and Obama's 2009 troop surge, Canada's tiny contingent of 2,800 soldiers kept the Taliban from re-taking Kandahar province. That involved what senior Canadian Forces commanders candidly described as a bloody, frustrating campaign of whack-a-mole. Canadian soldiers died at a force-size ratio twice the mortality rate of American soldiers in Afghanistan and in Iraq. But Canada held Kandahar. It took a 2007 British House of Commons defence committee report to point this out: "If Kandahar fell, and it was reasonably close run last year, it did not matter how well the Dutch did in Uruzgan or how well the British did in Helmand. Their two provinces would also, as night followed day, have failed because we would have lost the consent of the Pashtun people because of the totemic importance of Kandahar."

The significance was not lost on *London Times* columnist David Aaronovitch. If Canada's troops-out lobby had had its way and Canadian soldiers had been pulled out of Kandahar, the British would have been fatally exposed in Helmand, and any British withdrawal would have forced the Americans to rely solely on a futile air war. Pakistan would then fully revert to its duplicities, the Afghan government would collapse and there would be a spring in the step of every jihadist crackpot from Palestine to Malaysia. "That's before we calculate the cost to women and girls of no longer being educated or allowed medical treatment," Aaronovitch wrote in 2008. "And would there be less terror as a result?"

In Canada, this seemed to go over just about everybody's heads. During a pause in a lengthy afternoon briefing at KAF, I talked with battle group commander Lieutenant-Colonel Jerry Walsh. His soldiers had just pulled off a massive job called Operation Hydra, and he was tired. My questions led Walsh outside the usual military comfort zone, but he took a shot at helping me find the answers. "I don't believe Canadians understand what their sons and daughters are doing in Afghanistan, what progress is being achieved, how Canadian soldiers are received in the villages, what the Canadian flag means when a soldier enters a village, or how passionate Afghans are," Walsh said. "I don't think Canadians really believe how Afghans desperately want, for their own people, they really want peace."

In Canada, in March 2008, Parliament approved the recommendation by John Manley's panel that Canada's Kandahar mission be extended until 2011, when the international Afghanistan Compact was due for review. But then everything came to a standstill. The Manley panel had opened up the opportunity for a proper national conversation about what Canada should be doing in Afghanistan in the long run. Instead, the House Special Committee on Afghanistan endeavoured to shut the conversation down. The Opposition side, with half the committee's members, turned the committee into an exhibition chamber for every troops-out axe-grinder with a spurious or lurid allegation to make. Star-witness privileges were awarded to anyone with a trumped-up hypothesis implicating Canada in war crimes. Special consideration was given to insinuations that Canada was complicit in torture. With a year left to go in the Kandahar troop extension that Parliament had approved, nearly $18 billion of Canada's money spent and the lives of 139 Canadian soldiers lost, Prime Minister Harper allowed that, as far as he was concerned, after 2011 it was troops out: "We will not be undertaking any activities that require any kind of military presence, other than the odd guard guarding an embassy."

Parliament's mandate had obliged the Special Committee to travel to Afghanistan, to consult widely and to advise Parliament on how Canada should move forward. The committee was supposed to regularly report on Canada's aid and reconstruction programs in Afghanistan and on the Kandahar military mission. By the summer of 2010, with only months to go before the Kandahar extension expired, the committee had done none of these things. Nobody knew what was happening, least of all the Canadian Forces command in Afghanistan. Another thing Canadians didn't notice was that all of Canada's aid projects, all of Canada's commitments to help build an Afghan democracy, were in limbo. Just one marooned project was the Afghan-Canadian Community Centre (ACCC) in Kandahar City. The Canadian International Development Agency was a major funder, but CIDA was no longer sure what it was supposed to do.

The community centre was roughly equal parts college, vocational school, computer lab, library and free Internet café. It was graduating hundreds of Kandahari women out of their burqas and into well-paying jobs with degrees in English, business management and computer training. Many of the women were earning diplomas through online courses with the Southern Alberta Institute of Technology in Calgary. The centre was run by its founder, Ehsanullah Ehsan, a genius Johnny Appleseed of schools in the Pashtun Durand Line borderlands. He's probably the bravest man I've ever met. It was to his sanctuary of civility, learning and literature I was headed that day in the autumn of 2008 with Mad Max, the Afghan Mario Andretti. When we'd got stuck in that traffic jam coming into Kandahar City, Ehsan had called me on my cell phone. "Where are you? What is happening?" We're fine, I'd said.

The day I visited with Ehsan in the centre's rambling old house behind high whitewashed walls down a dusty back street, he'd just received another Taliban "night letter," the usual Taliban death threat. Ehsan said he would not repeat the foul language the letter contained. A few days before, on his own doorstep, the Taliban had shot and killed one of Ehsan's neighbours for the crime of working for a government electricity agency. A few days after we met, Ehsan was one of the first on the scene at the hospital to comfort those Kandahar schoolgirls who'd had acid sprayed in their faces as they walked to school.

Ehsan was one of thirteen brothers and sisters born to a well-to-do Pashtun family from the village of Shagoy, in Zabul province. The family ran a successful dried fruit business from their apricot trees and grape vineyards. It was all there for Ehsan's taking. But he walked away from it to devote his life to what he calls the cause of civilization. "Enlightenment, you know? All that beauty." He opened his first school in the Pashtun highlands on the Pakistan side of the border in 1995, when he was only twenty-five years old. He went on to open a network of schools in the borderlands, and in Balochistan, and in the Afghan provinces of Helmand and Kunduz.

After September 11, Ehsan decided to open a school here in Kandahar, the once grand and civilized city of almond groves, orchards and caravanserais on the trade route between the Mughal Empire and Persia. When Ehsan arrived in 2002, it was a broken and seething metropolis of roughly 750,000 people that had been the capital city of Taliban despotism. "I thought there was an opportunity to serve," he explained. By 2006, Ehsan still had only a few students, but after Canadian patrols started making their rounds through the city, his little school came to their attention. When Mitch Potter of the *Toronto Star* wrote an article about what Ehsan was up to, things started to get off the ground. Ehsan's school became the ACCC, a joint venture of sorts between Ehsan and Ryan Aldred, a Canadian reservist. Aldred ran the ACCC's fundraising efforts out of his home in Ottawa.

"I want to make a change," said Ehsan, the father of five young children. "I value freedom. I value civilization. And I would like to have that. But for that I have to work. If I try and if a few more try, then our country, our own country, will be similarly at once free and beautiful and peaceful and modern and as civilized as any nation."

You could not say that Ehsanullah Ehsan was in any way afflicted with the ailment George Orwell called "the sealing-off of one part of the world from another." How it had come to pass that so many Canadians were affected was a question James Murray of the Canadian Broadcasting Corporation helped me puzzle out one night at KAF. We stayed up late under the Kandahar stars to talk about it. A veteran Kandahar journalist, Murray was not shy about saying that a reasonable, well-informed person would have to conclude that the attention Canada's news media paid to Afghanistan was "a fucking disgrace."

Canadian journalists only rarely visited Afghanistan, Murray pointed out, except on brief "embed" tours with the Canadian Forces in Kandahar. During the years Canada was running KAF, hundreds of Canadian journalists were rotated through on military "embeds," though the assignments are nothing like the confinements within Canadian Forces propaganda that many people seem to think. That wasn't the problem. The problem was that few journalists stuck around very long. One who did was Matthew Fisher, the veteran foreign affairs reporter for the newspaper chain that owned the *National Post*. Fisher spent years at KAF, on and off, living in a tent. A few other reporters stayed in Kandahar long enough to produce, like Fisher, some solid, saucy and stunning journalism. Rosie DiManno of the *Toronto Star* comes to mind, as does the scrappy Christie Blatchford of the *Globe and Mail*, author of the splendid *Fifteen Days: Stories of Bravery, Friendship, Life and Death from Inside the New Canadian Army*.

The CBC's embedded journalist at KAF, James Murray doubled as the French-language Radio Canada correspondent and tripled as the part-time manager of the "pool" camera the CBC shared with Global TV. But he couldn't be everywhere all the time. Murray agreed that there was something astonishing about the lack of media presence in Operation Hydra, the extravaganza Lieutenant-Colonel Jerry Walsh had taken pains to explain to me. The operation had been as big as anything since the Battle of Panjwayi. Hardly any shots were fired, the Taliban ran away, and Operation Hydra was considered a smashing success. But just one Canadian reporter had gone out with the troops who swept through Nakhonay and Haji Baba in the operation. It was Jonathan Montpetit, from Canadian Press.

While I was making my rounds at KAF, the journalists embedded in the Ottawa press corps were amusing one another by crafting ever more tabloid-style shock and awe phraseology in their reports about the Special Committee on Afghanistan's "torture scandal" antics—bombshell revelations, incendiary disclosures, explosive testimony, you name it. At KAF, I couldn't find a single soldier of any rank, from the lowliest private to the most senior brigadier-general, who could make head or tail of it. When the soldiers at KAF talked about the country in the real world called Afghanistan, they spoke in the frightening, affectionate, profane, lively, bitter and warm language you would expect from soldiers. In Ottawa, everyone was talking about the gunpowder plots rattling Absurdistan.

It was bad enough that there were usually only three or four Canadian journalists in Kandahar at a time. Far worse was that the rest of Afghanistan—the entire country, in other words—was more or less ignored. Back in Canada, I had spoken with a senior and deservedly respected reporter with a major Canadian news organization who'd told me he had been in Kandahar several times, for weeks at a time, over a three-year period. He had not once found the opportunity to interview an Afghan woman. That's just one kind of opportunity that doesn't present itself to journalists embedded at KAF.

Now try to imagine what you would think about the United States of America if all you heard, saw or read came from the multimedia dispatches of three or four reporters riding around for years at night in the back of a police cruiser, through the most blighted and violent alleys of Detroit.

eight

THE ASHES OF THE OLD

IT WAS ON a cold spring night in 2010 at the Karakol Restaurant, an out-of-the-way place in the down-at-heels Afshar neighbourhood of Kabul's Karte Se district, that I fell into conversation with the Hazara intellectual Buddha Ahmedy, a thirty-one-year-old scholar of literature and philosophy and a prominent contributor to the eccentric Afghan journal *Republic of Silence*. We were sitting at a candlelit table, close to the pot-bellied stove to keep warm. It's not every day you get to meet a young, fiercely curious Afghan democrat who not only survived life as a refugee in Khomeinist Iran, but also got himself expelled from Imam Khomeini University in the Iranian holy city of Qom, and then from Tehran University, and lived to tell the tale in the bargain.

From a family of orchardists in a small village with a Turkic name that translates roughly as Burned Mountain, in Ghor province, Ahmedy said he was convinced he could remember his father's hands, even though he was only three years old during the anti-Soviet jihad when his father was murdered by the Khomeinist mujahideen front known as the

Army of Iran. Ahmedy's grandfather had been stoned to death during a Pashtunization frenzy. When the Taliban came, the slaughter of the Hazaras resumed, so Ahmedy's mother sent him to enrol in Islamic studies at Qom. "I was known as an isolated person there," Ahmedy told me. He got into trouble at Qom by trying to reconcile historical materialism with Islam. An avid student of the Torah and the teachings of Zarathustra, Ahmedy then began work at Tehran University on a Ph.D. thesis that examined the Quran as the historic literature of the Arab tribes. This caused his professors to worry. After they checked his records from Imam Khomeini University, Ahmedy was told to leave.

Inspired by the philosopher Walter Benjamin's notion of the sign, Ahsad Ahmedy took the name Buddha as a tribute to the giant Buddha statues of Bamiyan the Taliban infamously destroyed in the months before September 11, 2001. In his efforts to sort out the meanings of Afghan history and the currents underlying the absurd misapprehensions about Afghanistan abroad in the English-speaking world, Ahmedy had immersed himself in the neo-Marxist Frankfurt School of social theory and the dense ideas of the French psychoanalyst Jacques Lacan. He'd concluded that the Western world's misunderstanding of the Buddhas' destruction was itself a sign of a particular malaise that had lately come to cause him great concern. The enthusiasm in NATO capitals for a Taliban peace deal stemmed from that same deep malaise, he said.

The Taliban's destruction of the Buddhas was not simply an eruption of their rage against "satanic idols" owing to some demented reading of the Quran. It was because of their eyes, Ahmedy explained. The Buddhas' eyes were Hazara eyes. This is why the Taliban regarded the towering sixth-century monuments as such an abomination. The Buddhas stood as

208 / COME FROM THE SHADOWS

an affront to the Pashtun-chauvinist construction of Afghan history. Even King Nadir Shah, in the late nineteenth century, had fired cannon at the Buddhas in an effort to destroy them. This is where Ahmedy's concern about the Western malaise comes into it. "The reason it is impossible to negotiate with the Taliban is that the Taliban are the unconscious history of the Afghan people," Ahmedy said. "Negotiation is not possible when the subject is not self-aware."

Straightforward language problems also get in the way, because language can turn reality upside down. In the common lexicon of the liberal-democratic West, the revival of Talibanism after September 11 was an "insurgency." It doesn't help that anyone from the generation that came of age reading the term "insurgent" to mean the Nicaraguan Sandinistas, the Vietcong, or the Tupamaros of Uruguay will have the wrong brain synapses firing when they hear the term used in relation to Afghanistan. The same lexicon offers up "counter-insurgency" as a euphemism for the Cold War brutality of U.S.-backed police states. In Afghanistan, the revolutionaries are with the counter-insurgents, writes David Kilcullen, the brilliant Australian counter-terrorism strategist and senior U.S. State Department adviser, "while the insurgent fights to preserve the status quo." Ahmedy understood this perfectly. I never spoke with a Canadian soldier in Afghanistan who didn't understand it just as well.

But the topsy-turviness in the West's incoherence about Afghanistan, Ahmedy claims, comes from something deeper than language. Ahmedy's inquiries into violence and memory had led him to study the inside-out accounts of Afghanistan that prevail in the Western news media. He'd concluded that the problem involves a kind of fairy tale that requires the obliteration of memory, and it comes from the tragic incapacity at the core of liberalism itself to comprehend what we used to call "evil." Ahmedy's diagnosis is strikingly similar to the conclusion the American intellectual Paul Berman reluctantly reaches in his book *Terror and Liberalism*. Berman takes as a focal point the fatal error of Paul Faure's French socialists, who imagined that Nazism could be appeased, accommodated and reasoned with. Ahmedy takes as his starting point precisely the same mistake in the misapprehension that the Taliban can be reasoned with, when in fact Talibanism is a revolt against reason itself.

The affinities between European fascism and Pashtun chauvinism are not merely theoretical. They are proved by the real-world cross-pollination between 1930s-era Pashtunization and Nazi Aryanism. The Nazi-inspired pogrom in Balkh and the Nazi-Pashtunist joint venture to obliterate history and establish in its place the cradle of Aryanism were of a piece. That much is obvious, but the obliteration of memory rids the landscape of the traces of the obvious. The Pashtunization that Mohammad Gul Khan Momand carried out across northern Afghanistan included a systematic obliteration of non-Pashtun place names from Afghanistan's maps. Momand and his contemporaries went so far as to burn rare and ancient Farsi manuscripts that would prove the lie of a Pashtun Aryan history. The totalitarian seamlessness between the Pashtun tribal elite's collaborations with the Nazis in their fantasies about a cradle of Aryanism and with the Stalinists in their "national delimitation" campaign is also worth noticing. The pogroms and land seizures that began in Afghanistan in the 1930s were still going on in the 1970s. It is only because they were so brutally effective that a kind of "peace" prevailed in Afghanistan during those years. "In this process, government officials forcibly confiscated hundreds of thousands of hectares of fertile, cultivated and prime pasture lands from the local Uzbeks and Tajiks and distributed them among the Pashtun settlers," writes the anthropologist M. Nazif Shahrani. As for Talibanism, it is merely "the natural culmination of a long history of internal colonialism and a Pashtun dominated political culture."

Paul Berman, like Ahmedy, sees a crippling vulnerability at the bedrock of what most redeems Western liberalism—its rationality: "It was the belief that, in the modern world, even the enemies of reason cannot be the enemies of reason. Even the unreasonable must be, in some fashion, reasonable." Ahmedy reached his conclusions after taking into account the Taliban's elaborately produced videos that depict decapitation and dismemberment. Taliban terrorism is pornographic. It is its own punishment and its own reward. It is not the kind of terrorism that is merely a barbaric means to an end. It is an end in itself. It is the whole point. It is all-devouring, and it can't help itself. The most sincere peace-talk lobbyists will inevitably miss the point of Talibanism, because they can't help themselves, either. Berman explains why: "It was an unwillingness, sometimes an outright refusal, to accept that from time to time, mass political movements do get drunk on the idea of slaughter."

It is also true that the movement of history can turn on a dime, for the most surprising reasons. One the biggest untold Canadian stories in Afghanistan is the story of Grant Kippen, the chairman of Afghanistan's Elections Complaints Commission, who worked carefully and methodically within the bounds of Afghan law to nullify the stuffed ballot-box sweepstakes the 2009 election had become. While Abdullah Abdullah chose not to contest the presidency in the runoff that was ordered, he had this to say about Kippen: "Had it not been for the commission's efforts, we would have had no hope. There was a complaints commission that we could trust. They gave us hope." Kippen is close to a folk hero in Afghanistan. In Canada, hardly anybody knows his name.

In the fall of 2010, Canada dodged a bullet, thanks to Liberal Foreign Affairs critic Bob Rae. Fed up with the dysfunction and paralysis in Ottawa, Rae quietly set to work with several senior Conservatives who were fed up with Prime Minister Harper's blockheadedness about Afghanistan. With Liberal leader Michael Ignatieff's blessing, Rae and his Conservative allies managed an end run around the NDP, the Bloc Québécois and the usual parliamentary obstacles, relying on little more than the decency of old-fashioned statesmanship to guide the way. As a result, Canada did not pull its troops from Afghanistan but rather reassigned about 1,000 soldiers to a hands-on training program for the Afghan National Army, centred in Kabul. This was taken as a good sign by the Canada-Afghanistan Solidarity Committee. By the spring of 2011, Ottawa was looking at shifting at least some of its post-Kandahar efforts to Balkh province, and this came as especially welcome news to the human rights activists Abdul-rahim Parwani and I had met in Mazar-e Sharif. It was also good news for the young journalists I'd met in Mazar who'd told me their worries about the growing influence of radical mullahs like Mawlawi Abdul Qahir Zadran in the city. On April 1, 2011, rioters attacked a UN compound in Mazar, killing seven foreigners. Zadran was implicated in the incitements. The incident redoubled Balkh governor Mohammad Atta Noor's efforts to win Canada's help in beefing up the Afghan National Security Forces' capacity in the province.

Karzai's fevered hope of a peace deal with his Taliban "brothers" was still muddled. In a temper, Karzai had defenestrated Amrullah Saleh, the cerebral and deeply anti-Taliban chief of Afghanistan's National Directorate of Security. This allowed Saleh, who had served as Ahmad Shah Massoud's intelligence chief right up to the days before September 11, to be more candid about the implications of abandoning Afghan democracy and securing a cheap exit-strategy Taliban deal. "First, a massacre campaign will start," Saleh warned in a CBS television interview. "The human cost in this country will easily be up to two million people killed, at least. It will not be big news for Afghanistan. We are used to tragedies, throughout our history. But the cost for you will be bigger." Saleh, one the last Massoudists to hold senior office in Karzai's government, retreated to the Panjshir Valley to confer, to consult and to organize. But by that time, Berhanuddin Rabbani had taken up the post of Karzai's senior peace-talk envoy, of all things, in a "Nixon in China" gambit. Allah works in mysterious ways.

While the movements of a beast are not easily anticipated, the nature of the beast remains. The great dysfunction of Pashtun tribal politics is its susceptibility to a political economy that requires conquest, the extraction of tribute and subsidy, the abject submission of potential contenders and the ruthless elimination of rivals. Power sustains itself by the politics of blood and vendetta, the way of the gun and the cunning distribution of the spoils. Power expands by its voracious appetite for land and slaves and by its capacity for genocidal violence. A political economy like this tends to devour itself, because it inevitably produces a surplus value of barbarism. So it has to expand outwards. Like Nazism, and like Spanish and Italian fascism, it doesn't want to be reasoned with, and it is not easily contained.

This brings us back to the late Irish historian Fred Halliday's observation that the struggle in Afghanistan is to the twenty-first century's first decade what the Spanish Civil War was to Europe in the middle and late twentieth century. Historical analogies are always sketchy—the UN's forty-two-nation ISAF effort embraces twice as many countries as those that signed the formal anti-Nazi alliance of 1942—but the Canadian soldiers engaged in Afghanistan's anti-Taliban struggle deserve to be understood as the successors of the brave anti-fascists of the 1930s who fought in the Spanish Civil War. History rarely runs in straight lines, but when you look at the pedigrees of Canada's isolationist and pacifist "left," you also find a lineage that leads straight back to the 1930s, to the pacifism that George Orwell called "a bourgeois illusion bred of money and security."

By the late 1930s, Madrid's leftist government had been abandoned by the West's great democracies. The Spanish republic was left to fend for itself against several divisions of Spanish troops led by the fascist general Francisco Franco. Through his zealous appeals for them to see the confluence of fascist Catholicism and Islam, Franco successfully recruited 75,000 Arab mercenaries from Morocco. He was aided by another 75,000 soldiers, 660 aircraft, 150 tanks and a trove of munitions provided by Italian dictator Benito Mussolini. Germany's Nazi regime sent in a further 16,000 soldiers, 600 fighter and bomber aircraft and 200 tanks. And so it came to pass that roughly 1,700 Canadians sailed off to Spain to join with volunteer comrades in arms who came from the ends of the earth to take up the defence of the republic.

They say history is written by the victors, but that is not quite true. History is written by people who write. The

Canadian partisans in Spain had no Ernest Hemingway, Martha Gellhorn or John Dos Passos to valorize them. The Canadians had no W.H. Auden, Stephen Spender or George Orwell. But as it has been in Afghanistan, the Canadian contribution in Spain was out of all proportion to Canada's size. With a population ten times greater, the United States mustered only twice the number of volunteers in Spain. From a country with five times Canada's population, the British volunteers numbered only a few hundred more than the Canadians.

Unlike the British intellectuals, and unlike the core American contingent from the Young Communist League in New York, the largest single group of Canadians who fought in Spain came out of British Columbia's "slave labour" camps. The Canadian anti-fascist volunteers were workers, "far more proletarian" than the British or the Americans, the Spanish War veteran Irving Weissman recalled years later. The Canadians fought barefoot and ate oats out of the fields. "They were very, very working class. The overwhelming majority—it was stamped on them," Weissman remembered. The Canadians weren't ideologues, either. They fought from a gut instinct for solidarity. And just as the mortality rate among Canadian soldiers in Afghanistan far exceeded the death rate among American soldiers in Afghanistan or Iraq, at least 400 of the 1,700-odd Canadians who sailed to Spain never came home.

The story of the Canadians in Spain was never fully told, despite the Stalinist apologetics and labour-hall singalongs and revisionist hagiographies, until the pen was taken up by the young Canadian journalist Michael Petrou, in his 2008 *Renegades: Canadians in the Spanish Civil War*. As it happens, Petrou was with the Northern Alliance in the winter of 2001 as it roared across the Shomali Plains towards Kabul to send the Taliban packing. In a conversation shortly after his book was published, Petrou told me he agreed with the parallels. "The 1930s was a time when the left was capable of recognizing fascism," he said. "I find it frustrating that a lot of the left has failed to recognize real fascism in the world today. There is, unfortunately, a moral bankruptcy in broad sections of the left today, in its inability to recognize real fascism if it's opposed to the United States or whatever." It was not by accident, either, that Omar Samad, the former student activist who went on to become Afghanistan's ambassador to Canada, was an honoured guest at the Ottawa launch of Petrou's book.

There are also innumerable parallels between Spain and Afghanistan in the sordid alliances, geopolitical intrigues and the sinister great-power manipulations that go on behind the scenes. The story of the April 2009 Battle of Marefat High School is a case in point.

Odd as it sounds, the Khomeinist-inspired Shia "rape law" actually got its traction from the far-right Sunni bloc in Afghanistan's parliament, the Wolesi Jirga. The Sunni mullahs wanted their own Taliban-like marriage law, so they told the Iranian-backed ayatollah Mohammad Asif Mohseni: You go first; we've got your back; you can watch our back when our turn comes. An exhaustive review of the events that led up to the "rape law" fiasco undertaken by Lauryn Oates for the Afghanistan Research and Evaluation Unit, an independent think tank based in Kabul, reveals how Mohseni's Shia law was pushed through the Wolesi Jirga. It involved much backroom strong-arm work and a bait-and-switch job. The passage of the law was a botch-up from a parliament desperately in need of the basic rules and procedures the UN and the NATO democracies hadn't got around to helping Afghan democrats get established.

The geopolitical manipulations behind President Hamid Karzai's acquiescence to Mohseni in the "rape law" case were also directly tied to the April 2011 Afghanistan riots that led to the deaths of the UN workers in Mazar-e Sharif. Mohseni, whose followers arrived in a mob at Marefat High School in 2009, played a key role in the 2011 incitements, and Hamid Karzai played a role in the affair, too.

By 2009, on the sly, Tehran was pouring millions of dollars every year into a slush fund handled by Karzai's chief of staff, Umar Daudzai. The funds bought Iran favours from Karzai's palace, and allowed Karzai to buy favours from Afghan lawmakers and power brokers. Once you know that, it isn't surprising that when Mohseni asked Karzai to sign a personal-status law to impose the worst kind of Khomeinist marriage rules upon Afghanistan's minority Shias, Karzai did so, without even reading the law.

The April 2011 massacre at the UN compound in Mazar-e Sharif began with an Iranian propaganda initiative that sparked a series of bloody riots that left at least two dozen people dead across Afghanistan. The riots were nominally a reaction to a Quran burning staged by Terry Jones, an American Christian extremist. His stunt was almost completely ignored by both the American and the Afghan news media, but on March 24—the day before Karzai was set to visit Iran for bilateral talks—the Iranian foreign ministry, Iran's Lebanese proxy Hezbollah and Karzai's office issued simultaneous alarms about Jones's Quran burning. Iranian ministry spokesman Ramin Mehman-Parast said the incident was part of American "hegemonic plots." Karzai called for Jones's arrest and prosecution. The first Afghan protests were staged by the Shura-e Olama-e Shiia, the Shia religious council that Mohseni dominates. (You always know it's a Khomeinist event

by the telltale slogan, *Marg Bar Yahood*—Death to the Jews.)
The Kabul demonstrations were the first that most Afghans
had even heard about Jones's provocation. The incitements
and the hysterics then proceeded apace across the country.

Sinister propaganda played a role in the Spanish struggle of the 1930s, too. One of the lesser-known ploys involved
Canada's fabled Mackenzie-Papineau Battalion. The battalion actually began as a propaganda fiction. It was formed only
after Canadian volunteers arrived in Spain and discovered that
it didn't actually exist; they went on strike to force its establishment. But one of the starkest parallels between Afghanistan
and Spain, in a Canadian context, can be found in the direct
descent of the federal New Democratic Party's "anti-war"
politics from the disgraceful pacifism of its predecessor, the Co-
operative Commonwealth Federation, during the 1930s.

The CCF leadership consistently opposed recruitment to
the international brigades in Spain. In 1939, CCF founder
J.S. Woodsworth couldn't even bring himself to vote in favour
of Canada joining the Allies in the fight against the Nazis.
Many CCF rank-and-filers broke with the party brass and
headed off for Spain anyway, just as there were Liberals and
Conservatives among the volunteers who'd bucked their own
parties' prohibitions on recruitment to the brigades. The largest Canadian cohort of idealistic Communist Party members
arose from a pre-Bolshevik tradition, and there were also independent socialists, Trotskyists and free thinkers among the
Canadian volunteers. In Afghanistan, too, you'd find a surprising political diversity in the ranks of the Princess Patricia's
Canadian Light Infantry, the Royal Canadian Regiment and
the rest. You'd also find the same non-ideological gut instinct
for solidarity that had motivated the Canadian volunteers in
Spain. By September 11, in what had become of "the Left" in

Canada, that gut instinct just wasn't there anymore. It's not fair to generalize, but it's fair to say you'd be waiting a long time if you were expecting the West Point Grey Bolivarian study club and aromatherapy men's group to put its back into the fight.

Until September 11, 2001, the CCF leadership's pacifism was remembered in left-wing circles as a matter of grave error and shame, and it had been renounced by a long line of Canadian socialists and social democrats. After September 11, that same pacifism became a point of pride, a core feature of the left-wing identity, a value so central that to merely call yourself "anti-war" was to prove your claim to the honorifics "left-wing" and "progressive." By 2006, NDP leader Jack Layton had become J.S. Woodsworth's rightful heir and successor.

By 2011, there was another Canadian title Layton could rightfully claim. The May 2 federal election gave Stephen Harper the Conservative parliamentary majority he'd been hoping for, and the Liberal Party, led by the proudly interventionist Michael Ignatieff, was nearly obliterated. When the Bloc Québécois vote shrivelled, Jack Layton became leader of Canada's Official Opposition.

For all the parallels, there is also a critical distinction between then and now, between Spain and Afghanistan: the Spanish republic was lost. By 2011, the Afghan republic was still hanging on by the skin of its teeth, but opinion in the NATO capitals was bitterly divided. Do we push on, or do we cave in and cut a deal with the Taliban? The Obama White House was coming down squarely on the latter side. Lauryn Oates sums up the implications well in her polemic against neutrality: "There is only one side that history will forgive."

The Afghan cause is by no means hopeless. The struggle is occluded by the erasure of memory, by the sundering of subject peoples into shadows, and by the way Afghanistan's true stories are so often rendered false in their Absurdistan versions. But the democratic struggle is very real. By the spring of 2011, it was flowering again in Afghanistan, and it was erupting all over the so-called Muslim world: first Tunisia, then Egypt, then Yemen, then Libya, Bahrain, Syria, and Gaza. What had begun in Tehran in 2009 was now breaking out in mass pro-democracy protests in Tunis, Cairo, Damascus, everywhere. Hundreds of thousands of Arabs were pouring into the streets.

The Khomeinists and their Sunni Islamist counterparts were startled and confused. So was the "anti-war" movement throughout the English-speaking world. While the Canadian Peace Alliance was rallying against any NATO intervention in Libya, the Libyan revolutionaries were begging NATO for air strikes and arms drops. While activists on Canadian university campuses were preparing for another round of annual Islamist-friendly Israeli Apartheid Week seminars, Arab activists were girding for battles with Islamists bent on hijacking their revolutions. In Tunis, the placards read: "Nous sommes tous Musalmans, nous sommes tous Chretiens, nous sommes tous Juifs."

In Afghanistan, where democracy's young vanguard could be found in places like the hardscrabble Hazara city of Daste Barchi, thousands of young people were flocking to anti-appeasement, pro-democracy Facebook pages. One of the most popular Afghan Facebook groups explicitly described itself as anti-fascist. Fawzia Koofi, the young deputy speaker of the Wolesi Jirga, announced her candidacy for the 2014 Afghan presidential elections. And in April 2011, a new movement was born. The Basij-e-Melli (National Mobilisation) brought together Abdullah Abdullah and his supporters with

Amrullah Saleh, the tireless intelligence chief President Karzai had deposed in a fit of pique in 2010. The day Osama bin Laden was killed in Abbotabad, Pakistan, the Basij called for a celebratory rally. Three days later, on May 5, roughly fifteen thousand demonstrators gathered in Kabul. They wore green bracelets of the kind worn during the 2009 pro-democracy Iranian uprising. They chanted: "Death to the Taliban. Death to the suicide bombers." Saleh exhorted the crowds to fight any capitulation to Pakistan or the Taliban and mocked President Karzai's persistent references to the Taliban as his disaffected brothers. "They are not my brother, they are not your brother," Saleh told the cheering demonstrators. "Those are our enemies." The Massoudists were back.

As I write this, I can report that the doors of Marefat High School are still open.

Abdulrahim Parwani was especially cheerful during our visit to the school that spring day in 2010. Aziz Royesh, the school principal who had narrowly escaped Mohseni's rioters, was a veteran pro-democracy partisan. In the days when Abdulrahim was delivering his Massoudist newspaper by bicycle through the cratered streets of Kabul, Royesh was a mujahid, up in the mountains. The two of them talked old times while the students quietly attended to their studies, but at recess break, Abdulrahim and I ended up causing a noisy commotion in the school courtyard.

Girls and boys no older than Abdulrahim had been in the time of the white Volgas, no less curious or saucy, surrounded us. The fun was to test their English on us, and they spoke extremely well. Then they noticed my digital camera. Take a picture! Take a picture! They got a kick out of seeing themselves in the camera's view screen. We will take a picture of you now! So I handed over the camera and asked them what they wanted out of life: I will be a chemist; I will be a doctor; I will be a journalist; I will be a businessman. It went around like that in a perfectly matter-of-fact way.

Then Abdulrahim had the camera, and he was tugging at my arm with excitement, holding up the camera's view screen. It was a photograph that one of the kids had taken of the two of us. We were surrounded by young scholars, gazing into the middle distance at something Abdulrahim had been pointing at on the second-storey balcony that wrapped around the courtyard. He saw something uproariously funny about the picture. I couldn't see what it was. "See, I am just like Lenin, with all my comrades! In a poster, he is always pointing to something far away like that!"

The kids kept up their questions. How many Canadian soldiers are in Afghanistan? Does Canada make their soldiers come here, or can the soldiers decide? What do Canadians think about Afghanistan? Do you think Afghanistan will be rich like Canada one day?

Each one of them had the eyes of the Buddhas of Bamiyan.

NOTES

CHAPTERS I AND 5 rely almost wholly upon text sources for the evidence that upends the fictions of Absurdistan. Chapter 2 is drawn from my first-hand encounters in Afghanistan and relies heavily on text sources as well. The other chapters derive mostly from the notes I made on my visits to Afghanistan and my conversations with the people there. Unless otherwise made plain, the verbatim quotations in this book derive from those interviews, which have also informed a variety of articles, essays and opinion pieces I've written over the years for the *National Post*, *Vancouver Review*, *Democratiya*, *Z Word Magazine*, *Vancouver Magazine*, *Dissent*, *The Vancouver Sun* and HRS *Internasjonal* (Norway). Some interviews with key political figures were undertaken in the course of research for the Canada-Afghanistan Solidarity Committee's 2010 "Keeping Our Promises" report. Several of the Afghans who appear in Chapters 3 and 4 were featured in a series of essays I wrote for the *Calgary Herald* (in memory of the Canadian journalist Michelle Lang, who died in Kandahar December 30, 2009) and for the online daily *The Tyee*. Those essays derive from an exhibit series I undertook as a collaboration between the Canada-Afghanistan Solidarity Committee and the Funders Network for Afghan Women.

CHAPTER I: *Welcome to Absurdistan*

Epigraph: George Orwell, "Notes on Nationalism," *Polemic: A Magazine of Philosophy, Psychology & Aesthetics*, October 1945.

Intimidation, Iranian intrigue and Kabul's Khomeinist ayatollah, Mohammad Asif Mohseni: "The Struggle for Shi'ite Hearts and Minds," Parts I & II, *France 24*, May 14, 2009.

On the Afghan rape law controversy: Lauryn Oates, "A Closer Look: The Policy and Law-Making Process Behind the Shiite Personal Status Law," Issues Paper Series, Afghanistan Research and Evaluation Unit, September, 2009.

Iranian origin of "rape law" contents: "Statement of Groups of Iranian Women Supporting Afghan Women," *Canada-Afghanistan Solidarity Committee Bulletin*, April 15, 2009, http://afghanistan-canada-solidarity.org/content/statement-groups-iranian-women-supporting-afghan-women.

The Greg Mortenson Three Cups of Tea *scandal*: Jon Krakauer, "Three Cups of Deceit: How Greg Mortenson, Humanitarian Hero, Lost His Way," *Byliner Originals*, April, 2011.

Claims for the "bravest woman in Afghanistan": Malalai Joya and Derrick O'Keefe, *A Woman Among Warlords: The Extraordinary Story of an Afghan Woman who Dared to Raise Her Voice* (Scribner, 2009).

Ken Livingstone, al-Qaida as U.S. ally: "London Mayor Blames Bombings on West," Sky News, July 20, 2005.

"Graveyard of Empires" myth: Christian Caryl, "Bury the Graveyard," *Foreign Policy*, July 26, 2010.

Jack Layton's "six years of counter-insurgency" myth: Terry Glavin, "Fresh Start on Afghanistan Debate," *The Tyee*, January 23, 2008.

What the world thinks Afghans think: WorldPublicOpinion.org poll, "Global Poll Finds Widespread Belief that Afghans Want NATO Forces Out," University of Maryland Program on International Policy Attitudes (PIPA), July 23, 2009.

Myth of misogyny as unique to Afghan culture and history: Canadian Women
for Women in Afghanistan, Afghan Women in History synopsis,
http://www.cw4wafghan.ca; Ahmed Rashid, *Taliban: Militant Islam,
Oil and Fundamentalism in Central Asia* (Yale University Press, 2001);
Peter Levi, *The Light Garden of the Angel King: Journeys to Afghanistan*
(Readers Union, 1973).

Taliban "religion" foreign to Afghanistan, an aberration in Islam: Rashid, 2001.

Taliban as a multinational joint venture in jihadism: Rashid, 2001.

Afghanistan not plagued by chronic "insurgency": Thomas Barfield, *Afghanistan:
A Cultural and Political History* (Princeton University Press, 2010).

Pre-Reagan U.S. funding and arming of Islamist mujahideen in Afghanistan:
Robert M. Gates, *From The Shadows* (Simon and Schuster, 1996).

*Last days of the Najibullah regime, the U.S.-Soviet agreement on foreign troop
withdrawal and the Peshawar Accord:* Lester W. Grau, "Breaking Contact
Without Leaving Chaos: The Soviet Withdrawal from Afghanistan,"
Journal of Slavic Military Studies 20, no. 2 (2007); "Adrift in Soviet
Past: Kabul is left in the ruins of a crumbled empire," *Los Angeles
Times,* September 13, 1991; Human Rights Watch, "Blood Stained
Hands," July 2005, http://www.hrw.org/en/reports/2005/07/06/
blood-stained-hands-0.

*Origin of the Afghan Islamist groups, their internecine warfare and mercenary proxy
relationships with foreign powers:* Steve Coll, *Ghost Wars: The Secret History
of the CIA, Afghanistan and bin Laden, from the Soviet Invasion to September
10, 2001* (Penguin Books, 2004).

*The "deliberately deceptive journalism" and propaganda underlying the
legend of an Afghan welcoming of the Taliban:* Christian Bleuer, "The
Persistent Myth of Pre-Taliban Anarchy," *Ghosts of Alexander*
(blog), April 27, 2007, http://easterncampaign.com/2007/04/24/
the-persistent-myth-of-pre-taliban-anarchy/.

Taliban opium racketeering: The Century Foundation, "Afghanistan Watch,
Fact Sheet on Opium," November 2004; Raphael Perl, "Taliban and
the Drug Trade," U.S. Congressional Research report, October 5, 2001;
Gretchen Peters, "How Opium Profits the Taliban," U.S. Institute for
Peace, August, 2009.

Myth that the Taliban eliminated corruption: "Lifting the Veil on Taliban Sex
Slavery," *Time,* February 10, 2002; Ahmed Rashid, *Descent into Chaos:
The United States and the Failure of Nation-Building in Pakistan, Afghanistan,
and Central Asia* (Viking, 2008).

Myth that the Taliban and al-Qaida were former U.S. allies: Coll, 2001.

"Pashtunwali" and myth of Taliban entitlement to review evidence against Osama bin Laden: Rashid, 2001; "Taliban Met with U.S. Often: Talks Centered on Ways to Hand over bin Laden," *Washington Post,* October 29, 2001.

Final days of Taliban rule, post-2011 overthrow, U.S. reluctance to involve NATO: Grau, 2007; Rashid, 2008.

Myth of Afghan "quagmire," public opinion polls: See Appendix.

The UN/NATO/ISAF *"light footprint" calamity in Afghanistan, trends in U.S. commitment, the "insurgency," economic development and state-building:* Paul D. Miller, "Finish the Job: How the War in Afghanistan Can Be Won," *Foreign Affairs* 90, no. 1, January/February 2011.

NATO's *parsimonious Afghan commitment:* Anita Inder Singh, "Bankrolling Kabul," *The Guardian,* March 12, 2008.

Legacy of U.S. negligence, state-building aversion: Paul D. Miller, "Woodward's Missing Chapters," *Foreign Policy,* October 14, 2010; Rashid, 2008.

Conspiracy theories and "anti-Zionist" hysterics: See notes to Chapter 5. After September 11, the far-right journalist Eric Margolis consistently characterized the Taliban as a "religious anti-communist movement" fighting a "communist" post-911 regime in Kabul. He was a regular foreign affairs "expert" for CTV News and was routinely cited favourably and deferentially as an Afghanistan authority by a variety of avowedly left-wing columnists and writers from the purportedly progressive online daily *The Tyee* to the old socialist standard *Canadian Dimension.*

Capitulation to a "fascistic theocracy": James Laxer, "Why Canada Should Get Out Of Afghanistan," *Globe and Mail,* March 3, 2006.

Canadian loathing of U.S. president George W. Bush: Michael Adams, "Bash Thy Neighbour," *Globe and Mail,* October 19, 2005.

Canada's close-call House of Commons vote (149–145) to remain with the ISAF/ NATO *alliance in Afghanistan:* "Canada's Stay in Afghanistan Extended by Two Years," CBC News, May 17, 2006.

Troops-out a "misjudgement of historic proportions": Ban Ki-Moon, "Being in Afghanistan Is Dangerous, Not Being in Afghanistan Is More Dangerous," *Globe and Mail,* January 24, 2008.

Fred Halliday's parallel between the Afghan "war" and the Spanish Civil War of the 1930s: Danny Postel, "Who is responsible? An interview with Fred Halliday," *Salamagundi,* no. 150–51, 2005; Terry Glavin, "Our Generation's Spanish Civil War," *National Post* Full Comment, May 23, 2008.

CHAPTER 2: *The Children of Seth*

Linguistic origins of Balkh's first peoples: M. Paul Lewis (ed.), *Ethnologue: Languages of the World* (SIL International, 2009).

Afghan empires, ancient Balkh and literary traditions: Barfield, 2010; S. Frederick Starr, "Rediscovering Central Asia," *Wilson Quarterly,* Summer 2009; Bijan Omrani, "Afghanistan and the Silk Road: The Land at the Heart of World Trade," United Nations Assistance Mission to Afghanistan, background paper, n.d.; UNESCO World Heritage, Global Strategy, "Tentative Lists: City of Balkh (Antique Bactria)," Department of Historic Monuments, Ministry of Information & Culture, Kabul, 2004; Levi, 1973.

Zoroastrians: Major-General Sir H.C. Rawlinson, "Monograph on the Oxus," *Journal of the Royal Geographical Society of London* 42, 1851; L.H. Mills (trans.), *Sacred Liturgy and Gathas/Hymns of Zarathushtra,* (Sacred Books of the East, American Edition, 1898).

Buddhists and Barmakids: De Lacey O'Leary, *How Greek Science Passed to the Arabs* (Routledge & Kegan Paul Ltd., 1949).

Jewish Balkh: Encyclopaedia Judaica (The Gale Group, 2008).

Hiwi the Heretic: Eliezer Segal, *Ask Now of the Days that are Past* (University of Calgary Press, 2005).

Nestorians in Balkh and China: F. Hirth, "The Mystery of Fii-lin," *Journal of the American Oriental Society,* 30th Volume. Sajjad H. Rizva, "Avicenna (Ibn Sina) (c. 980–1037)," *The Internet Encyclopedia of Philosophy,* January 6, 2006, www.iep.utm.edu.

Afghan rulers' 175-year streak of dependency on foreign supports: Barfield, 2010.

Afghanistan and Nazi Germany: Milan L. Hauner, "Afghanistan Between the Great Powers, 1938–1945," *International Journal of Middle Eastern Studies* 14, 1982; Martin Ewans, *Afghanistan: A Short History of its People and Politics* (Perennial, 2001); "Encounters with Mohammed Gul Khan Momand," in Robert Byron, *The Road to Oxiana* (Picador, 1981).

The Nazi Foreign Bureau, Afghan affairs: Document 007-PS, "Brief Report on Activities of the Foreign Affairs Bureau of the Party from 1933–1943," The Avalon Project, Documents in Law, History and Diplomacy, Yale Law School, 1996.

Building a "cradle of Aryanism" in Balkh: R.D. McChesney, "An early 17th century palace complex in Balkh," *Muqarnas, An Annual on the Visual Cultures of the Islamic World* XXVI, 2009; R.D. McChesney, "Architecture and Narrative: The Khwaja Abu Nasr Parsa Shrine,

Part 2: Representing the Complex in Word and Image, 1696–1998," *Muqarnas: An Annual on the Visual Culture of the Islamic World* XIX, 2002; Akhror Mukhtarov, in McChesney, 2002.

Absorption of Nazi Propaganda in Shia Iran: Matthias Kuentzel, "Hitler's Legacy: Islamic Antisemitism in the Middle East," Invited Paper, Institution for Social and Policy Studies, Yale University, 2006.

Persistent crypto-fascism in Afghanistan: Soraab Balkhi, "The Degenerate Nature of the Neo-Nazi Afghan Mellat," *Afghan Outline,* 2007; Frank Clements, *Conflict in Afghanistan: A Historical Perspective* (ABC-CLIO, 2003).

Genocidal massacres during Taliban era: Michael Sheridan, "How the Taliban Slaughtered 8,000 People in Mazar-e-Sharif," *Sunday Times,* November 1, 1998; Human Rights Watch, "The Massacre in Mazar-e-Sharif," vol. 10, no. 7 (c), November 1998; Human Rights Watch, "Massacres of Hazaras in Afghanistan," vol. 13, no. 1 (c), February, 2001.

Taliban brutality, massacres and reprisal killings: Bureau of Democracy, Human Rights and Labor, "Country Reports on Human Rights Practices: Afghanistan," U.S. State Department, March, 2002.

CHAPTER 3: *A Tale of Two Cities*

Nick Meo, "Kabul was a fun city for foreigners; is it becoming the new Baghdad?" *Sunday Telegraph,* October 25, 2008.

Matt Walden, "Falling Short: Aid Effectiveness in Afghanistan, Agency Coordinating Body for Afghan Relief," ACBAR Advocacy Series, March, 2008.

Terry Glavin, "The New Kabul," *National Post,* November 13, 2008.

Terry Glavin, "A Choice of Comrades," *Democratiya,* Winter 2008.

Terry Glavin, "Unsung Heroes" series, *The Calgary Herald,* 2010.

Terry Glavin, "Heroes" series, *The Tyee,* 2010.

Murad Khane: Paul Kvitna, "Can Rory Stewart Fix Afghanistan?" *National Geographic,* June/July 2007.

Persecution of Afghan journalists: Sukumar Muralidharan (ed.), "Growth Under Adversity: Afghanistan Press Freedom Report, 2007–2008," International Federation of Journalists, 2008.

Mansoor Dadullah and the Mastrogiacomo/Naqeshbandi affair: Bill Roggio, "Former Taliban commander Mansoor Dadullah captured in Pakistan," *Long War Journal,* February 11, 2008.

"Nowadays, everyone is trying to get rich": Matthieu Aikins, "Last Stand in Kandahar," *The Walrus*, December, 2010.

Reconstruction progress: "Good News," The Ruxted Group, July 25, 2007; Paul D. Miller, "Finish the Job: How the War in Afghanistan Can Be Won," *Foreign Affairs* 90, no. 1, January/February 2011.

Comparison with Balkans: Anita Inder Singh, "Bankrolling Kabul," *The Guardian*, March 12, 2008.

CHAPTER 4: *Women's Work*

Mental health in Afghanistan: Ronald Waldman and Homaira Hanif, "The Public Health System in Afghanistan," Afghan Research and Evaluation Unit, May/June, 2002; "Country Profile Afghanistan— Mental Health and Substance Abuse," World Health Organization, n.d.; Ventevogel et al., "Mental health care reform in Afghanistan," *Journal of Ayub Medical College*, 2002.

Taliban "mining" landmines, continuing attacks on "de-mining" workers: Mine Action Coordination Center of Afghanistan (MACCA), www. mineaction.org/org.asp?o=17; Lynne O'Donnell, "Mines, bombs injure more Afghan civilians: ICRC," Agence-France Presse, April 14, 2010; UN Office for the Coordination of Humanitarian Affairs, "Afghanistan: Deminers in the Firing Line," IRIN Global, January 18, 2011.

Ongoing Taliban attacks on teachers, schoolchildren and schools: "Education under Attack 2010—Afghanistan," UN Educational, Scientific and Cultural Organization, February 10, 2010.

Basic indicators, women and children's health: UNICEF country reports, Afghanistan statistics, ongoing; Alexandra Reihing, "Child Labour in Afghanistan, Policy Innovations," Carnegie Council, June 20, 2007.

Talibs on Campus: Camelia Fard and James Ridgeway, "The Accidental Operative: Richard Helms's Afghani Niece Leads Corps of Taliban Reps," *Village Voice*, June 12, 2001; Carina Chocano, "Save the Children or the Buddhas Get It," *Salon*, March 22, 2001.

Women under Taliban rule: Sally Armstrong, *Veiled Threat: The Hidden Power of the Women of Afghanistan* (Penguin Canada, 2002).

American feminists who stood by Afghan women: Eleanor Smeal, "Why is the Feminist Majority Foundation Refusing to Abandon the Women and Girls of Afghanistan?" *Huffington Post*, July 15, 2009.

Sally Armstrong at UVic seminar: Terry Glavin, "Journalist Speaks Up for Afghan Women," *The Georgia Straight*, March 15, 2007.

Lauryn Oates: Terry Glavin, "Lauryn Oates' Fight for Afghan Women's Rights," *Vancouver Magazine*, October, 2010.

Against Neutrality: Sarah Chayes, "The Perils of Delivering Aid," *Globe and Mail*, August 15, 2008; Lauryn Oates, "Five Reasons Why I'm Not Neutral," *The Propagandist*, November 5, 2010.

President Hamid Karzai's "peace at any cost" plan: John Simpson, "Afghanistan's Karzai Moots Taliban Peace Scheme," BBC News, January 21, 2010.

Fawzia Koofi, *Letters to My Daughters* (Douglas and McIntyre, 2010).

The new generation of North American women's rights activists: Juliet O'Neill, "'Little Woman' from Canada raises big funds for Afghan teachers," *The Vancouver Sun*, July 18, 2010.

CHAPTER 5: *"If Ever a Country Deserved Rape"*

Remote Pashtun villagers thought Americans were Russian Soldiers: Daniel Carson, "Soldier Provides Glimpse into Afghan Mission," *New Herald*, July 8, 2009.

International Council on Security and Development poll results for September 11 questions: Report and poll results, "Afghanistan Transition: Missing Variables," ICOS, November 19, 2010.

Code Pink's deceptions: Aunohita Majumdar, "Code Pink rethinks its call for Afghanistan Pull-Out," *Christian Science Monitor*, October 6, 2009; Terry Glavin, "Peace at Any Cost," *Human Rights Service Internasjonal*, January 28, 2010; Lauryn Oates, "If NATO Abandons Afghanistan, Women Doomed," October 5, 2010, http://afghanistan-canada-solidarity.org/if-nato-abandons-afghanistan-women-doomed.

Andrew Potter and Joseph Heath, *Rebel Sell: Why the Culture Can't Be Jammed* (HarperCollins Canada, 2005).

Nick Cohen, *What's Left? How Liberals Lost Their Way* (Fourth Estate/ HarperCollins, 2007).

Michael Bérubé, *The Left at War* (NYU Press, 2009).

"Left-wing" anti-Afghan racism: Alexander Cockburn, "Press Clips," *Village Voice*, January 21, 1980; Lauryn Oates, "They're Not Worth It: The Afghan Barbarian Myth," *The Propagandist*, October 19, 2010.

Media hysteria, observed by Jason Elliot: Laura Miller, "The 'enemy' we barely know," *Salon*, September 19, 2001.

Noam Chomsky, "The New War Against Terror" (lecture transcript), *Counterpunch*, October 24, 2001.

Chomsky refuted: Laura Rozen, "Crying wolf, or doing their job," *Salon*, November 16, 2001.

Chomsky heralded in Al-Ahram: Faiza Rady, "A Silent Genocide," *Al-Ahram Weekly*, November 8–14, 2001.

The "most serious split within the left since the Soviet invasion of Hungary in 1956" refers to the aftermath of the Euston Manifesto, a declaration favouring muscular centre-left democracy and a liberal interventionist foreign affairs policy (both the author of this book and Lauryn Oates are signers). See: Keith Kahn-Harris, "An end to the left's decent split?" *The Guardian*, October 19, 2009.

Rick Mercer, *Talking to Americans* (CBC, 2001).

An especially moving account of the American Vietnam-era "draft dodger" experience in Canada: Jack Todd, *The Taste of Metal: A Deserter's Story* (Harper/Flamingo, 2001).

The absurdity of the left-Islamist courtships induced by September 11: Fred Halliday, "The Jihadism of Fools," *Dissent*, Winter 2007.

Shulamit Volkov, "Readjusting Cultural Codes: Reflections on Anti-Semitism and Anti-Zionism," *The Journal of Israeli History* 25, no. 1, March 2006.

Cultural code at work in Calgary protest against seal hunt, Canadian troops in Afghanistan and "siege of Gaza": "Protestors Rally across Canada to Speak Out Against Wars in Afghanistan, Iraq," Canadian Press, March 15, 2006.

Michael Moore as a latter-day P.T. Barnum: Jesse Larner, *Forgive Us Our Spins: Michael Moore and the Future of the Left* (John Wiley & Sons, 2006).

"Red" Tories: Ron Dart, *The Red Tory Tradition: Ancient Roots, New Routes* (Synaxis Press, 1999).

"Canadians are not 'warmongers,'" CTV News, September 10, 2006.

Moishe Postone, "History and Helplessness: Mass Mobilization and Contemporary Forms of Anticapitalism," *Public Culture* 18, no. 1, 2006.

Ely Karmon, "International Terror and Antisemitism—Two Modern Day Curses: Is There a Connection?" International Institute for Counter-Terrorism, February, 16, 2007.

Shalom Lappin, "How Class Disappeared from Western Politics," *Dissent*, Winter 2006.

For the "Cairo" conventions, pro-Islamist pseudo-leftism, the leadership and statements of Canada's "anti-war" movement, George Galloway at the Syrian fascist party's birthday celebrations, "anti-war" leaders celebrating with

Khomeinist officials, "Islam and The Left" convocations, etc., see: Terry Glavin, "The Cairo Clique: Anti-Zionism and the Canadian Left," *Z Word*, April, 2008; Terry Glavin, "With Friends Like These...," *Ottawa Citizen*, May 10, 2007.

Mohammed cartoons riots a Mossad plot: James Petras and Robin Eastman-Abaya, "The Caricatures in Middle East Politics," *Peacepalestine* (blog), February 25, 2006.

Embarrassing scene at "global progressive front" conference in Tehran: Terry Glavin, "What Iranian Dissidents Need—And Why They Deserve More from North America's Left," *The Tyee*, October 23, 2007.

Progressive Canadian Muslims decry the self-censorship of intellectuals: Terry Glavin, "Pull Back the Curtain of Fear," *The Georgia Straight*, March 16, 2006.

New Democrats gone "berserk": New Democratic Party of Canada, NDP Resolutions, 22nd Biennial Convention, Quebec City, September 8–10, 2006.

CHAPTER 6: *The Partisans*

A moving and carefully documented account of the 1978–80 period of the Stalinist tyranny in Afghanistan: Raja Anwar, *The Tragedy of Afghanistan: A First-Hand Account* (Verso, 1988).

The methodical elimination of Afghanistan's pro-democracy resistance during the "anti-Soviet jihad" period: Neamatollah Nojumi, "The Rise and Fall of the Taliban," in Robert D. Crews and Tarzi, Amin (eds.), *The Taliban and the Crisis of Afghanistan* (Harvard University Press, 2008).

The Islamist warlords and their war crimes, no evidence that atrocities committed against civilians were ordered by Massoud or his commanders: The Afghanistan Justice Project, "Casting Shadows: War Crimes and Crimes Against Humanity, 1978–2001," 2005.

Gulbuddin Hekmatyar: Human Rights Watch, "Blood Stained Hands" (report), July, 2005; Coll, 2004; Rashid, 2001; Rashid, 2008; Afghanistan Justice Project, 2005.

Ahmed Shah Massoud: Marcela Grad, *Massoud: An Intimate Portrait of the Legendary Afghan Leader* (Webster University Press, 2009).

The PDPA putschists as a function of the Ghilzai elites: Barfield, 2010.

Of the core PDPA leaders, "many had studied in America, and 14 of them had studied at just one American University—Columbia University in New York":

Adam Curtis, "Kabul: City Number One," Part 4, BBC News blog,
October 28, 2009.

*The convulsions of Afghan politics as a function of power struggles within the
Pashtun tribal elite:* M. Nazif Shahrani, "Taliban and Talibanism in
Historical Perspective," in Crews and Tarzi (eds.), 2008.

*The January 2010 London conference on Afghanistan, the objections Afghan
women's rights activists and Pashtun socialists raised regarding Taliban
reconciliation:* Terry Glavin, "Wrong Exit in Afghanistan,"
The Tyee, February 1, 2010.

Progressive Pashtuns and Pakistanis favour NATO intervention: Azizullah
Khan Khetran, "In Favour of Drone Attacks," *Pakistan Daily Times,*
November 6, 2010.

Lamani Brahimi in NDP eminent persons group: NDP Press Release,
"Next Steps in Afghanistan," March 17, 2009.

Lamani and "family values pact": "Islamic Bloc, Christian Right Team Up
to Lobby U.N.," *Washington Post,* June 16, 2002.

Brahimi and "womenfolk": Terry Glavin, "Surrender by any other name,"
National Post, February 9, 2010.

Taliban "manifesto": "Afghan call for ethnic cleansing," United Press
International, May 18, 2001.

"Former UN envoy Kai Eide explains why he held talks with the Taliban,"
BBC World Service, March 18, 2010.

CHAPTER 7: *The International Brigades*
Chris Wattie, *Contact Charlie: The Canadian Army, the Taliban, and the
Battle that Saved Afghanistan* (Key Porter Books, 2008).

British House of Commons, "Select Committee on Defence,"
Thirteenth Report, 2007.

David Aaronovitch, "No Retreat from the War on Terror," *Sunday Times,*
February 5, 2008.

Her Majesty the Queen in Right of Canada, represented by the Minister
of Public Works and Government Services, "Independent Panel on
Canada's Future Role in Afghanistan (John Manley, chair), Final
Report," January 2008.

Terry Glavin, "Reconstruction Seizes Up Amid Afghan Paralysis in
Ottawa," *National Post,* March 12, 2010.

Summary of Findings, Keeping Our Promises: "Canada in Afghanistan
Post-2011, The Way Forward," Canada-Afghanistan Solidarity

Committee, March 2010, http://afghanistan-canada-solidarity.org/
casc-report-keeping-our-promises.

Christie Blatchford, *Fifteen Days: Stories of Bravery, Friendship, Life and Death
from Inside the New Canadian Army* (Anchor Canada, 2008).

CHAPTER 8: *The Ashes of the Old*
King Nadir Shah's "Pashtunization" attempt to destroy the Bamiyan Buddhas:
Cultural Property Training Resource Afghanistan, "History of attacks
on the Buddhas: 12th through the 20th century," U.S Department of
Defense, U.S. Central Command.

David Kilcullen, "Counter-insurgency Redux," *Survival* 48, no. 4,
Winter 2006–2007.

Paul Berman, *Terror and Liberalism* (W.W. Norton, 2003).

Grant Kippen: Terry Glavin, "At Afghanistan's Crossroads Stands a Single
Canadian Traffic Cop," *National Post*, September 3, 2009.

Bob Rae: Campbell Clark, "Extension of Afghan Mission Result of Rare
Bipartisan Effort," *Globe and Mail*, November 18, 2010.

Interview with Amrullah Saleh, *60 Minutes*, August 1, 2010.

Talibanism as culmination of Pashtun domination and "internal colonialism":
Shahrani in Crews and Tarzi (eds.), 2008.

Afghanistan as the contemporary iteration of the Spanish Civil War: Michael
Petrou, *Renegades: Canadians in the Spanish Civil War* (UBC Press, 2008).

"Only one side that history will forgive": Lauryn Oates, "Five Reasons Why I'm
Not Neutral," *The Propagandist*, November 5, 2010.

Lauryn Oates, AREU Shiite Personal Status Law study, 2009.

April 2011 Quran-burning riots and Iranian role in provocation: Terry Glavin,
"The Massacre in Mazar-i-Sharif," *Dissent*, April 5, 2011.

Iran payola to Afghan presidential palace: Dexter Filkins, "Iran Is Said to
Give Top Karzai Aide Cash by the Bagful," *New York Times*, October
23, 2010; Dexter Filkins, "The Afghan Bank Heist," *The New Yorker*,
February 14, 2011.

Arab Spring: Terry Glavin, "Middle East Myths Drop Like Dominos,"
National Post, February 28, 2011.

Pro-democracy and Massoudist protests in Kabul: Jon Boone, "Afghans Protest
Against Taliban Peace Deal," *The Guardian*, May 5, 2011.

appendix

SOURCES ON PUBLIC OPINION

THE FOLLOWING IS a compendium of relevant focus group surveys, directed studies and public opinion polls undertaken in Afghanistan, as well as related data, accumulated during the decade following September 11, 2001.

1 *For a limited overview of trends discerned from Afghan public opinion surveys undertaken in the first half of the decade:* The Clingendael Institute Department for International Development, "Media, Public Opinion, and Peace Conditionalities in Post-Conflict Afghanistan—A Study Into Local Views on Donor Behaviour," December 2005.

2 Center for Economic and Social Rights, "Human Rights and Reconstruction in Afghanistan," May 2002.

3 National Democratic Institute of International Affairs, "Afghan Perspectives on Democracy: A Report on Focus Groups in the Kabul Area on the Eve of the Emergency Loya Jirga," May 2002.

4 Human Rights Research and Advocacy Consortium (HRRAC), "Speaking Out: Afghan Opinions on Rights and Responsibilities," November 2003.

5 National Democratic Institute of International Affairs, "A Society in Transition: Focus Group Discussions in Afghanistan," December 2003.

6 Asia Foundation/Afghan Media Resource Center, "A Survey of the Afghanistan Electorate—Democracy In Afghanistan," July 13, 2004.

7 Human Rights Research and Advocacy Consortium (HRRAC), "Take the Guns Away: Afghan Voices on Security and Elections," September 2004.

8   Center for Strategic and International Studies, "Voices of a New Afghanistan," June 14, 2005.

9   ABC News Poll, "Life in Afghanistan," December 7, 2005.

10 Program on International Policy Attitudes (University of Maryland)/ D3 System/Afghan Center for Social and Opinion Research, Kabul, "Poll of Afghanistan," January 11, 2006.

11 Asia Foundation/Afghan Center for Social and Opinion Research, "A Survey of the Afghan People" (reportedly the single largest and most comprehensive public opinion poll conducted in Afghan history), November 9, 2006.

12 Human Rights Watch, "The Human Cost: The Consequences of Insurgent Attacks in Afghanistan." April 2007.

13 Environics/D3 Systems/Afghan Centre for Social and Opinion Research, "2007 Survey of Afghans," October 18, 2007.

14 Integrity Watch Afghanistan, Torabi Delesgues, "Bringing Accountability Back In: From Subjects of Aid to Citizens of a State," 2008.

15 BBC, ABC, ARD Poll: Afghan Centre for Social and Opinion Research, "Afghan People Are Losing Confidence," February 2009.

16 Gallup Poll: Julie Ray and Rajesh Srinivasan, "Fewer Afghans See Corruption Increasing in Their Country," February 2010.

17 Gallup Poll: Julie Ray and Rajesh Srinivasan, "Taliban Increasingly Unpopular in Pakistan," March 2010.

INDEX

Army of Iran, 206
Aschiana, 78
Asefi, Humayun Shah, 57
Atrofi, Abdulhai, 166
Aurangzeb, 32
Azkiwa, Nasima, 51

Bakunin, Mikhail, 129
Bala Hissar, 37
Balkh Civil Society and Human
    Rights Network, 51
Balkh in the Late Middle Ages
    (Mukhtarov), 46
Balkh, province of, 36, 39
Balkh, town of, 30–38,
al-Balkhi, Hiwi (Hiwi the
    Heretic), 34
Balkhi, Soraab, 48
Bamiyan Buddhas, 45,
    207–8, 221
Bangash, Zafar, 148
Ban Ki-Moon, 26
Barfield, Thomas, 14, 179
Basij-e-Melli (National
    Mobilisation), 219–20
Battle of Marefat High
    School, 3–4, 215, 216
Battle of Panjwayi, 198
Bayqarah, Husayn, 32
Berman, Paul, 209, 210
Bérubé, Michael, 132, 136–37,
    138–39
bin Laden, Osama, 8, 11, 17,
    20–21, 74, 133, 134, 183, 220
Black, Dawn, 159–60
Blatchford, Christie, 203
Bleuer, Christian, 18–19
Blitzer, Wolf, 84
Brahimi, Lakhdar, 184, 185
Brumand, Asif, 40, 41
Bullard, Jeffrey, 123
Bush, George W., 121, 141
Byron, Robert, 45

Cairo anti-war conference, 151–52
Canada:
    in Afghanistan. *See* Canada's
        military role in Afghanistan
    anti-Americanism, 140–43, 147
    anti-war supporters, 125,
        147–54, 156, 157, 158, 218
    U.S. draft dodgers, 142–43
Canada-Afghanistan Solidarity
    Committee, 26, 38–39, 64, 107
Canada's military role in Afghanistan, 9,
    25–27, 39, 52, 112–13, 182, 211
    Battle of Panjwayi, 198
    journalists' failure to cover, 203–5
    Kandahar mission, 9, 39, 91,
        113, 146, 198–99, 200
    Operation Hydra, 204
    "torture scandal," 204
    withdrawal from, 39, 200
Canadian International
    Development Agency, 63, 201
Canadian Islamic Congress, 153–54
Canadian Jewish Congress, 155, 156
Canadian Labour Congress, 154
Canadian Peace Alliance (CPA),
    148, 149, 154, 219
Canadian Women for Women in
    Afghanistan (CW4WA), 108–9
Carter, Jimmy, 15
Caryl, Christian, 8
Case, Shirley, 111
Castro, Fidel, 153
Centres for Disease Control, 91
Central Asia Institute, 6–7
Chávez, Hugo, 153
Chayes, Sarah, 111
children, Afghan, 58, 77–78, 87,
    100, 171. *See also* girls, Afghan
Children's Development Bank, 78
Chomsky, Noam, 132, 133–35, 136
Clark, James, 148, 149
Clinton, Bill, 16
Cockburn, Alexander, 133, 134